Moments

OF INSPIRATION

A DAILY DEVOTIONAL

First Edition, 2018

Printed in the United States of America by:

A DIVISION OF
BAPTIST TRAINING CENTER PUBLICATIONS
A Ministry of:
Westwood Missionary Baptist Church
Winter Haven, FL
www.baptisttrainingcenter.org

Library of Congress Control Number: 2018955039

Holland, Rudy, 1946 -

     Moments of Inspiration / Rudy Holland.

     ISBN-13: 978-1-947598-07-2 (paperback)

     ISBN-10: 1-947598-07-4 (paperback)

     1. Religion - Christian Life - Spiritual Growth.

All Scripture quotations are taken from the King James Version

Moments

OF INSPIRATION

A DAILY DEVOTIONAL

Dr. Rudy Holland

A Division of BTC Publications
Winter Haven, Florida

What others are saying about
Moments of Inspiration:

Looking for something to uplift, strengthen and inspire you to meet the challenges of your day? I can highly recommend the God inspired messages from Pastor Rudy Holland. I have had the pleasure to experience his messages first hand, and now he has blessed us by making these powerful messages available as a daily devotional.

- Larry Cheatham

I was just a young freshman in high school when my pastor preached a series of messages on the book of Nehemiah. More than 35 years later I still recall the words I heard and still utilize the principles of spiritual leadership that he communicated so well. That pastor was Rudy Holland and to this day I still look forward to reading his daily devotional thought from the Bible. I know that you will benefit from spending a few moments in the Word of God, and that you will enjoy the personal anecdotes and God-given insights which Dr. Holland shares in this book.

- Pastor Tim Murr

My mornings usually begin with Brother Rudy's devotions, they are just what I need to start my day with the Lord. I am so thankful he takes time each morning to share because they are such a blessing. After reading them I feel like I have had a mini sermon. My late husband Dave looked forward every day to reading them too! It has also been my privilege to know Brother Rudy not just as my former pastor but also as my friend. My prayer is God will use this devotional to minister and bless others as it has done for me.

- Dreama Byer

Recently, I made the comment that I wish I could find a book of devotionals that were profound and that addressed the challenges of today. Thank God that Dr. Rudy Holland has been led to share his devotionals that speak to the hurting and to the heart of those who want a closer walk with God. Their scripture and application will give you a "spring in your step" for each new day.

- Patty Comer
Wife of Richard Comer,
Missionary to Latin America

Dedication

Behind any meaningful endeavor, there are those unseen and often unrecognized people that make the efforts a success. So is the case with PRH Ministries. When I retired from the Pastorate and began PRH Ministries, God have me a co-laborer who volunteered her services to help me with website, scheduling, travel arrangements, and a host of other other task needed to make this ministry functional. This young lady is Mrs Lewanda Spenser. For all the tireless hours freely given to this ministry, I proudly dedicate this devotional book to Lewanda Spenser. May God bless you for all your time and efforts given to PRH Ministries. (I Corinthians 3:9)

Dr Rudy Holland

1st Corinthians 10:13

ABOUT THE AUTHOR

Dr. Rudy Holland was born in Kenly, North Carolina to Rudolph and Ernestine Holland in 1946. He is the oldest of two siblings, Sandra Edwards and Diane Brown. His parents moved to Lynchburg, Virginia when he was 13. One special neighbor was Dr. Jerry Falwell who was also his pastor and mentor.

On April 1, 1965 Dr. Holland attended a revival meeting by Evangelist Lestor Roloff at Thomas Road Baptist Church. It was here he accepted Christ as his Lord and Savior. Shortly thereafter, he received the calling to preach.

He pursued his education with a B.A. in Bible from Tennessee Temple University. While attending Tennessee Temple he met and married his wife Doris in June 1967. Several years later they had two children Angie and Paul.

Dr. Holland was awarded the very first Doctorate of Divinity from Liberty Seminary by Dr. Jerry Falwell. He considers this to be a very distinguished honor.

His Ministry began back in 1970 where he started Berean Baptist Church, Berean Christian Academy and Berean Daycare. He pastored there for 19 years.

After Berean he spent the next 3 years evangelizing from 1989-1992. It was then he felt the Lord calling him to accept a Senior Pastoral position in Uniontown, Pennsylvania where he pastored 3 years.

Another door opened in Napa, California, so he accepted a Senior Pastor position there for 4 years before being led to Sanford, North Carolina as Senior Pastor. He retired after 15 years to pursue his PRH Ministries outreach.

PRH Ministries was started in honor of his son Paul, who loved the Lord and wanted to preach but through the trials of a brain tumor was unable to fulfill his dream. Dr. Holland set up PRH ministries as a legacy for Paul so through this ministry Paul's testimony would be shared.

Dr. Holland's theme of PRH represents Proclaiming The Word, Reaching The Lost and Helping The Hurting. With over 40 years of preaching, PRH Ministries is an extension of Dr. Holland's ability to Speak at Churches, Revivals, and Individual conferences.

During his Pastoral time Dr. Holland has spoken across America, several foreign countries, and been asked to speak at several Colleges and Universities. His passion is to help Pastors and Churches.

Other Accomplishments:

Served on Board of Directors with Baptist University of America, Tennessee Temple University and Davis College.

One of the founders of Virginia Assembly of Independent Baptist and Old Dominion Association of Christian Schools.

Instrumental figure in having a Church sponsored legislation passed in Virginia to protect religious liberties. House Bill 276 has been a model piece of Legislation for several states to guard against intrusive measures from state child care agencies into sponsored child development centers.

PREFACE

There are two men in the Bible of whom it is said that they walked with God. The first is Enoch. "And Enoch walked with God..." (Genesis 5:22). The second is Noah."...and Noah walked with God." (Genesis 6:9). Enoch is best known for going directly to be with the Lord without meeting death. Noah is best known for building an ark to save his family from the catastrophe of the flood. Now there are many others who walked with God and it is recorded in the Biblical record. However, it is only said of two men. Perhaps we could say that their lives had a special relationship with God. Both men evidently spent time with God. Walking with God speaks of our time spent with Him and a life that reflects quality time with Jesus.

In the early hours of the morning there is a dear friend of mine who walks with God and has put into print those personal hours in order that we could benefit from what God has taught him. Enoch is known for not dying. Noah is known for saving mankind by building an ark. Rudy Holland is known for his endurance that has been an example of joy as he has faced numerous challenges through the home-going of his precious son Paul, the numerous illnesses in his family and those occasions when he has been falsely accused. His strength has been the relationship that he has with God. Rudy knows what it means to walk with God.

I personally have learned much from him. It is easy to talk about Rudy the educator, the pastor, the revivalist, the evangelist, the husband, father, and grandfather. However, we are able to go deeper with him in this volume that reminds of a relationship we can have with God that takes us deeper. These devotional thoughts spent in the early hours of a day with a man who walks with God will be refreshing for all of us. Read them carefully and prayerfully and you and I will begin to understand to a fuller degree what it means to walk with God. Thank you, Rudy, for sharing these intimate times with your readers. I trust we will apply these lessons to our lives as you learned and modeled them for us.

Dr. Dino Pedrone

January 1

I first want to wish each and everyone of you a Happy New Year. I pray each you experience the blessing of God throughout the year. New Year's Day sometimes comes on a Sunday, making it the **first** day of the year as well as the **first** day of the week. In any event, it is the **first** day of the rest of our lives. As I pondered this thought of firsts, I thought of the first words in the Bible. They seem to set the course for all of the firsts in our lives. Note those first words in Genesis: "*In the beginning God.*" The verse does not stop there, but for today we will just consider these four words. Every year should begin with God in our lives. Acknowledging God in our future and seeing God in our past is an essential to fulfilling His plan for our lives. Yes, it is necessary for us to begin this year with a surrendered will to our God. This journey through the coming year begins with a recognition of God **today**. This is the **first** day of the rest of your life. Give this and every day you live as a day to serve the Lord. As we begin a new year, may each of us give this year of our lives to the Lord. May we serve and live for Him throughout these next 12 months and beyond. May we begin by giving today to God. On the first day of the week we should acknowledge our God by being in His house and worshiping Him. Go to a good Bible-preaching church and begin your week with a worship experience with God's people. Today marks the first day of the rest of our lives. May we live each day, one day at a time for the Savior. Remember: "*In the beginning God.*" May God be in all our beginnings! God bless and Happy New Year!

January 2

The single best indicator of true devotion can be summed up in the word **sacrifice**. Most of us shy away from sacrifices that truly cost us anything. We tend to give God out of our abundance but never to the point of sacrifice. As I read through the Bible I note just how often altars were built and sacrifices offered. As Abram journeyed to the land that God had for him, he regularly built an altar. In Gen. 12:7 we see that as Abram received the promise from God for the land, "*there builded he an altar unto the Lord, who appeared unto him.*" Abram then traveled to a mountain east of Bethel, "*and there he builded an altar unto the Lord, and called upon the name of the Lord*" (Gen. 12:8). These altars were places of sacrifice and worship. As we journey through life to a place called heaven, we need to build some altars. We need to have places and times where we offer sacrifices to our God. These sacrifices are not to provide salvation for us, but are offerings of love and appreciation for the ultimate sacrifice made on the cross by Jesus for us. They are places of worship where the Lord appears to us and we call upon His name. Our sacrifices may be sacrifices of praise; sacrifices of our time, our talents, or our treasures. We lay these on the altar of sacrifice for our Lord. These altars are places of worship. They may be in the church, a designated place in our home, or as you walk and enjoy God's creation. Wherever our altars are, they are an essential to our relationship with our God. My thought for today is that we don't forget to build some altars along life's way. They are altars of sacrifice and worship to the Savior. God bless and have a great day.

January 3

Men and women at their best are still flesh; they are still human. Abram, whose name was later changed to Abraham, is called "the father of the faithful." He is the patriarch of the nation of Israel. However, he was just a man still living in sinful flesh. As we journey through the book of Genesis we do not go far before we have an account of Abram sinning. We read of this in Gen. 12:10-20. I believe Abram's denial of Sarai being his wife and allowing her to be taken by the pharaoh to be one of his wives was preceded by a wrong decision. That wrong decision was to go to Egypt. Gen. 12:10 states, "*And there was a famine in the land: and Abram went down into Egypt to sojourn there; for the famine was grievous in the land.*" Though it seems reasonable that Abram would seek to go to a place where he could escape the famine, I find no indication that God led Abram to go to Egypt. Egypt was a pagan land and was not on the route Abram had been traveling. Throughout the Bible it is a picture of the world that is in conflict with the things of God. When we are faced with situations that seem impossible to us, we must be careful that we do not follow the leading of the flesh and fail to trust God. I can honestly say that I have experienced the progression of a wrong choice that leads to even worse choices. Abram chose to go to Egypt instead of staying the course that God had for him. That one decision led him to the place of the embarrassing decision of lying about Sarai being his wife. Today I challenge each of us, in spite of our circumstances, to follow the leading of God in our lives and not be swayed by the adversities of life. God bless and have a great day.

January 4

I have heard many people justify bad decisions by saying, "My decisions only hurt me." The truth is that every decision of life affects the lives of our families, our friends, and other people. As the poet John Donne said centuries ago, "No man is an island." We see an illustration of these truths in Genesis 12, where Abram lied about Sarai being his wife. The Pharaoh took Sarai to be one of his wives but then discovered the truth. "*The Lord plagued Pharaoh*," according to verse 17, and Sarai was no doubt embarrassed as she and Abram were "sent away" in verse 20. It was fear that caused Abram to make the decision to lie. Verses 11-12: "*And it came to pass, when he was come near to enter into Egypt, that he said unto Sarai his wife, Behold now, I know that thou art a fair woman to look upon: Therefore it shall come to pass, when the Egyptians shall see thee, that they shall say, This is his wife: and they will kill me, but they will save thee alive.*" That fear was reflected in Abram's words to his wife in verse 13: "*Say, I pray thee, thou art my sister.*" We all need to recognize the consequences of our sins on the lives of others. Good decisions bless the lives of others, while bad decisions can bring heartache and trouble in the lives of others. Replace fear with faith. God can take care of us, even if we find ourselves in Egypt. Remember, though, that Abram's first wrong decision was to go to Egypt. Sin is progressive and the consequences are inevitable. We can make our choices, but consequences are often beyond our control! God bless you and may each of us make good decisions today.

January 5

I never cease to be amazed at the loving kindness of our God. In Genesis 13, Abram returned from Egypt to Bethel, which means "the house of God." This was the very place he had left to go to Egypt. We read in chapter 12 of him building an altar at Bethel, and again after his sin in Egypt and his return to what Gen. 13:4 called "*the place of the altar.*" It is also worthy to note that God had blessed Abram materially in spite of his failures: "*And Abram was very rich in cattle, in silver, and in gold*" (Gen. 13:2). I want to encourage all who have left God's plan for their lives in exchange for the things of the world (Egypt is a picture of the world). I would suggest the following: **Return** to the place of blessing. It will be the exact place where you left the will of God. It was at Bethel that Abram decided to go down to Egypt, and it was to Bethel he returned. For some of us it may be a return to church; for others a return to having that quiet time with the Lord or the place of service He has given us. Define your Bethel and return. **Recognize** your need for God in your life. In both instances at Bethel, it is written that Abram "called upon the name of the Lord." We all need regular times of acknowledgements of our dependence upon God. When there is a famine in our lives, God can feed us. We do not need to flee to the world for our needs. God is our source; He will take care of us. **Rejoice** in the blessing of a loving and gracious God. He desires to bless us, and His grace is extended to all and any that will return to Bethel. God bless you today and have a great day!

January 6

The character of a man is often best reflected by his reaction to conflict. In Gen. 13:5-18 we read of a conflict between Abram's herdsmen and those of his nephew, Lot. Notice verses 8-9. "*And Abram said unto Lot, Let there be no strife, I pray thee, between me and thee, and between my herdmen and thy herdmen; for we be brethren. Is not the whole land before thee? separate thyself, I pray thee, from me: if thou wilt take the left hand, then I will go to the right; or if thou depart to the right hand, then I will go to the left.*" Abram gave Lot the choice of the land. Though Abram was the elder and could have decided for himself what land he would take, he allowed Lot to make his own decision. This was a gracious and humble act. I am reminded of the words of the Apostle Paul in Phil. 2:3. "*Let nothing be done through strife or vainglory; but in lowliness of mind let each esteem other better than themselves.*" This truly was the attitude of Abram toward Lot. It was Dr. Lee Roberson, longtime pastor of Highland Park Baptist Church in Chattanooga and founder of Tennessee Temple University, who had the words "Live for others" written on a 3x5 card taped to his desk. This was his own personal reminder to esteem others better than himself. A gracious and humble spirit will gain you the favor of God. Though from a human perspective Lot chose the better of the lands, in the the end it was Abram who received the greatest blessing. Lot's choice brought him defeat and great loss. God honors and blesses a humble and generous spirit. God bless you and have a great day!

January 7

Consistency is the evidence of spiritual maturity. We could define this consistency as faithfulness. As I look at the life of Abram, there is one thing that stands out. Everywhere he went, Abram built an altar. When he came to Bethel on his journey to the land God had promised him, he built an altar (Gen. 12:8). After the bad decision to go to Egypt and his lie about Sarai being his wife, he returned to Bethel to the place of the altar (Gen. 13:4). After he separated from Lot and his herdsmen: "*Then Abram removed his tent, and came and dwelt in the plain of Mamre, which is in Hebron, and built there an altar unto the Lord*" (Gen. 13:18). As I think about the faithfulness and consistency of Abram, I am reminded of I Cor. 15:58. "*Therefore, my beloved brethren, be ye stedfast, unmoveable, always abounding in the work of the Lord, forasmuch as ye know that your labour is not in vain in the Lord.*" The altar was a place of sacrifice. It was a place of worship. Building an altar required service or effort. Today I challenge each of us to be faithful and offer our lives as "*a living sacrifice, holy, acceptable unto the God, which is your reasonable service*" (Rom. 12:1). May we be faithful to attend the place of worship. This can be, and all of us need for it to be, a church where we are fed spiritually from the Word of God and we enjoy the fellowship of other believers. All of the above require effort or service, but I want to found faithful, consistent in my relationship with my Savior. God bless and have a great day.

January 8

We all have had those in our lives who we felt "did us wrong." Maybe they took advantage of us in a financial deal or they spoke evil of us or they were just disrespectful and treated us harshly. Whatever the case, we felt wronged by this person or persons. How we respond to the needs of these persons will speak volumes as to our relationship to God. I am reminded of the words of the psalmist who said in Ps. 35:10, "*Lord, who is like unto thee, which deliverest the poor from him that is too strong for him, yea, the poor and the needy from him that spoileth him?*" Oh, but you say, "You do not know what he said about me or what he did to me!" It really does not matter; we are to reach out to the hurting regardless of their treatment of us. By the way, according to Prov. 25:21-22 our best retaliation to mistreatment is to do right to those that mistreat us. "*If thine enemy be hungry, give him bread to eat; and if he be thirsty, give him water to drink: For thou shalt heap coals of fire upon his head, and the Lord shall reward thee.*" We never should do good to get revenge, but doing good will be used of God to convict those that are guilty of wrong treatment of you. We read of Abram rescuing Lot, his nephew who had taken advantage of him, in Genesis 14. When Lot was captured Abram could have said, "Serves him right; he is getting what he deserves." But Abram rescued Lot and his possessions. According to Gen. 14:16, "And he brought back all the goods, and also brought again his brother Lot, and his goods, and the women also, and the people." May God give us the spirit of Abram. May we seek to bless our enemies and manifest the spirit of Christ. God bless and have a great day.

January 9

Did you ever question the promises of God? If you have not, you are a blessed and an unusual person. No, I have never questioned God's power nor His integrity, but I have questioned how and when His promise would become a reality in my life. So it was with Abram in Genesis 15. God had promised to make of Abram a great nation. He had promised to bless Abram's seed, yet Abram had no son. It seemed impossible to Abram that there could be a nation from his loins if he had no son. The statement of Abram's concern is found in Gen. 15:3. *"And Abram said, Behold, to me, thou hast given no seed: and lo, one born in my house in mine heir."* In verse 4 God reiterated His promise and in verse 5 God showed Abram the land that would be his and his seed. My thought for today is that we hold fast to the promises of God. When I retired from the pastorate, God gave me a promise from Isa. 42:19. *"Behold, I will do a new thing: now it shall spring forth: shall ye not know it? I will even make a way in the wilderness, and rivers in the desert."* I have had moments when I questioned how and when this new thing would come in my life, but all along the way God has given indications of His provisions and plan. I claimed that promise more than three years ago and am still claiming it. I have not arrived in the promised land. I do not see the way, but my God has the way planned and the provisions for the journey will be made available as needed. Today I must live this day and trust God for the future. God never fails to keep His promises! God bless and have a great day.

January 10

"God said it; I believe it; that settles it." I have heard this quote from many speakers, but never really thought about it until I recently read Gen. 15:6. Though I had read this verse many times and had noted that it is quoted four times in the New Testament (Rom. 4:1-3; 9-10; 19-24 and Gal. 3:5-7), I never really gave deep thought to its meaning. The verse is Abram's response to the promise of God for there to be a great nation to come from him and the promise of a land that was to be for that nation. Abram had done nothing to deserve the promised blessings. As a matter of fact, Abram had sinned when he lied to the pharoah in Egypt about Sarai not being his wife. But as Rom. 4:3 says, he "*believed God.*" He did not just believe there was a God. Abram believed what God had said. In other words, Abram trusted the promise of God to be true. He placed his faith in that promise. My thought for today is you and I are saved by faith. That means we are saved by believing God's promise to save us on the merits of Jesus' shed blood on the cross. It also means we live the Christian life believing the promises of God. More than just **believing in God**, we **believe God**. "God said it" is the **promise**; "I believe it" is to **possess** that which is promised; "that settles it" is the **positive assurance** of God's Word. I once heard Charles Stanley say, "The hardest thing I find to do in my Christian life is to believe God." My challenge for us today is for each of us to believe God!! Believe His promises! God bless and have a great day.

January 11

My nature is to be impatient. I have a tendency to get ahead of God and make decisions that are unwise. If I do not see how God is going to provide, I will begin to plan to help God with the program. The end is always less than good. Often, I see the hand of God working a little later to meet the need that I thought was up to me to obtain. As I read Genesis 16 I see Abram and Sarai faced the same temptation to get ahead of God. God had promised to bless the seed of Abram, but he and Sarai had no son, so Sarai offered her handmaiden, Hagar, to Abram to bare him a son (v. 1-3). It was not long after Hagar conceived that she lost respect for Sarai, who then blamed Abram. In verse 5 are the words of Sarai to Abram: *"the Lord judge between me and thee."* She was telling him to let the Lord decide which of them was right. The truth is that both were wrong, Sarai for offering Hagar and Abram for accepting the offer. Regardless, the outcome was not good. Broken relations. From that decision would come a nation of people that would be a thorn in the side of the nation of promise that would come from the "seed" of Abram. From the loins of Ishmael would come the the Islamic nations that have long sought to destroy the Israelites. If Abram had only waited, God had a plan. He would provide Abram and Sarai a son, Isaac. My challenge for today is that we wait upon the Lord. We must in faith wait patiently for God's time and God's plan for our needs to be met. To get ahead of God only brings hurt and disappointment. I close with the admonition of Isa. 40:31. *"But they that wait upon the Lord shall renew their strength; they shall mount up with wings as eagles; they shall run, and not be weary; and they shall walk, and not faint."* God bless you today. Be still, wait patiently and watch God work!

January 12

A short time ago I conducted a funeral in Roanoke, Va., for a dear friend. It was a few years after the homegoing of her husband. As I pondered what to say in the service I remembered a very low time in my life and ministry. During that time this couple invited my wife and me to dinner, and at the meal they presented each of us with an enveloped containing a check. I was instructed to use the money given me to begin our new ministry and the funds given to my wife were for our living expenses during the early days of that ministry. God has always put the right people in my life at just the right time. A few years ago, God placed people in our lives to help us launch PRH Ministries. Today, there are people who hold my hands up in our ministry as prayer partners and those who financially support our ministry. God has placed National Center for Life and Liberty in my life to give me an opportunity to help preserve the religious liberties of churches and Christians. God uses people to bless us. We are His conduits to bless others. There are times that God wants to use us to be that conduit, to be that source of blessing to someone. I have not deserved the help and support of others. Only by the grace of God and the goodness of God's people have I been so richly blessed. My personal challenge is that I be the person who reaches out to hurting people to bless them. As these and many others have been friends to me, I want to be a friend to others. The circumstances of need are not for me to judge. I am reminded of the exhortation of Prov. 17:17. "*A friend loveth at all times, and a brother is born for adversity.*" God uses people to bless us, but God also desires to use us to bless others. God bless and have a blessed day.

January 13

As a teenager, I once told my dad that everyone was bleaching their hair blond. My dad did not take favorably to me doing this. When I informed him of the fad of the day and that everyone was participating, he informed me, "Not everyone. You are not, so there is at least one who will not be bleaching his hair." I thought this was a bit unfair, but I complied. Through life I have looked back to that time and realized my dad was teaching me that just because everyone is doing a particular thing, I do not have to be a part of it. While bleaching one's hair was certainly not a sin, it was my dad's decision and I was to obey. There are things that, while accepted in society, our Heavenly Father deems wrong and identifies as sin. Just because it seems that "everyone" is doing it does not make it right. Abram's problem with Hagar and Ishmael began when he complied with a known custom at that time and had a woman other than his wife bare him a son (Gen. 16:1-5). You see, everyone was doing it. It was the accepted practice of the day. I hear many couples that live together out of wedlock say, "Everyone is doing it." Regardless of the accepted practice of the day, it is still sin in the eyes of God. His values have not changed and do not change just because everyone is doing it. A number of practices that are accepted today are rejected by God in His Word. The result in Abram's life was not good. Abram's people, the nation of Israel, are still suffering from that decision. Regardless of whether we understand the commandments of the Lord, or even if the world rejects God's rules, we are to obey. The Bible says in Isa. 55:8, "*For my thoughts are not your thoughts, neither are your ways my ways, saith the Lord.*" God bless and have a great day.

January 14

God is a God of confirmation and provides us with reminders of His promises in our lives. It is interesting to note just how many times God confirms His promise to give Abram and his seed a land and to make a great nation through him. In the first 16 chapters of Genesis this is done at least four times (Gen. 12:1-3, 13:14-17, 15:4-18, 17:1-8). Could it be that God knew Abram would need the reminders to remain enlightened to the presence and power of God in his life? It could have been that God reminded Abram to keep him encouraged in his journey to the land. God has not changed and neither has man. We all need to be reminded of the power and presence of God in our lives. There is an interesting passage of scripture in II Peter 1:4-9. Verse 4 says, "*Whereby are given to us exceeding great and precious promises ...*" The subsequent verses include a list of things we are to add to our faith: "*virtue ... knowledge ... temperance ... patience ... godliness ... brotherly kindness ... charity.*" Then the warning in verse 9: "*But he that lacketh these things is blind, and cannot see afar off, and hath forgotten that he was purged from his old sins.*" However, God has provided us reminders of His promise of the forgiveness of sin to us. He has given us His Holy Spirit to live in us. According to Rom. 8:16, "*The Spirit itself bears witness with our spirit, that we are the children of God.*" We also have written Word of God to assure us of His promises (I John 1:9). Then there are circumstances of life where God shows up and meets a need or performs a miracle that again proves to enlighten us to His presence and power and to encourage us in our journey in this life. My challenge is for each of us to draw upon these reminders to help us through life's journey. God bless and have a great day.

January 15

God is never, never late fulfilling His promises, but our impatience causes us at times to think they will never be fulfilled at all. Consider the promise of Christ's return for His bride, the church. To some this has been promised for so long that it seems only to be a cliché in the pastor's sermon. But I assure you that Jesus is coming! It may be today, it may be tomorrow or may be years from now, but He is going to return just like he promised. Jesus said in John 14:3, "*I will come again.*" Though some doubt and some laugh at the promise, the time will come. Jesus will return "*and the dead in Christ shall rise first: Then we which are alive and remain shall be caught up together with them in the clouds, to meet the Lord in the air: and so shall we ever be with the Lord*" (I Thess. 4:16-17). Just as God gave Abram and Sarai a son in **His** time, so will our Lord return in **His** time. The birth of Isaac came at the most unlikely time in the lives of Abram and Sarai. They both were well past the years of child bearing, yet God kept His promise. The birth of a son was doubted by Sarai, and Abram even laughed at the thought of them having a child (Gen. 17:17), but in due time God made it happen. My thought for today is that we do not lose hope in the promises of God. We should live every day looking for the coming of the Lord. This could be the day of promise for us. It could be the day Jesus returns; may we not be as Abram and doubt the promise. God bless you today and "*look up, and lift up your heads; for your redemption draweth nigh*" (Luke 21:28).

January 16

Isn't it amazing how God communicates His purpose to us and gives us continuing reminders of His will for our lives? In Genesis 17, God gave two continuing reminders of His covenant to bless Abram and make a great nation from his seed. God changed Abram's name to Abraham (v. 5) and Sarai's name to Sarah (v. 15). He also ordered the circumcision of Abraham and all other men of his family (v. 11-14). God once again confirmed His covenant with Abraham. The Lord has also given us reminders of our relationship with Him. The first is that of baptism, which is to be the first act of obedience for a believer. The act of baptism **does not** save: "*For by grace are ye saved through faith*" (Eph. 2:8). The waters of baptism do not wash away our sins: "*... and the blood of Jesus Christ his Son cleanseth us from all sin*" (I John 1:7). Baptism is an outward act confirming that which has taken place in the life of one who has trusted Jesus as Savior. If you are a believer and have not followed Jesus in water baptism, you should do so. Another reminder of God's promises to us is His church. Every first day of the week we gather in church to worship our God. This continuing practice is not only that we might worship Him and be instructed in His Word but to serve as a reminder of His promises to us. We all need to be reminded of God's covenant with us as His children. Baptism and the church serve as reminders of His promises to us. God bless and have a great day.

January 17

"Come on in and make yourself at home. We'll have dinner (or supper) in a little while." I can still hear these words coming from my grandmother as friends came in the house for a visit. There was always a meal or snack served to visiting guests in my grandmother's house. I understand that times have changed, but the Christian grace of hospitality is still much in demand. Hospitality is defined as "the friendly and generous reception and entertainment of guest, visitors, or strangers." The Apostle Paul listed it as a spiritual gift in Rom. 12:13, where he wrote, "*Distributing to the necessity of the saints; given to hospitality.*" Due to the differing lifestyles and circumstances of each of our lives, I will allow that each of us will show hospitality in differing ways. I do suggest that there are some who have the spiritual gift of hospitality, but surely all of us need to show hospitality according to our abilities and opportunities. We see an illustration of hospitality in Genesis 18. Three men came to visit Abraham in the plains of Mamre. These were not just ordinary men, but were sent from God to deliver a message. Abraham showed the men hospitality by feeding and welcoming them. We as Christians need to be friendly and generous toward others. Our hospitality may encourage some struggling brother or sister, or it may be the thing that would enlighten some sinner to the love of Jesus for them. May each of us be hospitable to someone today.

January 18

We serve the God of the impossible. Today you may be facing what seems to be an impossible situation, but nothing is impossible with God. When the messengers from the Lord gave Abraham the news that his wife Sarah would bear a son, she laughed. It was humanly impossible for Sarah to bear a child because of her age. The response from God in Gen. 18:14 still applies today: "*Is any thing too hard for the Lord?*" God does not always answer our needs the way we think they should be answered, but it is never because He does not have the ability to answer. There is no problem He cannot solve, no need He cannot meet, and no situation He cannot control. I am reminded of the words of Jesus to His disciples in Matt. 19:26. "*With men this is impossible; but with God all things are possible.*" These two verses should be a daily reminder of the greatness and power of our God. I pose this question to you right now: "*Is any thing too hard for the Lord?*" With confidence I can answer: "*With God all things are possible.*" We serve an awesome God. May we look beyond our human abilities and see the omnipotent (all-powerful) God that we serve. May our confidence be in Him and not in ourselves. Give Him praise today for His mighty power! God bless and have a blessed day!

January 19

The value of our testimony can never be over emphasized. Jesus referred to His people as *"the salt of the earth"* (Matt. 5:13) and *"the light of the world"* (Matt. 5:14). There is no better example of the righteous having a preserving ability or characteristic than what is recorded in Gen. 18:16-33. The wickedness of Sodom and Gomorrah, where Abraham's nephew Lot had moved with his family, had come before the Lord and they were destined for His judgment. Abraham negotiated with the Lord that if ten righteous people could be found in those cities, that judgment would be spared. But not even ten could be found and both cities were destroyed. Many lessons can be learned from this account, but the one that I want us to note today is the value of our testimony. Could it be that God would spare our country His judgment if only there remained a faithful remnant of the righteous? I wonder how you and I would be measured in the eyes of the Lord. Would we be listed among the righteous? My challenge for us today is that we take account of our testimonies. Are we being *"the salt of the earth"* and *"the light of the world"*? Much more than our personal destiny may be depending on our testimony. May God help each of us to be found faithful and to be righteous in His sight today. God bless and have a great day!

January 20

This is an important date in America. Every four years on this date an elected president is sworn in and begins the official duties of that office. The leadership of America has an effect on the entire world and has a lasting effect on our country. Even if this is not an inauguration year, today is a good day for us as Christians to note our responsibilities. We are reminded in I Tim. 2:1-2, "I exhort therefore, that, first of all, supplications, prayers, intercessions, and giving of thanks, be made for all men; For kings, and for all that are in authority; that we may lead a quiet and peaceable life in all godliness and honesty." Our first responsibility is to **pray** for those in authority — for our President and all others in positions of leadership. I have prayed for previous presidents as well as our current one regardless of whether I agree with their policies. My prayers are in obedience to a much higher power. "*The king's heart is in the hand of the Lord, as the rivers of water: He turneth it whithersoever He will*" (Prov. 21:1). I will also **promote** the areas of the presidents' agenda that reflect Biblical morality. I have dedicated my ministry to the protection of religious liberty and the freedom of our churches to the preach the Gospel. As a part of the National Center for Life and Liberty, I am well aware of the attacks on the church to quiet our message. There is an attempt to force acceptance of the immoral or amoral upon the church. As Peter stated in Acts 5:29, "*We ought to obey God rather than men*." But I would hasten to remind us that the decisions of our leaders will largely determine the moral compass of our society. As the wisest earthly leader of all wrote in Prov. 14:34, "*Righteousness exalteth a nation: but sin is a reproach to any people*." God bless you today and God bless America.

January 21

Many of us would alter the course of our lives had we known the end of our journey. The decisions of today determine our destiny. Nowhere do we see this truth played out more than in the life of Lot, whose desire for wealth led him to choose the land around the wicked cities of Sodom and Gomorrah. In Genesis 19 he was shown grace from God when two angels were sent to instruct him to leave the cities, which God was going to judge because of their wickedness. Even as Lot was leaving Sodom, his wife became a pillar of salt (Gen. 19:26) because of her disobedience to the instructions given by the messengers of the Lord. Then Lot's two daughters committed incest with their father (Gen. 18:30-38). This all began with Lot's decision to move to what seemed to be the best land, the most productive land, and the best opportunity for wealth. We should be careful to make all of our decisions within the will of God for our lives. We must seek His guidance in every decision of life. The desire for wealth and pleasure has been the first step to the destruction of many well-meaning people. Wealth is not bad in and of itself, and neither is pleasure, if within the will of God. I would rather live in poverty in the presence of God than with wealth in the midst of wickedness. The progression of sin is real and always takes us to an undesired and unexpected end. My prayer today is that we might seek God's will for our lives and not seek to choose our own way. God bless and have a great day!

January 22

Just when you think you are doing so well spiritually, you are tripped up by some sin that has been a problem throughout your Christian life. Can you identify with that? I am reminded of the words of Heb. 12:1. "*Wherefore seeing we also are compassed about with so great a cloud of witnesses, let us lay aside every weight, **and the sin which doth so easily beset us**, and let us run with patience the race that is set before us ...*" (emphasis mine) Abraham's besetting sin was fear. He feared for his life due to the beauty of Sarah his wife. In Gen. 12:10-20 he lied to the pharoah in Egypt, who he feared would kill him and take his wife for himself. Again in Gen. 20:1-12 Abraham did the same thing in his dealings with Abimelech. Each of us should strive to identify "*the sin which doth so easily beset us.*" For some it may be the fear of man, as it was with Abraham. This fear causes you to deceive or manipulate others thinking it is for your own good or protection. For some it may be an addiction. Others may wrestle with the sin of immorality or lust. Whatever the sin that trips you up in your walk with the Lord, it can only be conquered through an admission of your weakness and a repentant spirit. Our victory is in Jesus! The Apostle Paul, after dealing with the weakness of the flesh, concluded in Rom. 7:24-25, "*O wretched man that I am! who shall deliver me from the body of this death? I thank God through Jesus Christ our Lord. So then with the mind I myself serve the law of God; but with the flesh the law of sin.*" Simply stated, to deal with that sin which entangles us so easily we must recognize it, repent of it, and rely on the Lord for victory. God bless and have a great day!

January 23

Great truths are often hidden in few words. Two short phrases in Gen. 21:1 jump off the page to my attention: "*And the Lord visited Sarah **as he had said**, and the Lord did unto Sarah **as he had spoken**.*" These statements reference the promise of God that Abraham and Sarah would have a son. Though Abraham was 100 years old and Sarah was 90, God gave them a son, just like He said. As I read the words "*as He said*" and "*as He had spoken*" I was encouraged. God promises are **certain**. He never fails to keep His promises. They are not dependent upon **circumstances**. The ages of Abraham and Sarah would naturally prohibit them from having a child, but all things are possible with God. If He said it, it will happen just as He spoke it. We can **cling** to that in times of doubt or trouble. We need to know the promises of God. They are written for us in the Bible and He never fails to keep them. It is our responsibility to hold fast to the promises of God as we face the trials and tribulations of life. Many Christians live discouraged because they do not know His promises. Others question God rather than waiting for His time and and His way of keeping His promises. Live today with confidence that God will do "*as He said*" and "*as He had spoken*." God bless and have a great day.

January 24

The words of that old spiritual, "God wants you 100 percent; 99 percent won't do, won't do," come to mind as I read through Genesis 22. In this chapter we see God testing the faith of Abraham. God had given Abraham and Sarah a son of promise. Now God was telling Abraham, "*Take now thy son, thine only son Isaac, whom thou lovest, and get thee into the land of Moriah; and offer him there for a burnt offering upon one of the mountains which I will tell thee of*" (Gen. 22:2). Later in the chapter we see that God did not allow Abraham to offer Isaac, but provided a substitute for a sacrifice. However, the test for Abraham was the mental agreement to give the darling of his heart to the Lord. Though Abraham knew God had promised Isaac to be his seed to be used to bring about God's promises to him, Abraham was willing to obey and to trust the Lord. I doubt God will ever make a request of us as He did Abraham, but He does desire that we offer to Him whatever He may ask. I recently was at a missions conference where the pastor asked if anyone felt the call of God to be a missionary. I wondered if there were those in that congregation who sensed that call but felt that the sacrifice was too great for them to go. There are times when God call us to places or positions that may seem strange or impossible. Our responsibility is to trust and obey. The call of God may appear to be a great sacrifice, but God has a "*ram caught in a thicket*" (Gen. 22:13) prepared for you. Could it be that God is calling you to take a step of faith today and trust God for what seems to be an impossible sacrifice? Do not fear; God has a plan and purpose for those that will trust Him and give 100 percent of themselves to Him. God bless and have a great day!

January 25

One of my favorite verses in the Bible is Gen. 22:8, "*And Abraham said, My son, God will provide himself a lamb for a burnt offering: so they went both of them together.*" These were the words spoken by Abraham to answer a question posed by his son Isaac in the previous verse. "*And Isaac spake unto Abraham his father, and said, My father: and he said, Here am I, my son. And he said, Behold the fire and the wood: but where is the lamb for a burnt offering?*" Abraham not only answered his son but also made a prophetic statement. There was coming a day when **God would provide Himself** to be the **sacrifice** for you and me. Jesus was our "*ram caught in a thicket*" — our substitute who died in our place. It was God who sent Jesus to die for our sin. The hope of our salvation was **planned** by God the Father and **provided** by God the Son. Hallelujah, what a Savior; what a salvation! Let us give praise and glory to God today for our salvation. It is totally dependent upon what He has done for us. We can truly say that it is all about Him and because of Him. God bless you today and have great day!

January 26

The names of God, and especially the compound names, describe the character of God. The Bible says in Gen. 22:14, *"And Abraham called the name of that place Jehovahjireh: as it is said to this day, In the mount of the Lord it shall be seen."* The meaning of "*Jehovah-jireh*" is "God will provide." Abraham gave that name to the place where God provided a ram to be sacrificed as a substitute for his son Isaac. This compound name for God is a reminder to all of us of the very character of God — that He is the source of all our needs. He is the provider of our **salvation**. He is the provider of my **substance** (daily bread). He the provider of the **strength** to face the trials and tribulations of life. If we walk in obedience and faith, God will surely be our Jehovah-jireh! From personal experience I can testify that God will and does provide my every need. When I retired from the pastorate I did not know where or how I would ever have an effective ministry to churches and pastors. Looking back over the first two years of that ministry I can truly see and report to all that God is my Jehovah-jireh. To Him be all glory and praise! In one year I spoke in 50 churches and went on mission trips to Lithuania and the Philippines while also participating in 16 seminars with Attorney David Gibbs III and the National Center for Life and Liberty. All of these opportunities came from the hand of God. He is my Jehovah-jireh! To see God as Jehovah-jireh we must obey His command and trust Him, even when it does not seem reasonable. My challenge for me and you today is for us to claim God as our Jehovah-jireh. God is our provider! God bless and have a great day!

January 27

Death always comes too quickly. Regardless of the number of years one may live, they are always too few. As a pastor I have conducted the funerals of people of all ages. Regardless of the age of the deceased, those left were always filled within grief. In Gen. 23:1-2 we read, "*And Sarah was an hundred and seven and twenty years old: these were the years of the life of Sarah. And Sarah died in Kirjatharba; the same is Hebron in the land of Canaan: and Abraham came to mourn for Sarah, and to weep for her.*" Though Sarah was 127 years old, her death brought sorrow to Abraham. Death is **unescapable**. It is an appointment that all of us will keep. We are reminded in Heb. 9:27, "*And as it is appointed unto men once to die, but after this the judgment.*" Regardless of age or physical condition, death is **unexpected**. Though we mentally know the time has come for a loved one or friend to die, emotionally it is a shock. In light of these facts, surely we must live every day as if this could be our last day. We also must cherish every day we have with family and friends. They will not always be here and neither will we. We must live every day with a genuine concern for the salvation of others. We never know when this day may be our last day to share the Gospel with them. Live every day as if it will be your last day on earth — for surely, if Jesus does not return, one day will be our last day. God bless and have a great day!

January 28

According to Prov. 18:22, "*Whoso findeth a wife findeth a good thing, and obtaineth favour of the Lord.*" I believe God puts a man and a woman together to be man and wife. The only marriages ordained by God are between a man and a woman. It is imperative that Christians marry Christians. God has a particular woman for each man and it is our responsibility to find God's choice for our spouse. When we marry in the will of God it is truly "a good thing." We find an example of God providing a wife for Isaac, the son of Abraham and Sarah, in Genesis 24. It is interesting to see how God prepared the hearts of Rebekah and Isaac to be brought together as man and wife. God is interested in the details of our lives. Most of you who are reading this have already made your choice of a mate. However, we have a responsibility to teach our children and grandchildren to seek God's choice for their lives. It is not about beauty or physical appearance and it is not about position or wealth. The choice of a husband or wife is about following God's will. God has a plan for every life, and that includes the person each of us is to marry. In a time when nearly 50 percent of all marriages end in divorce, may we take seriously the sanctity of marriage. May we teach our children and grandchildren to seek God's choice for their mates. God bless and have a great day.

January 29

What do you do when your heart is broken and life brings you disappointments? I recall being very discouraged in my first year of college. I did not want to admit it, but I was homesick. I had not been able to secure a job and the bills were mounting. I was feeling like quitting. I will never forget going to chapel and hearing a preacher from Atlanta speak. His message was titled, "I Think I Will Just Go On Anyway." The speaker was Dr. Raymond Hancock. After hearing the message I resolved to not quit, but just go on anyway. I cannot remember all of the message, but I remember the decision not to quit. Years later I had the privilege to get to know Dr. Hancock. He spoke at my church and I spoke at his church several times. That message I heard in college became the title of a book of sermons written by Dr. Hancock. Let me encourage you, no matter what your situation in life, to just keep on keeping on for the Lord. Abraham buried his wife Sarah and mourned for her. No doubt she was the love of his life. But in Genesis 25 we see that Abraham took another wife. I do not suggest that everyone should marry after the death of a spouse, but I do suggest that regardless of your lost or difficulty you must decide to just go on with your life. It may be that the hurt will never leave, but life is to be lived for Jesus until He returns for us or we go to be with Him. Today I encourage you to just go on anyway. Don't quit living. Don't quit serving the Lord. God is not finished with you. He has a plan for the remainder of your life. God bless and resolve today to just go on anyway.

January 30

We all admire great people. As we consider the life of Abraham surely he stands out as one of the great people in the Bible. His testimony of a man of faith, obedience, and perseverance is spoken of some 60 times in the New Testament. However, the commentator Clarke wrote of Abraham, "Reader, while you admire the man, do not forget the God that made him so great, so good, so useful." God has allowed me to know some great Christian men and women but I must always remember that they are what they are because of their faith and the grace of God. There are inseparable truths demonstrated throughout the Bible. One is the responsibility of man to obey God, live by faith, and surrender our lives to Him. The second is the sovereignty of God. God blesses whom He chooses to bless and He raises up whom He will. At the appointed time we all die. The only thing that matters is not our position in life but our preparation for eternity. The Bible says in Gen. 25:8, *"Then Abraham gave up the ghost, and died in a good old age, an old man, and full of years; and was gathered to his people."* Death is the great equalizer in life. From the great to the lowly, all of us will die. Only our faithfulness, our obedience, and service to God will matter at the end of our days. My thought for today is that we do not spend our time worrying about our position in this life, but be more concerned with our preparation for eternity. May we let God determine our place of prominence in this life and may we only focus on our obedience to His will for our lives. The greatness of our life does not depend upon the positions we hold, but rather on our obedience to His will. His plan and His place for us is our seat of greatness. God bless and have a great day!

January 31

I love to preach and teach the Word of God. When presenting Biblical truths, I often apply them to our daily lives. One Biblical principle I emphasize frequently is that God is in control. I often quote or read Rom. 8:28 as a reminder that no matter what happens in our lives God has a plan and God has a purpose for everything that comes in our lives. *"And we know that all things work together for good to them that love God, to them who are the called according to his purpose."* Not all things that happen to us are good. However, God takes the good and the bad things and desires to use them for **His glory** and **our good**. As I have recently had two messed-up knees and not been able to get around as I wish, the truth I have preached had to be practiced. I have always found that preaching is much easier than practicing. God puts our faith to the test through the trials and tribulations of life. We say that we believe God is in control, but when the unexpected problems come we often ask why. My friend, I write these thoughts for all of us but especially for myself. I once heard a nationally-known preacher say, "The hardest thing for me to do as a Christian is to believe the Bible." He did not doubt the inspiration of the Scriptures. He was just saying that when the test of faith comes, we must remind ourselves that God is in control. Whatever you are going through today, it is for God's glory and will ultimately work together for your good. "Lord, help me to believe and forgive me for my unbelief" should be our prayer. God bless and have a great day.

February 1

I remember my pastor speaking of another pastor, who had made some bad decisions and had lost his ministry, as one who had "sold his birthright for a mess of pottage." For the satisfaction of the moment, this man had forfeited the blessings of God on his life. The analogy used by my pastor came from the account in Gen. 26:29-34 of Esau giving his birthright, as the firstborn son, to his brother Jacob for a bowl of pottage (soup). I have witnessed more people than I care to to think about who have forfeited the blessings of God for the satisfaction of the moment. Some have made bad moral decisions and lost family or ministry. Others have made decisions to satisfy an addiction only to lose family and health. My thought for today is that we always consider the consequences of our actions. If the desire of today is going to bring heartache tomorrow, just say no to your desire. We must remember that our tomorrows will be determined by the decisions of our todays. Hold fast to the blessings that God has given you. Do not allow a moment of weakness to cause you to lose those blessings. God is a God of forgiveness and grace, but the consequences of bad decisions are often irrevocable. I pray that it will never be said of one of us, "He sold his birthright for a mess of pottage." God bless and have a great day.

February 2

Just because we go through difficult times, it doesn't necessarily mean we are out of the will of God. I recall in the early days of our ministry desiring to open a child development center at our church. We faced opposition on every side. The neighbors objected to our having the CDC. The city required a change in zoning and there were those in the church who questioned the Biblical mandate of providing childcare at the church. One dear Christian lady came to me with the observation, "If we are having such a difficult time, maybe God does not want us to have a childcare ministry at our church." She was not being critical but only trying to help. My response? "Maybe because we **are** having difficulty, it is God's will and Satan is trying to hinder the work of God." We do not need to go down into Egypt just because there is a famine in our own land. Gen. 26:1-2 says, *"And there was a famine in the land, beside the first famine that was in the days of Abraham. ... And the Lord appeared unto him [Isaac], and said, Go not down into Egypt; dwell in the land which I shall tell thee of."* Be sure to follow Jesus through the difficult times of life. Do not fear the famines. God has a plan and will make a way. By the way, we opened that child development center and it grew to minister to more than 100 children. It was a blessing to many families and to the church. After more than 45 years that ministry is still actively serving the church and the community for the glory of the Lord. I am glad we did not abandon the cause in the midst of opposition. God bless you today and remember that He is our source for every need of life. Have a great day!

February 3

If you want to know what is wrong with the youth of today, just look in the mirror. The attitudes and actions of this generation are a reflection of the past generation. Abraham lied twice about Sarah being his wife. In Gen. 26:7 we read about Isaac doing the same thing with Rebekah. What did Isaac learn from Abraham? He learned fear — the fear of man — instead of how to trust God in the times of need. I believe our youth seek wealth and pleasure because their parents have made wealth and pleasure the focus of their lives. Too many parents never think of emphasizing God in their daily decisions, and their children grow up never considering the will of God for their lives. I suggest this is why we have such a shortage of young people entering the ministry or surrendering to go to the mission field. We, as parents and grandparents, need to be conscious of the things we teach by example to our children and grandchildren. They need to see **faith** demonstrated in our lives. Faith is the antidote to fear. They need to see **faithfulness** lived in our lives — faithfulness to God and to His church. They need to learn the **fruits of labor**. Ambition and self-reliance are learned from youth. Learning to work for what you have is the antidote for an entitlement attitude. May God help us to pass on to the next generation the character that will please God and bless their lives.

February 4

There are times when we find the will of God difficult to accept. In Genesis we see this very truth illustrated. Regarding the births of Esau and Jacob, Gen. 25:23 says, *"And the Lord said unto her, Two nations are in thy womb, and two manner of people shall be separated from thy bowels; and the one people shall be stronger than the other people; and the elder shall serve the younger."* Despite this stated promise from the Lord that the younger Jacob would be blessed and Esau, the oldest, would serve him, Jacob took advantage of Esau and acquired his birthright (Gen. 25:30-34). Then in Genesis 27 we read of Jacob and his mother Rebekah deceiving Isaac to get the blessing intended for Esau. As I read of the plot of Rebekah and Jacob to steal the blessing intended for Esau, I continued to think of the promise of God, *"and the elder shall serve the younger."* All the deception and trickery were so unnecessary! God had given the promise. They only had to wait for Him to fulfill it. Though we will never know how or when God would have brought the promise to pass, we can rest assured He did not approve of the methods used by Jacob and Rebekah. Accepting the promises of God as a certainty, and being willing to accept His will as perfect for us, will always require faith and often require patience. His will never demands deceit or manipulation. We must learn to *"wait upon the Lord"* (Isa. 40:31). He will provide in His time and according to His plan. I know of times in my life I have gotten ahead of God. In every case it brought hurt and an unwanted result. When Esau found out that Jacob had stolen his blessing, he desired to kill Jacob (Gen. 27:41). Don't try to gain the blessings of God through the efforts of the flesh. May God give us patience to wait for His time and His plan for our blessing! God bless and have a great day.

February 5

Whatever God allows to come in your life, use it for His glory! If life gives you lemons, make lemonade! First, use your experiences of life to become all God wants you to be. Second, enjoy life and allow God to take your trials and tribulations and used them for your good as well as for His glory. The message I preach more than any other is "Five Lessons I Have Learned From Tragedy." This is a testimonial message about the illness and death of our son Paul. Often when I travel to a church to speak, the pastor will ask me to share this message to encourage his people. When our little six-year-old son, who seemed in perfect health, was diagnosed with a brain tumor, I could not see how anything good could come from his illness or the circumstances surrounding it. Looking back over the years, I can see how God used our son's illness to shape my life and my ministry. I can truly say that God has received glory from the life and testimony of our son. I am only the voice that speaks our son's message and shares the abundant grace and mercy shown to our family during the 26 years of his illness. My thought for all of us today is summed up in II Cor. 1:3-4. *"Blessed be God, even the Father of our Lord Jesus Christ, the Father of mercies, and the God of all comfort; Who comforteth us in all our tribulation, that we may be able to comfort them which are in any trouble, by the comfort wherewith we ourselves are comforted of God."* Perhaps someone reading this is going through or has gone through some difficult days. Give your grief and trials to Jesus. He will use them to bring glory to His name and He will bless you with joy and peace in the midst of your circumstances. God bless and have a blessed day!

February 6

God shows up in the most unexpected places. In the opening verses of Genesis 28 we read about Jacob being sent away to find a wife of his own people. While making his way to *"Padanaram, to the house of Bethuel"* (v. 2), he rested. While asleep he dreamed of the promises of God to bless him and make a great nation of him and give him the land surrounding where he lay. When Jacob awoke he said in verse 16, *"Surely the Lord is in this place; and I knew it not."* As we go through life God shows up when we do not expect Him. He shows up to guide us. He shows up to strengthen us. He shows up to bless us. Keep a keen eye open today to see God work in your life. He may come in an unexpected way. He may come at an unexpected time or place. But He always shows up for His children. Jacob named this place Bethel, which means "House of God." It became a reminder to Jacob and others who followed him of the presence and promises of God. Take note in your life of the "Bethels" — the places where GOD showed up in your life. God bless and have a great day!

February 7

"I do not like to go to a church where they are always talking about money!" As a pastor I have heard those words many times. Yet the Bible speaks often of the use of money — as far back as Abraham, who gave a tithe to the priest Melchizedek (Gen. 14:20). Later, in Gen. 28:22, Jacob said these words at the place he named Bethel: *"And this stone, which I have set for a pillar, shall be God's house: and of all that thou shalt give me I will surely give the tenth unto thee."* The practice of tithing can be traced throughout the Scriptures. There are some who believe that tithing is only an Old Testament practice, and that the New Testament standard is "grace giving." Even if you conclude that grace giving is the standard for the church, I contend that surely we would not give less under grace than the tithe that was required under the law. But it is not my intention to debate that issue in these pages. I would simply challenge all of us to recognize that returning a portion of what God has given us serves several purposes. Yes, it surely finances the ministries of the church. However, there are deeper and more personal reasons to give of our material wealth to the Lord. First, giving is an acknowledgement of **God's ownership** of all He has given us. Everything I have, all my earthly goods and wealth come from God. When I tithe or give sacrificially I acknowledge God as my source of all things. Second, giving is an act of **worship**. We worship Him with our tithes and offerings. God blesses those who worship Him. I close with Luke 6:38. *"Give, and it shall be given unto you; good measure, pressed down, and shaken together, and running over, shall men give into your bosom. For with the same measure that ye mete withal it shall be measured to you again."* God bless and have a great day!

February 8

The hearts of men have never changed. Deceit and deception have always been a problem in the hearts of human beings. As I read Genesis 29 I was reminded of the depravity of all men. Jacob had deceived Isaac, his father, and then he became the victim of deceit. He labored seven years for the hand of Rachel in marriage only to be deceived and given Leah, Rachel's sister to marry. He then had to work another seven years for Rachel. The statement in Rom. 3:23 — *"For all have sinned, and come short of the glory of God"* — is proven true in every life, every day. Surely not all of us engage in deceit as recorded in these chapters, but we all must beware of the weakness of our flesh and the sins that so easily become a part of our lives. Sometimes we are the victim of other's misdeeds, and at times we are the guilty ones. My thought for today is that we guard our lives from sin. We are told in Ps. 119:11, *"Thy word have I hid in mine heart, that I might not sin against thee."* The first step to prevent committing sin is to daily read and memorize the Word of God. Jesus said in John 15:3, *"Now ye are clean through the word which I have spoken unto you."* Second, be ready to confess your sin. We are instructed in I John 1:9, *"If we confess our sins, he is faithful and just to forgive us our sins, and to cleanse us from all unrighteousness."* Third, live a surrendered life to the Holy Spirit that dwells within you. Rom. 8:2 reminds us, *"For the law of the Spirit of life in Christ Jesus hath made me free from the law of sin and death."* May God help each of us to live victoriously over sin today! God bless and have a great day.

February 9

I have had the privilege of being in the presence of some people who really blessed me — people whose relationship with God seemed to bring blessing to those around them. I recall my college roommate. He was the son of missionaries and truly lived an example of the Christian life before me. I was a young Christian and needed mentoring in the things of the Lord. He taught me to daily spend time with the Lord. He was constantly looking for the answers for his needs from God. His faith was something I had never witnessed. I was blessed to have been in his presence as a young believer. Jacob had been with Laban for several years. Jacob had taken wives and had children while with Laban. God had blessed him, but it was time for him to return to the land of his father. According to Gen. 30:27, *"And Laban said unto him, I pray thee, if I have found favour in thine eyes, tarry: for I have learned by experience that the Lord hath blessed me for thy sake."* My challenge is twofold today. First, seek the company of those who will be a blessing to you. The blessing may not be one of material or monetary value; It may be encouragement or instruction. I am what I am largely due to the investments made by others in my life. Our ministry is what it is due to those who have blessed us with prayers, encouragements, and financial support. I thank God for those who have blessed me and my ministry. Secondly, seek to **be** a blessing to someone today. You may able to speak a word of encouragement, or to lend a helping hand to someone today. Look for that opportunity to bless someone today. God bless you and have a great day.

February 10

    Not every day is a day without trouble. There are times in our lives when **nothing** seems to be going right. We all have days when we need to be reminded that our strength, hope, and peace in the midst of the storms of life come from the Lord. I have never been sick or had to hospitalized. God has blessed me with good health, although I have had and do have sickness in my family. Many of us struggle with financial problems. Others are struggling with broken hearts resulting from broken relationships. Still others weep over family or friends that are the victims of addictions. Today we all should be reminded to seek the Lord in the time of our trouble. I wish to give you just a few verses to help you through the difficult times, and I challenge you to search the Scripture for those verses that give you hope and help in your time of need. My life verse, upon which I have rested my hope in the hour of my deepest need, is I Cor. 10:13. *"There hath no temptation taken you but such as is common to man: but God is faithful, who will not suffer you to be tempted above that ye are able; but will with the temptation also make a way to escape, that ye may be able to bear it."* Consider the exhortation of the psalmist in verses such as Ps. 18:6. *"In my distress I called upon the Lord, and cried unto my God: he heard my voice out of his temple, and my cry came before him, even into his ears."* Or you may claim the promise in Ps. 34:4. *"I sought the Lord, and he heard me, and delivered me from all my fears."* God is greater than my circumstances. He desires to comfort us and to give us the strength for the challenges of the day. God bless and have a victorious day.

February 11

"Times have changed." I have heard this statement often from attorney David Gibbs III at legal seminars we conduct across the country, introducing the need for churches to be diligent in having their documents of governance (constitution and bylaws) up to date and considering how we minister in today's society. Lawsuits are filed every day against churches and Christians unlike anything we would have dreamed of in years past. After Jacob had served in the house of Laban for 20 years he was married with children and his fortunes had increased. But when it was time for him to return to his father's house, according to Gen. 31:2, *"And Jacob beheld the countenance of Laban, and, behold, it was not toward him as before."* Times had changed. We must be sensitive to the changing times in our lives. For over 40 years I was a pastor at a church, but now I travel and speak in churches and work with National Center for Life and Liberty. My ministry is still to proclaim the Word of God, but now I seek to help and bless churches around the country. Times have changed in my life and ministry. It may be that God has a change for your service for the Lord. Follow His leading. Change is not always bad. As churches and believers, we cannot change our doctrine, but there are times we must change our methods — not for the sake of change, but because "times have changed" and God has a different path for us to follow. May God give us wisdom and a willingness to change as we seek to win men and women to the Savior! God bless and have a great day.

February 12

The sayings of men from the Bible are sometimes not in keeping with the original intent of the sayings. For example, men have often used the words of Gen. 31:49 as a parting gesture or a statement of kindness or blessing: *"The Lord watch between me and thee, when we are absent one from another."* But they were originally said by Laban during a time of conflict with Jacob, who had left along with livestock and other possessions of Laban. They were agreeing to disagree, and Laban was literally asking God to be their judge, even as they were to be apart. It is good for us to let God be the judge in the times of conflict in our lives. Laban had the power to take revenge, but God stopped him (Gen 31:24). When there are conflicts with others, we first need to determine what Jesus would do or what God would have us do. In other words, let God be the judge. God will and can watch between us and our accusers, even if we are apart. The New Testament instruction is found in Rom. 12:19. *"Dearly beloved, avenge not yourselves, but rather give place unto wrath: for it is written, Vengeance is mine; I will repay, saith the Lord."* Forgive those who have mistreated you. Ask God to be the judge in the conflict and leave the results to Him. God bless you and have a great day.

February 13

My Dad often quoted this old country saying: "The chickens always come home to roost." What he meant was that the deeds of your past will catch up with you. In Jacob's life the chickens certainly came home to roost. In Genesis 32 when fleeing from Laban he found himself facing his brother Esau. Years earlier Jacob had left home in a hurry after stealing Esau's birthright and receiving the blessing their father Isaac intended for the older brother. There was great animosity in the heart of Esau toward Jacob, and after more than 20 years they faced each other again. The chickens had come home to roost; Jacob's sin had found him out. We see his state of mind in Gen. 32:7. *"Then Jacob was greatly afraid and distressed ..."* My thought for today is that we should face the consequences of our actions in the time of our transgression. The Biblical remedy for healing broken relationships is found in the words of Jesus in Matt. 18:15-17. It has been my experience that most issues can be reconciled when the instruction of verse 15 is followed: *"Moreover if thy brother shall trespass against thee, go and tell him his fault between thee and him alone: if he shall hear thee, thou hast gained thy brother."* If the relationship is still broken after that, the next two verses give instructions to follow from there. In short, it is best to face the situation and not put it off. Eventually, the chickens will come home to roost. God bless and have a great day!

February 14

To my wife, Doris, I wish a Happy Valentine's Day! This is the day we acknowledge those we love. I thank God for my wife! I truly can understand the words of Prov. 18:22. *"Whoso findeth a wife findeth a good thing, and obtaineth favour of the Lord."* These are sad days in America regarding marriage. In 1950, 78 percent of all adults in America were married. Today that number is only 48 percent. Cohabitation is becoming the norm. The Bible is clear that men and women are to marry, and cohabitation is a sin. God performed the first marriage in the Garden of Eden, and Jesus performed His first miracle at a wedding (John 2). There are numerous verse in the Bible declaring the sanctity of marriage, such as Heb. 13:4-7, Gen. 2:22-24, Eph. 5:22-23 and many others. I noted some 30 references from one source that declare God's intent for man to marry. All of us should honor our spouses. Every day should be a day of sharing a loving relationship, but Valentine's Day is a special day to say "I love you" to a wife or husband. Take time today to speak words of affection to your spouse. If possible do something special for your valentine. God will bless the home where Biblical principles are followed. In Prov. 18:22 we are reminded that those who marry *"obtaineth favour of the Lord."* God bless you today and may we ever preach and practice the sanctity of marriage.

February 15

When life seems rough, often things are not as bad as we think. As Jacob traveled to the home of his father, his greatest fear was to meet Esau. After all, had not Jacob deceived and tricked Esau out of his birthright and a blessing from Isaac their father? Jacob anticipated the worst. But read Gen. 33:4 and see what happened when the two met. *"And Esau ran to meet him, and embraced him, and fell on his neck, and kissed him: and they wept."* This greeting was not what Jacob had expected! As I read this account, I thought how many of us may be surprised with the response of those we think harbor ill feelings against us. The broken relationships in life can be and should be mended. My challenge for us today is to seek to restore those broken relationships in our lives. Things are often not as bad as we think. We may be surprised at the response of that one we feel has hard feelings toward us. We must go with the right attitude. If we have offended our brother or sister, we must seek forgiveness. If we have been offended, we must forgive the one that has offended us. Life is too short to carry bitterness and resentments in our hearts toward others. Seek to restore those broken relationships in your life. God bless and have a great day.

February 16

The consequences of compromise can often be as bad as disobedience. We see an example of the consequences of compromise in Genesis 34. According to Gen. 31:3, *"And the Lord said unto Jacob, Return unto the land of thy fathers, and to thy kindred; and I will be with thee."* The Lord made it clear again in verse 13: *"I am the God of Bethel, where thou anointedst the pillar, and where thou vowedst a vow unto me: now arise, get thee out from this land, and return unto the land of thy kindred."* But in chapter 33 we see that Jacob went to Shechem, not Bethel. Because of that, this is what happened to his daughter Dinah in Gen. 34:2. *"And when Shechem the son of Hamor the Hivite, prince of the country, saw her, he took her, and lay with her, and defiled her."* Later in the chapter her brothers avenged her by killing Shechem and Hamor, taking the dead men's wealth as they went. Verse 30: *"And Jacob said to Simeon and Levi, Ye have troubled me to make me to stink among the inhabitants of the land ..."* The opening verses of Genesis 35 describe Jacob's journey to Bethel, where God told him to go in the first place. It is better to obey God completely and not compromise our obedience to Him. We can avoid many heartaches and much trouble if we follow the leadership of God for our lives. Short cuts or evasion to doing the will of God often brings hurt and embarrassment. Let us hear God today. May we heed His leading and avoid the hurts of compromise. God bless you and have a blessed day!

February 17

On this date in 2017 I underwent surgery to repair a torn meniscus in my knee. The night before the procedure, the last thing I read was a message from a friend who was praying for me. The first message I saw the next morning was the same thing from another friend. I thought of how blessed I am to have so many people praying for me. I never want to take for granted the prayers of my friends. Thank you for praying! As I went in for the procedure knowing that there would be some down time to allow for healing, I thought of Ps. 46:10. *"Be still, and know that I am God: I will be exalted among the heathen, I will be exalted in the earth."* I also considered how blessed I am and have been with good health over the years. This is so minor compared to the health problems of so many. God has blessed me and I give Him praise for that today. My thought for today is that I must pray for others as they have and are praying for me. Sometimes we are more engaged in seeking prayer for ourselves than we are to pray for others. The prophet Samuel said, *"Moreover as for me, God forbid that I should sin against the Lord in ceasing to pray for you ..."* (I Sam.12:23) I also rest on the promise of Rom. 8:28. *"And we know that all things work together for good to them that love God, to them who are the called according to his purpose."* Whether minor or major surgery or any other circumstance, God has a plan and is in control. We must praise Him for all the blessings of life. Today's bumps in the road must not rob us of the reality of the goodness of God and His bountiful blessings to us. God bless you today and have a great day.

February 18

It is never too late to return to the place of blessing. For Jacob there was a special place, Bethel, where he encountered God (Gen. 28:12-17). It was at Bethel that God confirmed to Jacob that he was heir to the promises God had made with Abraham — the promise of a land; a promise of a people to come from his loins; and a promise of God's presence to be with Him. When Jacob left the house of Laban, God told him, *"Return unto the land of thy fathers, and to thy kindred; and I will be with thee."* (Gen. 31:3) Jacob did not go to his father's house, but went instead to Shechem, a pagan land (Gen. 33-34). It was in Shechem that Jacob's daughter was defiled by the son of Hamor the Hivite, and the sons of Jacob avenged their sister by killing the sons of Hamor. Jacob's failure to obey God had brought tragic results. But God is good, even when we fall or fail. According to Gen. 35:1, *"And God said unto Jacob, Arise, go up to Bethel, and dwell there: and make there an altar unto God, that appeared unto thee when thou fleddest from the face of Esau thy brother."* Some of us may need to return to the place of blessing. Maybe we have made some bad choices. God still calls for us to return to Bethel! He has not forgotten nor forsaken you. Bethel awaits our arrival and there we will find the presence of our God. May today we go back to Bethel in our lives. God bless you and have a great day!

February 19

Have you noticed the congregations of most churches are aging? There are not a lot of young couples in the average church. I read that only 4 percent of millennials (ages 18-30) attend church. The article I read gave several reasons for the failure of millennials to make church a priority in their life. Rather than analyze the reasons for a lack of church attendance, I want to give a personal observation supported with a Biblical illustration. Regardless of the struggles within our society, we live in a culture of comfort. Most people, and especially millennials, have very few needs. They have homes to live in (often with parents), food to eat, and clothes to wear. They are too young to have experienced the **real** world, but they think they are doing all right, so why go to church? There will come a time for many of them when their only hope is God and the church! When Jacob came to an awful situation in his life, the message that came to him was, *"Arise, go to Bethel and dwell there: and make there an altar unto God"* (Gen. 35:1). The word "Bethel" means "house of God." It was a special place in the life of Jacob. The church was a **special** place for many of today's millennials as they grew up. Only now, as they are older, have they determined church is not relevant to their lives. Bethel was also a place of **surrender** in the life of Jacob. Gen. 28:21 ends with the phrase, "then shall the Lord be my God." These were the words uttered by Jacob after his encounter with the Lord. Bethel was a place of **safety**. Gen. 35:5 says, *"And they journeyed: and the terror of God was upon the cities that were round about them, and they did not pursue after the sons of Jacob."* It would be best if millennials honor and support the house of God, but my observation is when life deals them a blow greater than they or their parents can handle, they will return to their "Bethel," the house of God.

February 20

Have you ever noticed how God confirms His will in our lives with particular events? As a young preacher I often wondered if I was doing what God wanted in the place of God's choosing. I so wanted to be in God's will for my life. Now that I am just north of 70, I still desire to do and be what God wants with my life. As I read through the life of Jacob, I notice how often God reminded Jacob of His plan for his life — whether it was in a dream (Gen. 28:11-22) or an encounter with the angel (Gen. 32:22-32). In Gen. 35:10 we see that God changed his name from Jacob to Israel. This name was to be a reminder of the covenant God had made with Abraham and Isaac was now passed to Jacob. God has never spoken to me in a dream and I've never wrestled all night with an angel, but God has given confirmation that I am in His will. God speaks to us today through **His Word**. When I was seeking God's will concerning the Lord's call for me to preach, it was Paul's words to Timothy in I Tim. 1:12-14 that He used to confirm His call upon my life to preach His Word. God will often confirm His will through **the words of others**. I recall seeking advice from my Bible professor, Dr. Porter, and his words of wisdom confirmed God's calling in my life. "Young man if you can do anything other than preach and be happy, do it," he said. "If you are only satisfied to preach, then preach." After 50 years, only preaching satisfies my deepest desire for my life! Lastly, evaluate the **work** of your life. Will it bring glory to the Savior? If you are undecided about God's plan for your life, search the Scriptures, seek Godly advice, and be sensitive to the results of your choices in life. God bless you today as you serve Him!

February 21

Envy, according to the definition offered by a Google search, is "a feeling of discontent or resentful longing aroused by someone else's possessions, qualities, or luck." Envy is often synonymous with jealousy. In either case it is a sin that is the first step toward a greater transgression. Most acts of theft begin with feelings of envy. Many acts of violence have their roots in jealousy. We see in Genesis 37 an illustration of the fruits of envy. Of the twelve sons of Jacob, Joseph, the youngest was his favorite. Gen. 37:3 tells us, *"Now Israel loved Joseph more than all his children, because he was the son of his old age: and he made him a coat of many colours."* Jacob's attitude toward Joseph created an envious spirit in the hearts of Joseph's brothers. Verse 4: "And when his brethren saw that their father loved him more than all his brethren, they hated him, and could not speak peaceably unto him." All of us should strive to guard our hearts against envy or jealousy. Sad to say, but this a sin of many pastors and other Christian leaders. One identifier of their envy is they cannot speak well of the successes of others. They always seem to find the negative in the ministry of those that are leading larger or more successful ministries. I also see this sin in the lives of believers of every walk of life. I hear their envious spirit as they speak negatively about others that have been blessed or have a position in life greater than them. The answer to envy? *"Not that I speak in respect of want: for I have learned, in whatsoever state I am, therewith to be content"* (Phil. 4:11). Success and happiness are not found in positions of life or material prosperity. They are the fruits of being where and what God has planned for your life. Envy is actually an expression of one's discontent with God's plan and purpose for one's life. God deliver us from an envious spirit and jealous heart! God bless and have a great day!

February 22

Sin will take you farther than you wanna go,
Slowly but wholly taking control.
Sin will leave you longer than you wanna stay;
Sin will cost you far more than you wanna pay.

Those words, written by Harold McWhorter in a song made famous by the Cathedrals among others, convey my thought for today. In Genesis 37 is the account of Joseph being the favorite son of Israel and his dreams of becoming the head and ruler of his brothers. Verse 11: *"And his brethren envied him; but his father observed the saying."* Their envy grew into malice, as evidenced in verses 19-20 when Joseph went to check on his brothers at their father's request. *"And they said one to another, Behold, this dreamer cometh. Come now therefore, and let us slay him, and cast him into some pit, and we will say, Some evil beast hath devoured him: and we shall see what will become of his dreams."* Reuben, the eldest, stopped them from killing Joseph. Instead he was thrown into a pit and then sold to a caravan of Ishmaelites headed to Egypt. Who would have thought that the sons of Israel, the brothers of Joseph, could ever be so cruel and sinful? The story serves to remind us that great transgressions are often the fruits of attitudes of envy or jealousy. I remember well the warning of the little cliché: "Sow a thought, reap an act; sow an act, reap a habit; sow a habit, reap a destiny." Beware of your attitude toward others. Your attitude will ultimately define you actions and your actions will define your destiny. God bless you today and have a great day.

February 23

Each day of our lives is a stepping stone to lead us to God's ultimate place for our lives. When we are mistreated or when we endure trials and tribulations we often cannot see God's intended purpose. As I read of the treatment of Joseph by his brothers, I think of the song "Trust His Heart" written by Babbie Mason. The words of the chorus are:

> **God is too wise to be mistaken;**
> **God is too good to be unkind.**
> **So when you don't understand,**
> **When you don't see His plan,**
> **When you can't trace His hand — Trust His heart.**

Maybe today, some of us are experiencing abuse or mistreatment from others. It could be that our circumstances seem impossible. We ask, "Why, God?" But we receive no answer. It could be that God is moving you to an unexpected place of blessing. It could be that He desires your trust and your loyalty regardless of your circumstances. He wants us to "trust His heart" even when we cannot "see His plan." Little did Joseph know that the pit was a stepping stone to the palace (Gen. 37-41). I would remind each of us of the words of Isa. 55:8. *"For my thoughts are not your thoughts, neither are your ways my way, saith the Lord."* Even when the adverse circumstances of life are the result of my own poor choices or have been brought about by the hand of others, God has not forsaken me. He uses everything in my life for my ultimate good and for His glory. Today I may not understand His plan, but I will trust His heart! God bless and have a great day.

February 24

In life we can find ourselves in the most awkward places. So it was with Joseph. After being sold to a traveling caravan and carried to the land of Egypt, he was sold as a slave to Potiphar, one of Pharaoh's top officers. In Gen. 39:2 we read an amazing and comforting word: *"And the Lord was with Joseph, and he was a prosperous man; and he was in the house of his master the Egyptian."* In this verse I see three things. First is the **presence** of the Lord. Though Joseph was in a foreign and wicked place, God was with him in that place and at that time in his life. Second is the **prosperity** of Joseph. God's blessings are not restricted by circumstances. Though Joseph was a slave in the house of an Egyptian, God prospered him. God can bless you right where you are. Third is the **place** where Joseph found himself. He was in a hostile environment and a different culture; the Egyptians did not worship the God of Joseph. There is no doubt Joseph felt out of place, yet the Lord was with him. No matter the place we are in or the circumstances in our life, **God is with us.** We may feel alone, but He is there. In the midst of the storms of life, He is there. We must also remember that **God can bless us** regardless of the circumstances of life. Wherever you are today, God is with you and He can bless you. Be comforted today with those promises. God bless and have a great day.

February 25

"If a job is worth doing, it is worth doing right." We all have heard that phrase often over the years, but the principle is taught in the New Testament. Col. 3:17 says, *"And whatsoever ye do in word or deed, do all in the name of the Lord Jesus, giving thanks to God and the Father by him."* As I read Gen. 39:1-6 I see an example of Godly character. Though a slave to Potiphar, Joseph's testimony showed that God was with him, and his master saw this. Verses 4-6: *"And Joseph found grace in his sight, and he served him: and he made him overseer over his house, and all that he had he put into his hand. And it came to pass from the time that he had made him overseer in his house, and over all that he had, that the Lord blessed the Egyptian's house for Joseph's sake; and the blessing of the Lord was upon all that he had in the house, and in the field. And he left all that he had in Joseph's hand; and he knew not ought he had, save the bread which he did eat. And Joseph was a goodly person, and well favoured."* My thought for today is that we not allow bitterness or resentment to come into our lives. Though we may be mistreated and taken advantage of, each of us must still be an example before others. There is no doubt that Potiphar worshiped idols and did not know Joseph's God. It was Joseph's testimony and hard work that impressed Potiphar. God moved in the Egyptian's heart, but it was Joseph's positive attitude in a time of adverse circumstances that God used to speak to Potiphar. It could be that some of us are the victims of circumstances that have been perpetrated upon us. May God give us grace and strength to take the opportunity to live a testimony of His grace before others regardless of our circumstances. God bless and have a great day!

February 26

It is reported by attorney David Gibbs III that 80 percent of all accusations made against church leaders and workers are vastly exaggerated or are untrue. The sad thing is that the accusation is usually believed or at least places a shadow over the accused. This matter of false accusations is not new. In Genesis 39:7-21 is the account of Joseph being seduced by Potiphar's wife. Joseph did not yield to the temptation, but Potiphar's wife falsely accused him. Potiphar believed her and Joseph was thrown into prison. Think of the life of Joseph — from the the pit where he had been placed by his brothers for no reason but their envy and jealousy, to the palace where he served as a slave, to the prison. If anyone had reason to be depressed and discouraged, surely it was Joseph! However, according to verse 21, *"But the Lord was with Joseph, and shewed him mercy, and gave him favour in the sight of the keeper of the prison."* My thought for today is that we be aware of temptation and flee from it. However, do not be surprised if along life's journey you are accused, though innocent, of some wrong. The best approach to an accusation is to answer it and live on. Do not allow the accusations of others to rob you of your joy or purpose in life. Rest in the promise that the Lord is with you and will bless you. Beware of defending yourself. My pastor was criticized unjustly, and I told him that I was going to his defense. His instruction to me has helped me through my ministry and life: "Do not defend me! My enemies will not believe you and my friends do not believe the accusations." Let God be our judge today. He can bless us regardless of our circumstances. Even in a prison, God has a plan and a purpose. Praise God for His mercy and grace. God bless and have a great day!

February 27

Isn't it amazing how quickly good deeds can be forgotten? Any person can do a good deed with no reward in mind, but the person who receives the benefit forgets the kind gesture. So it was in the life of Joseph, in prison unjustly after being falsely accused by Potiphar's wife of inappropriate behavior. The butler and the baker of Pharaoh's house were sent to the same prison as Joseph, who through the power of God interpreted their dreams. The butler was restored to his position (Gen. 40:21) while the baker was hanged (Gen. 40:22), both happening just as Joseph said they would. Joseph had only one request of the butler: *"But think on me when it shall be well with thee, and shew kindness, I pray thee, unto me, and make mention of me unto Pharaoh, and bring me out of this house"* (Gen. 40:14). That did not happen, as verse 23 points out. *"Yet did not the chief butler remember Joseph, but forgat him."* It was two years later, in a time of national crisis, that the butler finally remembered him (Gen. 41:9-14). We cannot place our fate in the hands of men. Even those we help often forget us in our times of need. Do good to others without expectation and remember that God is our rewarder. I also would challenge each of us to not forget those that have blessed us. I never want to be as the butler and enjoy the blessing that comes from others without being a blessing to them if possible. Never allow the disappointments that come from others to govern your attitude. God will repay, and He will bless you in His time, just as He did Joseph. God bless you and may you seek to be a blessing to someone today.

February 28

You are where you are today so you can be a blessing to others. The journey of life may seem hard, but God has a place for you that you may be a blessing to someone. Joseph traveled through some difficult years, but at 30 years of age he was promoted to a place of honor and power in the land of Egypt (Gen. 41:46). A great famine had come to Egypt and the surrounding countries. Joseph had interpreted Pharaoh's dream, predicting the coming years of famine and thus preparing for it (Genesis 41:15-40). The last verse of Chapter 41 says, *"And all countries came into Egypt to Joseph for to buy corn; because that the famine was so sore in all lands."* God had put Joseph in a position to be a blessing to the people of Egypt and other lands as well. Wherever you are in life, God wants to use you to be a blessing to others. Joseph was a blessing to the butler when they were in prison, to the pharaoh and to the people of Egypt. He was a blessing to many people in foreign lands and ultimately to his own family. Today I challenge you look for opportunities to be a blessing to others. It is worth noting that as Joseph blessed others, God blessed him. We should not do for others just to get something, but as we do for others we will receive from Him. *"Give and it shall be given unto you"* (Luke 6:38) is a principle that extends far beyond the giving of material wealth. If we give kindness, we will reap kindness. If we give love, we will reap love. Simply stated, be a blessing and you will be blessed. God bless you and remember to bless someone today. God has placed you where you are to be a blessing to someone. Have a blessed day!

Restoration or reconciliation is always better than revenge. The story of Joseph in Genesis 42-46 unveils many illustrations of God's love for us. Joseph has been called "the greatest picture of Jesus and His grace found in the Old Testament." Surely there are many types of Christ found in the narrative of the life of Joseph. When reading Genesis 42 I was impressed that he, having been offended years earlier by his brothers, sought reconciliation rather than revenge. God seeks a restored relationship with us through the sacrifice of Jesus, His Son. All of us have offended the God's holiness, as is made clear in Rom. 3:23. *"For all have sinned and come short of the glory of God."* We deserve judgment, but God offers grace to all who will receive. Rom. 10:13 says, *"For whosoever shall call upon the name of the Lord shall be saved."* God seeks restoration and reconciliation with sinful man rather than revenge. *"But God commended His love toward us, in that, while we were yet sinners, Christ died for us"* (Rom. 5:8). My prayer is that everyone reading this has received by faith God's offer of salvation. Though all of us are sinners, God desires a relationship with us. He does not seek revenge for our transgressions. Each of us should have the same forgiving attitude toward those who sin against us as Joseph had toward his brothers and Jesus has toward us. Christ taught us in Matt. 6:12 to pray, *"And forgive us our debts, as we forgive our debtors."* May God give each of us a forgiving attitude toward those that have sinned against us. God bless and have a great day!

March 2

As I read the last nine chapters of Genesis I am reminded of the old saying, "What goes around comes around." The brothers of Joseph had deceived their father, Jacob. They sent Joseph away on a caravan, then dipped Joseph's coat in blood to convince Jacob his favorite son was dead (Gen. 37:31-33). Joseph went to Egypt as a slave and eventually rose to the second-highest office in the country. A great famine came to his homeland and to Egypt. But Joseph had prepared for the famine and had grain stored. Now his brothers had to go to Egypt to buy grain, not knowing they must face Joseph. When Joseph saw his brothers, he did not reveal himself to them but deceived them. They had been guilty of deception and would now be victims of deception. The difference was that they would be recipients of blessing, not evil as was Joseph. The consequences of unconfessed sin continue to bring chastisement. It had been 22 years since the brothers placed Joseph in the pit and sent him away with the caravan. They still had to face their sin. As the saying goes, "The wheels of justice grind slow, but they grind ever so fine." My challenge for us today is that we deal with the sin in our lives daily. We are assured in I John 1:9, *"If we confess our sins, He is faithful and just to forgive us our sins, and to cleanse us from all unrighteousness."* We are also warned in Gal. 6:7, *"Be not deceived; God is not mocked: for whatsoever a man soweth, that shall he also reap."* God bless and have a great day!

"Blood is thicker than water." That old saying suggests that family relationships will always take priority in the lives of people. Unfortunately, that is not the case today. One off the saddest things I have dealt with as a pastor is broken relationships among family members — brothers and sisters who will not speak to each other, or parents estranged from children. The list goes on and on. "Oh, you just do not know all they have done to me." Have they thrown you in a pit and left to die? Have they sold you to a caravan to be carried to a foreign land? These are a few of the things Joseph experienced at the hands of his brothers. Yet, when his brothers had need and Joseph had the ability to help them, he extended a heart of forgiveness and a hand to help them. Don't misunderstand me; there are consequences for sin. There are times we must establish boundaries even for those we love. However, we **must** maintain a heart of forgiveness and be ready to extend a hand of help. Joseph revealed himself to his brothers and offered to bring them and their father, Jacob, to Goshen and take care of them (Gen. 45:1-10). How could Joseph forgive his brothers? How could he pledge to care for them who had sought to do him such harm? In that passage there are three references by Joseph of God's plan for good.

Verse 7: *"And God sent me before you ..."*

Verse 8: *"So now it was not you that sent me hither, but God ..."*

Verse 9: *"God hath made me lord of all Egypt ..."*

His brothers' actions were sinful and wrong, but God is bigger than the evil actions of others and can turn wrongs to right if we trust Him! Guard your attitude toward those, even family, that have mistreated you. God is in control. God has a plan. Be sure your heart is right and your hand is ready to reach out to those that have hurt or disappointed you. God bless and have a great day.

March 4

There are times we find it difficult to believe how the unexpected has come our way and God has blessed us beyond our imaginations. Consider what must have gone through Jacob's mind when his sons brought word that Joseph was alive. The Bible tells us that when he heard the news, according to Gen. 45:26, *"And Jacob's heart fainted, for he believed them not."* In the following two verses Jacob was convinced: *"And they told him all the words of Joseph, which he had said unto them: and when he saw the wagons which Joseph had sent to carry him, the spirit of Jacob their father revived: And Israel said, It is enough; Joseph my son is yet alive: I will go and see him before I die."* I have used this text for an Easter message, with the thought that God has sent evidences (wagons) to provide proof that our Savior lives. One of those evidences is **the testimony of the witnesses** (I Cor. 15:1-8). Another is the **testimony of an empty tomb.** The bones or grave of the founders of other religions can be found, but not so of Jesus because He is alive. There is also the **testimony of the church.** Did you ever wonder why we worship on Sunday rather than the Sabbath, which is Saturday? The reason the church, the body of Christ, worships on Sunday is as a reminder that our Savior lives! God often sends "the wagons" as evidence of great blessing. He did for Jacob and He has done it for us with the resurrection of our Savior. Watch for the wagons in your life! God bless and have a great day!

March 5

**"Only one life, twill soon be past;
Only what's done for Christ will last."**

Those two very familiar lines are from a poem by C.T. Studd, who served as a missionary nearly 40 years in China, India and Africa until his death in 1931. Born into a wealthy family and one of England's top cricket players in his youth, he gave away nearly all of his earthly possessions and chose to invest his life in what really matters. Today's thought of the brevity of life and living with eternity (heaven) in mind was prompted by my reading of Genesis 49, which describes Jacob giving his last blessing to his sons. Verse 33 says, *"And when Jacob had made an end of commanding his sons, he gathered up his feet into the bed, and yielded up the ghost, and was gathered unto his people."* His life was over. If Jesus tarries His coming, we all will die just as he did. *"And as it is appointed unto men once to die, but after this the judgment"* (Heb. 9:27). It is said of me that I am retired, and it is true that I have retired from being a pastor. However, with life so short and heaven so real I must serve the Lord as long as I have health and opportunity. My challenge for us today is that we live every day as if it might be our last, for of a certainty one day will be our last. At the end of life, only what we have done for the Savior will matter. God bless and live for Jesus today and every day!

March 6

God does not recognize time as we do. The Bible says in II Pet. 3:8, *"But, beloved, be not ignorant of this one thing, that one day is with the Lord as a thousand years, and a thousand years as one day."* In His eyes our circumstances are but an event in our short lives. As we come to the close of the book of Genesis, we read of Joseph's words to his brothers regarding their evil treatment of him. This reflects his understanding of the sovereignty of God in his life. Note Gen. 50:19-20. *"And Joseph said unto them, Fear not: for am I in the place of God? But as for you, ye thought evil against me; but God meant it unto good, to bring to pass, as it is this day, to save much people alive."* The actions of Joseph's brothers and the way they treated him was horribly wrong. However, a gracious and sovereign God can take the worst of man's actions and use them to accomplish His purpose. May we learn to trust God even when the circumstances of life seem to be so unfair and unjust. God knows the future and has a plan for our lives. Our responsibility is to be, as Joseph, submissive to the Lord regardless of the circumstances of life. It could be that God has an unexpected purpose for your life. As Prov. 3:5-6 admonishes us, *"Trust in the Lord with all thine heart; and lean not unto thine own understanding. In all thy ways acknowledge him, and he shall direct thy paths."* God bless and have a great day!

March 7

The final verse of Genesis says, *"So Joseph died, being an hundred and ten years old: and they embalmed him, and he was put in a coffin in Egypt."* Reading this passage I am reminded not only of the **brevity** of our lives, but of the testimony of the **blessed** life of Joseph. His life blessed others. His legacy was that he had suffered many injustices in his life, but he never allowed them to bring bitterness or resentment in his life. He left behind a testimony of a forgiving spirit. Joseph also left a legacy of faithfulness to his God. From a New Testament perspective, we would say that this was a man who truly lived like Jesus. What an example for us to follow in our Christian lives. Joseph was not perfect, but he is truly an example of godliness for us. What kind of legacy are we leaving? When someone speaks your name after you are gone, what will come to their mind? Those thoughts are a major part of your legacy. When I think of those I have known in the ministry who have died, I immediately think of some influence they had on my life. When I think of my pastor, Dr. Jerry Falwell, I think of his great faith and love for people; when I think of Dr Lee Roberson, my thoughts go to his unwavering stand for the Gospel and his vision to reach the world with the Gospel. These are but two examples of many. For what will you and I be remembered when we are dead? We are building those memories as we live. May God help us to leave legacies that honor and glorify our Savior! God bless and have a great day.

March 8

As we begin the National Center for Life and Liberty seminars, David Gibbs III often says, "Times have changed!" I think all of us can agree with that. A nation that once acknowledged God, and whose values were based upon the moral standards of the Judeo-Christian ethic, has become a nation that rejects the God of the Bible and is quickly becoming an amoral (**no** morals) nation. What has changed? I would suggest that our nation suffers from the same dilemma as the nation of Israel in the beginning of the book of Exodus. According to verse 8 of the first chapter, *"Now there arose up a new king over Egypt, which knew not Joseph."* I would suggest that in America we have had many elected officials who *"knew not"* the God of the Bible. Because we the people elect our rulers, we must accept the responsibility for the decline of our nation. Therefore, we can conclude that we have a population which also does not know Him. The hope of the nation is a return of the people to the God of the Bible. We must seek to elect leaders who will protect our religious liberties. Every week I speak to churches whose religious liberties are being challenged. We the people **must** stand up and speak up or we will become the slaves of the modern-day Egyptians. I do not suggest that every leader will be or needs to be a born-again believer, but I do suggest that every elected official must seek to maintain the Biblical values upon which this nation was built. May God give each of us the courage to challenge the evil of our day and declare, as in Ps. 33:12, *"Blessed is the nation whose God is the Lord."*

March 9

More than 500,000 abortions are performed each year in the United States. This procedure is done in the name of women's health. I would suggest it is done for the sake of sexual freedom — abortions allow people to engage in sex without the consequence of having a child. The fact that an unborn fetus is a living person goes unnoticed, and the fact we are taking more than 500,000 innocent lives annually fails to be considered in our society. There was a time in the history of the nation of Israel when the king of Egypt ordered all the male babies be put to death by the midwives (Ex. 1:15-22). We gasp at the thought of such cruelty, yet we have grown insensitive to the evil of our day. We just accept the fact that abortion is the right of the woman with no consideration of the rights of the unborn. My thought for today is that we as Christians must stand for life. Some took that stand in Egypt: *"But the midwives feared God, and did not as the king of Egypt commanded them, but saved the men children alive"* (Ex. 1:17). Wouldn't it be wonderful if every Christian medical worker — whether doctor, nurse, or medical assistant — would say, "No, I will not perform abortions"? Wouldn't it be good if we the people refused to allow our government to use our tax money to take the lives of the unborn? May God help us to have the courage of those Jewish midwives. God bless you and have a great day!

March 10

Sometimes I wake up early in the morning and just feel the need to have the presence of God to be real in my life. There's no particular problem, just the feeling that I need time with Him. Yes, there are physical needs in my life and my wife's life. There are financial concerns and challenges in the ministry. However, these are ongoing concerns. There is also the need at a particular hour for a fresh touch from God to encourage and enable me to continue serving and living for Him. At that time my thoughts go to Ps. 105:4. *"Seek the Lord, and his strength: seek his face evermore."* One great need of my life is to be reminded of the **presence** of God. Though it may not always feel that way, He is present with us. Today's challenges will not be faced alone. God will be there! I must rest in His **power**. Nothing is too hard for our God. No problem, no need, and no challenge is beyond His ability to handle. He is the all-powerful God. There may be someone reading this today who feels all alone and helpless. My challenge for you today is to follow the admonition of Isa. 55:6. *"Seek ye the Lord while he may be found, call ye upon him while he is near."* We may not always understand why we face the difficulties of life, but we can always rest in the **promise** of Isa. 55:8. *"For my thoughts are not your thoughts, neither are your ways my ways, saith the Lord."* So today, let each of us acknowledge His presence, draw upon His power, and claim His promises for today. God is with us, His power will sustain us, and His promises will enable us. God bless and have a great day!

I had only been a Christian a few weeks when, at a testimony meeting at a youth camp, I was approached by a lady who said to me, "Rudy, I believe God is going to call you to preach. I am going to pray for you every day that God will use you to preach His Word." That lady kept her word and prayed for me daily. While in college, I received letter with a one-dollar bill enclosed, with the words, "I pray for you daily." Several years later, at a special day at the church I had founded and was pastoring, I had this lady attend and I recognized her for her faithfulness to pray for me. There are countless numbers of people who have had a major role in the successes of our lives. Many will go unnoticed and even unknown in this life. They are the reason for many of our successes and for the blessing of God in our lives. One of the heroes of the saving of the life and the rescue of baby Moses was his sister, most likely Miriam. This sister was given the responsibility of watching the basket with baby Moses at the edge of the river. According to Ex. 2:4, *"And his sister stood afar off, to wit what would be done to him."* It was this sister who saw Pharaoh's daughter take the child from the water's edge and approached her about getting a Hebrew woman to nurse and care for the baby (Ex. 2:7-8). It was this unnamed sister who got Moses' mother to care for her son in the palace of the pharaoh. Praise the Lord for those unknown prayer partners, those hidden hands of help, and those who speak on our behalf. Many of us are what we are and blessed because of those unknown and unseen people that intercede on our behalf. Thanks to all the prayer warriors and other supporters in my life. May God help each of us to be a silent blessing to someone today!

March 12

It is never right to do wrong to do right. Sin is always sin! However, it has always amazed me how God can take the evil deeds of man and weave a good result from them. We saw this in the life of Joseph — sold by his brothers to a caravan that took him to Egypt, where God promoted him to a place of authority to be used to provide for the nation of Egypt and his own family. In Ex. 2:11-12 we read of Moses killing an Egyptian in a moment of anger. This act of violence was brought about by his seeing the mistreatment of his brethren. *"And it came to pass in those days, when Moses was grown, that he went out unto his brethren, and looked on their burdens: and he spied an Egyptian smiting an Hebrew, one of his brethren. And he looked this way and that way, and when he saw that there was no man, he slew the Egyptian, and hid him in the sand."* When Moses' sin became known, he had to flee from Egypt for his life. It is interesting to note that it was later, **after** Moses' sin, when God called him to be the deliverer of his people (Ex. 3:10). It reminds me of the wonderful grace of our loving Lord. No, sin is **never** right, but God can take the vilest of sinners and cleanse them and use them for His glory. God can take the failures of our lives and use them to put us in the place of usefulness. Yes, a confession and repentance of our sin is required, but there is forgiveness and there is place of service for every believer. God has a plan and place for you who have failed or fallen. Look for that burning bush in your life (Ex. 3:2) to find God's plan for you. God bless you today and remember that He loves you and has a plan for your life!

What is God's calling for your life? "But I am not called to any particular place of service," you say. It is my opinion that every child of God has a place of service in the work of God. Not all are called to preach. Not all are called to sing, but all are given a place of responsibility in the work of God. We are all members of His body. We are reminded by the Apostle Paul in Eph. 5:30, *"For we are members of his body, of his flesh, and of his bones."* Every part of the body — every member — has a function, so I conclude every believer has a function in the body of Christ. Our place of service is to be determined by the Lord. Some may feel they are physically unable to serve, but the greatest place to serve is as a prayer warrior, to intercede on behalf of others who may be serving and to pray for the lost. There is a work for all to do. Some receive a special calling from God to a particular work. So it was with Moses. In Ex. 3:1-10 God called him from a burning bush to be the deliverer of Israel from Egypt. I have never had a "burning bush" experience, but I have had the experience of knowing the call of God in my life, which is to preach His Word. What is God calling you to do? What place of service has He given you? Some are called to go; some are called to give; some are called to graciously serve as teachers or helpers. There are some who are given the ministry of prayer. There are many other places of service. You must find God's place for you and fulfill His calling for your life. As Henry Blackaby said, "Find out what God is up to in your life, and join Him!" God bless you today and have a great day!

March 14

The excuses of man pale in comparison to the power of God. Moses offered a series of excuses to God for not returning to Egypt to deliver the people of God from their bondage (Ex. 3:11-4:20). This passage reminded me of how men fail to see the truth that "where God guides, God provides." God never calls us to a task without equipping us for that task. When I felt God was calling me to preach, I thought I could never stand and speak in front of a congregation. I felt so unworthy, so inhibited, and so lacking in knowledge — yet I knew God was calling me to preach. In the early days of my ministry, I would study all week, and on the morning I was to speak, I would get up early and go to another room and preach my massage as I stood before a mirror. I even gave an invitation, and it was amazing the results of those sermons in that bedroom before that mirror with Jesus and me. Remember the words of the Lord to Moses in Ex. 4:1112. *"And the Lord said unto him, Who hath made man's mouth? or who maketh the dumb, or deaf, or the seeing, or the blind? have not I the Lord? Now therefore go, and I will be with thy mouth, and teach thee what thou shalt say."* God answered every objection of Moses with a demonstration of His power. The Lord reminded Moses that He made him just the way he was and could use him to do His will. If God is calling you to a particular task, trust Him to provide the power to do His bidding for your life. He knows your weakness, but His power is greater than than your inabilities or weakness. God knows you and God will provide for His callings in your life. God bless you today!

March 15

Someone has said, "Excuses are a lie stuffed into the skin of the truth." As I read the excuses that Moses gave to God as to why he should not go to Egypt to deliver the people from bondage, I am reminded of the excuses I have heard over the years why people could not serve the Lord. Moses questioned his **position** in Ex. 3:11. *"Who am I ..."* Maybe Moses wondered if the pharaoh would know who he was or maybe this was a statement of humility. The Lord assured him in verse 12, *"Certainly I will be with thee."* Always remember in the work of God, it is not about who we are, but who He is. Moses questioned his **preparation** in Ex. 3:13. *"What shall I say unto them?"* God answered in verse 14 by instructing Moses to call the people's attention to Him. *"Thus shalt thou say unto the children of Israel, I Am hath sent me unto you."* Our success in serving the Lord is not dependent upon what we know, but Who we know! In Ex. 4:1 Moses questioned the **perception** of others. *"But, behold, they will not believe me."* God responded by giving Moses supernatural power, turning his rod into a serpent (v. 3-4). His hand became leprous and then was cleansed (v. 6-7). The work of God must always be done with the power of God. Moses questioned his **public speaking** ability in Ex. 4:10. *"O my Lord, I am not eloquent ..."* God reminded him in verse 11 that He made Moses and He could enable Moses to speak. *"Who hath made man's mouth?"* The only ability needed to serve our Lord is availability. God will enable us for His calling in our lives. Moses concluded in Ex. 4:13 that God had the **wrong person**. *"O my Lord, send, I pray thee, by the hand of him whom thou wilt send."* He told the Lord to send someone else, and this made the Lord angry (v. 14). God wants you and me, not someone else. May God help us to lay aside our excuses and obey his leading and calling in our lives today. God bless and have a great day!

March 16

The burden of the ministry or calling of God is often made lighter or easier with help from others. As Moses made his excuses in Exodus 4 for not going to Egypt to lead his people out, God provided Aaron to assist him. In verse 10 Moses said, *"... but I am slow of speech, and of a slow tongue."* Here is what God said about Aaron in verse 16: *"And he shall be thy spokesman unto the people: and he shall be, even he shall be to thee instead of a mouth, and thou shalt be to him instead of God."* It has been my experience that God has always placed an "Aaron" in my life at the right time to assist me in the work God has given me. Pastors and other Christian leaders often need that. When we ask God for help, He will often send that help through another person. When Moses tried to use his own lack of eloquence as an excuse, God sent Aaron to be his spokesman. In my ministry I also have made excuses to keep me from doing the will of God, but He has always provided the helping hands, the giving hearts, and the personal help for me to do His will. When I was a pastor, God gave me loyal capable assistants to carry out His work. As I travel and speak, God has given me partners to support our ministry. I do not think we should ever underestimate the place of service of the Aarons in our lives and ministry. Today I give thanks to God for those He has placed in my life to remove my excuses not to fulfill His calling in my life. God bless you and have a great day!

For the most part, leaders of nations through history have not been sensitive to Christian values. There are exceptions and thank God for those leaders. But often even leaders who profess to be Christian are persuaded to compromise Biblical convictions. It is worthy to note that Moses grew up in the palace of Egypt with the only Godly influence being his mother. By Exodus 5 we see that God chose and sent Moses to Egypt to deliver His people from bondage. He was greeted by a ruler who knew neither him nor his God. Verses 1-2: *"And afterward Moses and Aaron went in, and told Pharaoh, Thus saith the Lord God of Israel, Let my people go, that they may hold a feast unto me in the wilderness. And Pharaoh said, Who is the Lord, that I should obey his voice to let Israel go? I know not the Lord, neither will I let Israel go."* As Christians, we must live for God regardless of the circumstances of society. Though we must and should pray for those in authority, we should not let their lack of obedience to the Word of God sway our commitments to the Lord. I thank God for the conservative and even Christian positions of some of our political leaders, but regardless of a ruler's position, we must stand for Biblical principles. As Peter said in Acts 5:29, *"We ought to obey God rather than men."* I am not advocating that we break the law if it is possible for us to live within the law, without violating our faith. However, as Christians we must obey God, even it means persecution. May God give us courage to live for Him and the wisdom to stand for Biblical values. God bless you and have a great day!

March 18

Recently I was thinking about the words of Jesus in Matt. 19:26. *"... with God all things are possible."* I feel sure those words characterized the feelings of Moses and Aaron when they first appeared before Pharaoh in Exodus 5. These words of Jesus have been my strength many times in almost 50 years of ministry. There are times that I know only God can give me the strength to continue. There are times only God can provide my needs. But every time I needed strength, God gave an abundance of His strength. When the need was great, it is God who met the need. When Moses and Aaron could not persuade the pharaoh to let the people go, God did. Today you may be facing what seems to be impossible. Remember, *"With God all things are possible."* Even the heart of a king can be changed by our God! Your need and your circumstance are not too hard for our God. Please pray for for our ministry's financial support. These are always lean months, but God will and has already begun to meet our needs. Surely I can say, *"but with God all things are possible."* Thank you for your prayers! God is good all the time, and all the time God is good! God bless, and I covet your prayers.

Sometimes things get worse before they get better — at least that is the way it seems. However, things are not always as they seem to be. God sent Moses to be the deliverer of the Israelites. Pharaoh increased their burdens by taking away the straw they needed to make the bricks they were to make (Ex. 5:6-19). In verse 21, we read of the murmuring of the Israelites against Moses and in verses 22-23, we see Moses complaining to God. The Lord's response in Ex. 6:2 is noteworthy. *"And God spake unto Moses, and said unto him, I am the Lord."* With that statement God reminded Moses, "I **know**, I **care**, and I am **in control**." Today, your burden may be heavier than usual. Do not fret; He is still Lord. He knows all about your burdens, He cares about you, and He is in control. I have found that when I am overwhelmed with the cares of this life, I find strength to face another day without straw, in knowing that **He is Lord.** You may not be able to see the light at the end of the tunnel of your trouble, but you can rest assured that God has a plan and purpose for the road you are traveling. It would not be long, and these same burdened Israelites would be leaving their bondage with the riches of Egypt in their possession (Ex. 12:35-36). I close with the chorus of a familiar gospel song written by Bill and Gloria Gaither:

> *Hold on my child, joy comes in the morning;*
> *Weeping only lasts for the night.*
> *Hold on my child, joy comes in the morning;*
> *The darkest hour means dawn is just in sight.*

Hold on today because **He is still Lord**. God bless you and have a great day!

March 20

There is already enough preaching in America today to convert every soul and bring every believer to spiritual maturity. The problem is, as stated by Jesus in Matt. 13:13, *"... because they seeing see not; and hearing they hear not, neither do they understand."* Moses had the same problem with the Israelites. The Bible says in Ex. 6:9, *"And Moses spake so unto the children of Israel: but they hearkened not unto Moses for anguish of spirit, and for cruel bondage."* We need to heed the message of the Word of God — not just hear it, but heed it. Believe His promises regardless of your circumstances. God is bigger than your problems and more powerful than the rulers of this world. The Israelites saw the demonstrations of the power of their God. They beheld the breaking of their bondage and the crushing of the heart of the king of Egypt. We also can believe His promises for us today. He is the same God today as He was in the days of Moses. We just need to not only hear His word but heed it. May we let our actions today reflect our faith in the promises of God for our lives. May we have a living relationship with Jesus that assures us of His promises. In the words of a song written years ago by Paul Rader:

> **Only believe, only believe.**
> **All things are possible if you'll only believe.**

God bless you today and have a great day.

At a mission conference I attended a year or two ago I heard a message that stayed with me. The text was the second chapter of Jonah and the emphasis was on prayer. It is true that Jonah prayed in a time of trouble in his life, **but he prayed**. It was after his prayer that the Lord delivered him from the belly of the great fish. As I listened to the message, I thought of the many times in my life that, in the midst of trouble, I had cried out to the Lord. I also thought that if Jonah had prayed before he fled from the will of God, he could have escaped the storm and avoid being in the belly of a great fish. My thought for us today is that we pray **before** we find ourselves in the midst of trouble. Now if you find yourself in the "belly of a great fish," by all means pray. My pastor said often, "Nothing of eternal value is ever accomplished apart from prayer." The Lord said in Jer. 33:3, *"Call unto me, and I will answer thee, and shew thee great and mighty things, which thou knowest not."* All of us need to renew our commitment to pray. You should pray for God to save the lost, pray for strength to live for Him, pray for God to provide your every need, but most importantly, **seek Him** through prayer. I once read of a great man of God who prayed, "Lord, I come to you in prayer to ask for nothing. I come only to seek you." The Bible says in Isa. 55:6, *"Seek ye the Lord while he may be found, call ye upon him while he is near."* God bless you today and have a great day!

March 22

God's plan is often opposed by the world. We should not think it odd that we face opposition to the preaching of the Gospel. Moses' announcement to Pharaoh from God, "Let my people go," was sternly rejected. Even in America, a nation founded upon Biblical principles, Christians are opposed on every hand. We are restricted as to where we can pray or preach and are maligned for our beliefs. As I read through Exodus 7-12, I am reminded of the words in II Chr. 20:15 to Judah and King Jehoshaphat as they faced a great battle: *"Thus saith the Lord unto you, Be not afraid nor dismayed by reason of this great multitude; for the battle is not yours, but God's."* The distractions that come from the world should cause us not to quit, but to give the battle to the Lord. It may be that your battle today is personal and spiritual in nature. Your help and victory will come as you give your conflict to the Lord. God can change any situation and bring deliverance. Moses and Aaron faithfully obeyed the Lord, and He brought the deliverance of the nation. All He requires of us is faithfulness. May we determine today to arise out of our attitudes of defeat and discouragement and just keep serving the Lord, knowing that the battle is not ours, but God's. Sunday School teacher, keep teaching. Preacher, keep preaching. Servant of God, keep serving. Do not let the opposition of the world or Satan stop you. God is on your side and He will give the victory. God bless and just keep on keeping on for the Lord.

There are ten plagues recorded in Exodus 7-12 that came upon the land of Egypt. These plagues came at the time Moses was seeking to deliver the Israelites from the bondage of the Egyptians. Their purpose was to answer Pharaoh's question in Ex. 5:2, *"Who is the Lord, that I should obey his voice to let Israel go? I know not the Lord, neither will I let Israel go."* Each plague directly challenged one of the gods of Egypt, and together they proved the God of Israel to be greater than all of them. I challenge you to read Exodus 7-12 and note the **awesome** power of the God of Israel, remembering that the God of Israel is **our** God. Our God is greater than all and any adversary. Our God can change the direction of a person's life, a family, a church, or even a nation. There are times when I feel all hope is lost in our country to ever return to the Christian values of our heritage. Then I read Exodus 7-12 and realize that with Him all things are possible. The path to deliverance is not always easy, but the destination is worth the trip. Do not lose hope for your family, your church and our country. God is greater than the gods of this world. As we read of the wonders performed by our God throughout the Scriptures, may we never forget the exhortation of Heb. 13:8. *"Jesus Christ the same yesterday, and to day, and for ever."* He can do it again! He can set His people free. God bless you and have a great day!

March 24

The world and Satan will always offer God's people compromises — opportunities of partial obedience to the will of God. In Exodus 7-12 God sent Moses and Aaron to lead the nation out of Egypt's bondage, but Pharaoh refused to allow the people to leave, so God had sent various plagues to encourage Pharaoh to let the people go. Pharaoh offered three compromises, each of which is similar to what Satan and the world offers us to keep us from complete obedience to the Lord. The first compromise: **You can go, but not too far.** The Bible says in Ex. 8:28, *"And Pharaoh said, I will let you go, that ye may sacrifice to the Lord your God in the wilderness; only ye shall not go very far away: intreat for me."* Many Christians still live very close to the things of this world and have not separated themselves. Refer to Rom. 12:2 as our instruction for complete obedience. The second compromise: **You can go, but you cannot take your family.** Pharaoh's directive in Ex. 10:9-11 was that the men could go, but the children were to remain in Egypt, a picture of the world. I am amazed how Christian parents today allow their children to live so worldly. Their music, their dress, their language, etc., are far from being Christlike. The parents may have left Egypt, but they have left their children in Egypt. The third compromise: **You can go but leave your fortunes.** According to Ex. 10:24, *"And Pharaoh called unto Moses, and said, Go ye, serve the Lord; only let your flocks and your herds be stayed: let your little ones also go with you."* Today, Satan convinces us that we need to leave our money and wealth in the world. Complete obedience includes a separated life from the world, a commitment to have a Godly family and an acknowledgement that my wealth comes from the Lord. May God keep us from the compromises of the world and Satan. God bless and have a great day!

March 25

My mother lives in a memory center in Lynchburg, Va., and is nearly 90 years young. Though she does not have recent memory, she is very healthy for her years. Each of us should remember to honor our parents regardless of their health. I do not see my mother as often as I like or should. No, she will not remember that I was with her. However, I will know that I was there. In Eph. 6:2-3 we are reminded by the Apostle Paul, *"Honour thy father and mother; which is the first commandment with promise; That it may be well with thee, and thou mayest live long on the earth."* Honor them with your presence. Parents are blessed by just the presence of their children. As a parent, I know how much it means to just see and be with my children. Honor them with your praise. There are no perfect parents, just like there are no perfect children. However, as children we need to acknowledge the sacrifice of our parents for us. I praise my mother for always praying and desiring that I be a preacher. She never told me of her prayers and desire for me to preach until the night I called home to tell her and Dad of my decision to prepare for the ministry. I can still hear her telling me over the phone, "Well, it does not surprise me. When I sat in that rocking chair and rocked you as a baby, I prayed that God would make you a preacher." I give my Mom praise for that and for her prayers down through the years of my ministry. May God give us Godly parents that raise their children for the Lord!

March 26

Do you ever wonder why God's people are so despised by the world? Throughout the Old Testament and even today we see how rejected and persecuted are the Jews. We see a similar attitude toward Christians. Attorney David Gibbs III suggests we are rejected and despised because we teach and believe there is **only one way** to be saved. Acts 4:12 tells us, *"Neither is there salvation in any other: for there is none other name under heaven given among men, whereby we must be saved."* As God was preparing to deliver the Israelites from the bondage of Egypt, he gave instruction to Moses for the people to slay the lamb and apply its blood upon their door post. As the death angel passed through the land to smite the firstborn of every house, the houses with the blood would escape the judgment of death. According to Ex. 12:13, *"And the blood shall be to you for a token upon the houses where ye are: and when I see the blood, I will pass over you, and the plague shall not be upon you to destroy you, when I smite the land of Egypt."* There was **only one way** to escape the plague. Despite all the concern for political correctness, we must not forget there is only one way for men to be saved. The way of salvation is through faith in the shed blood of the Lamb of God, Jesus. He died upon a cross to shed His blood that we might be saved. He is the only way to salvation! His blood is the only payment for sin. This makes it imperative that we get the message of salvation to all people. May God help us to share this message with others today. God bless and have a great day!

The Bible is the written revelation of Jesus. Consider the description in this poem. The author is unknown.

I see my Lord in the Bible
Whenever I chance to look
He is the theme of the Bible
The center and the heart of the Book
He is the rose of Sharon, He is the Lily fair
Yes, whenever I open the Bible
The Lord of the Bible is there
He, in the book's beginning gave the earth its form
He is the ark of safety to bear the brunt of the storm
The burning bush in the desert
The budding of Aaron's rod
Yes, when I open the Bible, I see the Son of God
The lamb upon Mount Moriah
The ladder from earth to sky
The smitten rock of the desert
The shepherd with staff and crook
Yes, whenever I open the Bible
I see the Lord in the Book
He is the seed of the woman
The Savior virgin-born
He is the Son of David
Whom men reject with scorn
The Lord of eternal glory
Whom John the apostle saw
The light of the celestial city
the Lamb without spot or flaw
The Bridegroom coming at midnight
For whom His people look
Yes, whenever I open The Bible
I see my Lord in the Book!

If you want to meet Jesus, you can meet Him in the pages of the Bible! God bless and have a great day!

March 28

There are some things we should never forget. As God prepared to deliver the Israelites from the bondage of Egypt, He instructed them in Ex. 12:14, *"And this day shall be unto you for a memorial; and ye shall keep it a feast to the Lord throughout your generations; ye shall keep it a feast by an ordinance for ever."* To this day, the Jewish people observe Passover every year as an eight-day festival. It is a reminder of God's deliverance of their people from Egypt. As Christians, we also have days of celebration to remind us of God's deliverance of us from our sin. We celebrate Christmas as reminder that God sent His Son, born of a virgin, to be our Savior. We celebrate Easter to remind us that though Jesus died on a cross for our sin, on the third day He arose from the dead and is alive to save us from our sin, so we can have a personal relationship with a living Savior. Memorials are important! They keep alive those things God has done for us. I would suggest that there are times in our lives we should memorialize, like the day you received Jesus as your Savior. Now I know there are some who do not know the day, and that is OK as long as you know the Savior. I know the day, the hour, and the place where I received the Lord as my Savior (April 1, 1965). I recall the day I answered the call of God to preach His Word (Jan. 25, 1966). There are some other special days such as my wedding anniversary (June 24, 1967) along with the birthdays of my wife, children and grandchildren. What are some of the days of memorial in your life? Think of them today and recall the blessings of God in your life. We cannot live in the past, but the past can encourage us for today! God bless you and have a great day!

It has been said, "God always pays, but not always on Friday." He pays in judgment for sins and disobedience, but He also pays in blessings and keeping His promises. It could be that today you wonder if your life will ever be better. You have prayed, you have sought for blessing, but still you carry a heavy burden. As I read of the deliverance of the Israelites from Egypt in Exodus 12, I am reminded that they had been in Egypt for more than 400 years — most of those years as slaves to the Egyptians. They lived without the finer things of life and served under the heavy hand of their oppressors. But **pay day** had come! After the Lord sent the death angel to every home that did not have the blood applied to the door post, Pharaoh ordered the Israelites to leave, and the Egyptians were glad to see them go. Notice verses 35-36: *"And the children of Israel did according to the word of Moses; and they borrowed of the Egyptians jewels of silver, and jewels of gold, and raiment: And the Lord gave the people favour in the sight of the Egyptians, so that they lent unto them such things as they required. And they spoiled the Egyptians."* The Israelites collected back wages for those many years of slavery. Pay day had finally come! God always rewards His people in His time and in His way. Surely we all have had times when we felt God had forgotten us. We felt enslaved to the circumstances in our lives. Just hold on; as Ps. 30:5 proclaims, *"Weeping may endure for a night, but joy cometh in the morning."* Jesus' death and His shed blood on the cross not only redeem us from the slave market of sin but assure us of His blessings upon our lives. In His time and in His way our Heavenly Father will reward us as His children. Remember, "God always pays, but not always on Friday." God bless you and have a great day!

March 30

Today is my mother's birthday. She was born in 1928. Each time I am able to visit her at this time in our lives, my thoughts go to the brevity of life. Years come and go and time seems to fly by. Even Jesus recognized the value of time. He said in John 9:4, Jesus said, *"I must work the works of him that sent me, while it is day: the night cometh, when no man can work."* In the past few years as I see my mother dealing with dementia, I have been made aware of the value of the time I have to serve the Lord. My ability to serve can end with death or with the loss of physical or mental ability. Today I give God praise for health and the ability to serve the Lord. I do not want to waste a day. I know the night is coming when I cannot work! Each of us needs to evaluate our days. How are we living the days that God has given us? We must enjoy the day and make the most of every day. I will always remember the words of my pastor to me when I was a young pastor: "Never worry about making money. You can always make more money. Worry about time; you cannot make more time." Our most precious gift is time — time to live, to love, and to serve our Savior. The Bible says in Ps. 118:24, *"This is the day which the Lord hath made; we will rejoice and be glad in it."* God bless and have a wonderful day!

"God is even interested in how you brush your teeth." This is a quote from one of my college professors. He was illustrating the love and concern that God has for us. He cares about **every** aspect of our lives. Yes, He cares when we hurt, when we have great need, and when we face difficult circumstances. But He also cares about the simplest of needs in our lives. I recall as a pastor praying for a parking place as I would be making hospital calls. Many times I was on a tight schedule and needed to park and make the calls. I knew that God is interested in the details of our lives. I was reminded of the concern of God for the details in my life as I read in Exodus 13 the instructions given to the Israelites as to their observance of the the Passover. Verse six: *"Seven days thou shalt eat unleavened bread, and in the seventh day shall be a feast to the Lord."* Today the observance of Passover is given to detail, to teach, and to remind the people of God of their deliverance from Egypt. The Passover is also a beautiful picture of our salvation and the sacrifice of the Savior for our sins. We need to include God in every aspect of our lives. Seek His plan for your daily life. I have found that if I acknowledge Him in the insignificant things of life, it is easier to include Him in the important things. In Matt. 10:29-30 Jesus said, *"Are not two sparrows sold for a farthing? and one of them shall not fall on the ground without your Father. But the very hairs of your head are all numbered."* If God cares about a sparrow falling, and if God numbers the hairs on our head, surely He cares about every aspect of our lives. That means I should include Him in every decision of my life. God bless and have a great day.

April 1

Today is April Fool's Day. On this date in 1965, Satan got fooled! It was a Thursday and I was a senior in high school. Our family attended Thomas Road Baptist church in Lynchburg, Va. The church was having a revival with evangelist Lester Roloff. When I got home from school, my mother asked if I would join the family and go to the revival with them. I was not saved and had no interest in the things of God. After much pleading from my mother, I agreed to go to the revival. It was there that I received Jesus as my Savior. I will never forget standing at my seat during the invitation wanting to go forward but fighting it. I felt the hand of my mother on my hand that was gripping the pew, and I heard her broken voice say through her tears, "If you want to go, I will go with you." I stepped out, followed by my mother, and went to a counseling room where I was led to Christ by an old deacon named Bro. Mayberry. As my mother stood behind me, I could feel her tears falling on my back as I invited Jesus into my life. **Praise God for His glorious salvation!** We should never forget the hour of our salvation. You may not recall the day nor the date, but surely you must remember the experience of receiving Jesus Christ as your Savior! The experience of receiving Christ not only changed my destiny from hell to heaven, but it changed my life. After 50-plus years, it is still **real**. Every day I walk with the Savior. I haven't always lived as I should, but I have never lived a moment without being His child. I continue to live knowing Heaven is my home! Today I give Him praise for His unspeakable gift of salvation. If you do not know Jesus as your Savior, you can receive Him today. According to Rom. 10:13, *"For whosoever shall call upon them name of the Lord shall be saved."* God bless you and have a great day!

April 2

How quickly we forget the blessings of God as we move from one trial to another in this life. The nation of Israel had just experienced a great miracle of being set free from the bondage of slavery. They left Egypt with their coffers full of its wealth, led by the presence of God which manifested itself by a *"pillar of cloud"* during the day and a *"pillar of fire"* at night (Ex. 13:21). In Exodus 14 we read about Pharaoh and his chariots pursuing the children of Israel. It is interesting to note their response as the chariots came near (v. 10-12). **They were afraid**. Verse 10: *"And when Pharaoh drew nigh, the children of Israel lifted up their eyes, and, behold, the Egyptians marched after them; and they were sore afraid ..."* **They attacked Moses.** In verse 12 the people cried to Moses, *"For it had been better for us to serve the Egyptians, than that we should die in the wilderness."* We live in a world of trouble, and our deliverance from the consequences of sin does not remove us from the pursuit of the Pharaohs of this world. It has been my experience that, in this life, we move from one spiritual or physical challenge to another. But the God who saved us from sin is big enough to part the waters of the seas for us, just as He did for the Israelites. God continuously desires to show Himself mighty to us who follow Him! I also want to warn us against blaming our trials and tribulations on others. How often I have heard church members blame the pastor for the problems in the church. This is not to say that leaders are not responsible for many unfortunate circumstances. However, God is greater than the mistakes of others. Moses had made no mistake; he was simply following the leadership of God. Yet the people blamed him for their circumstance. Trust God, even if the chariots pursue you. Do not be quick to cast blame on others for your trials. It could be that you are about to see a miracle like the parting of the Red Sea! God bless and have a great day!

Have you ever felt totally helpless and hopeless? Surely that was the way the Israelites felt as they faced the Red Sea before them and the chariots of Egypt behind them. I recall a few times in my life when, humanly speaking, I was helpless and hopeless. It was at these times that my faith was made strong. The strength of faith comes through the test and trials of life. It is when there is nothing you can do that God shows up and does for you. Notice the Lord's instruction to the people of Israel through Moses in Ex. 14:13. *"Fear ye not, stand still, and see the salvation of the Lord."* He told them to *"stand still"* and do nothing but **wait** on the Lord. Too often we want action immediately. We rush to act when God says to wait. The command to "see the salvation of the Lord" was a directive to **watch** God work. When you are standing still, the remedy that comes is undeniably from the Lord. Verse 14 begins, *"The Lord shall fight for you."* The battles of life are not ours to fight. God will fight our battles if we are in His **will** and if we **wait** on Him as we **watch** Him work. The words given to Moses in the hour of Israel's helplessness and hopelessness are appropriate for our lives today. May we examine our lives today to be sure we are where God wants us to be, in His will. If trouble comes, let's not be quick to act, but wait on the Lord! Maybe a quiet time of prayer and fasting may be the action you need to take at this time of trial in your life. Then, watch God work. Obstacles can be removed, enemies can be destroyed, with escape and victory just ahead. Simply stated, when all else fails and there is no hope nor help in sight, trust God. The God of Moses and the Israelites is our God! God bless and have a great day!

April 4

Men frequently question the awesome power of God. There are skeptics who do not believe the account of the parting of the waters of the Red Sea. One writer suggested that the place where the Israelites crossed was but a mere stream. My response to that is an even greater miracle must have occurred for the entire Egyptian army to drown in just a shallow stream. But the account of the waters parting and the people walking between the walls of water on dry ground is exactly how it happened. The chariots of the Egyptian army were stuck in the midst of the sea and the walls of water crashed down upon them, just as recorded in Ex. 14:2431. But do we believe our God is able to do great and mighty works today? Is He truly the same God who led Israel out of Egypt and parted the Red Sea, delivering the Israelites and destroying the Egyptian army? I am glad to report that He is! Remember the words of the Apostle Paul in Eph. 3:20. *"Now unto him that is able to do exceeding abundantly above all that we ask or think, according to the power that worketh in us."* We must never limit God. He might have a Red Sea experience in store for you today — a blessing of deliverance that is above all that you could ask or think. God still has the power to part the waters, if He chooses to do so. Let's look beyond our limitations to the infinite power of our God. The Bible says in Ex. 14:30, *"Thus the Lord saved Israel that day out of the hand of the Egyptians; and Israel saw the Egyptians dead upon the sea shore."* This could be your day of deliverance. God has not changed. He is still the sovereign God of the universe. God bless you and have a great day!

April 5

What do you do after God has blessed you? How should you react when God has just delivered you from a great burden or trial? Our answer can be seen in Ex. 15:1-21 in the response of Moses and the the Israelites after being delivered from Pharaoh and his army. They had just seen a miracle. The waters of the Red Sea parted, and the entire nation of Israel walked across on dry ground. They witnessed the destruction of the Egyptian army as it tried to cross the sea between the walls of water. God had blessed them; they had been delivered from their enemy. So Moses led the people in a time of praising the Lord. Verse 1: *"Then sang Moses and the children of Israel this song unto the Lord, and spake, saying, I will sing unto the Lord, for he hath triumphed gloriously: the horse and his rider hath he thrown into the sea."* In the following verses we read of singing, dancing, and the playing of instruments, all in praise to their God. All of us ought to spend more time **praising** the Lord and less time **pouting** about the disappointments of life. Look around today and see the mighty hand of God defending and providing for you. Intentionally give Him praise today for the blessing he has bestowed upon you. Follow the admonition of the old hymn, "Count your blessings, name them one by one, and it will surprise you what the Lord has done." God inhabits the praises of His people (Ps. 22:3). If you want to spend time in the **presence** of the Lord, enter into a time of **praise!** Rehearse, as Israel did, what God has done for you and give all praise and glory. God bless you today and have a great day!

April 6

The Christian experience begins with a deliverance from the slave market of sin. It continues as a journey to the place of victory and blessing. The book of Exodus illustrates our salvation in the deliverance of Israel from Egyptian slavery. It records the journey of the Israelites to the promised land, a place of blessing. The journey of the Israelites offers many lessons for us as we make our spiritual journey in this life. The promised land is not Heaven, but a picture of the place of victory and ultimate blessing for the believer in this life. (When the Israelites entered the promised land, there were still conflicts and battles. There are **none** in Heaven.) The Apostle Paul declared in I Cor. 10:11 about the Old Testament, *"Now all these things happened unto them for ensamples: and they are written for our admonition, upon whom the ends of the world are come."* The Bible says in II Tim. 3:16, *"All scripture is given by inspiration of God, and is profitable for doctrine, for reproof, for correction, for instruction in righteousness."* There is much to learn from the pages of the Old Testament and the characters and circumstances described in its pages. Look at the latter part of Exodus 15. The children of Israel were just three days into their journey and they had found no water. When they finally found water, it was bitter and they could not drink it. But God told Moses to cast a certain tree into the water and it became sweet. It is important to learn that the Christian journey is a bittersweet experience. God can take the bitter waters of Marah in our lives and turn them sweet. Today I challenge you to search the Scriptures and learn of the awesome power of our God. God bless and have a great day!

April 7

God is a God of balance — He balances the hard times with the good times. We often view life from only the bitter times and overlook the the sweet and blessed times in our lives. The Israelites' first stop for water was at Marah. The bitter water was made sweet by Moses' obedience to the Lord in casting a tree into the water (Ex. 15:23-26). The second station in their journey was a place called Elim. Verse 27: *"And they came to Elim, where were twelve wells of water, and threescore and ten palm trees: and they encamped there by the waters."* As I read this verse I was reminded of the Elim Home for Alcoholics, a ministry of Thomas Road Baptist Church in Lynchburg, Va. This was a place where those in the "desert" of a life of addiction could find an oasis of help. Have you ever noticed how God places the "Elims" in our lives? As we travel this spiritual journey, there are times and places of refreshing along the way. Thank God for the spiritual oases that are provided for us. There are also those oases along life's way that are times and places of physical refreshing for us. Be on the lookout for places of spiritual refreshing or physical rest. They are very necessary in our lives. My wife finds the seashore an oasis for her. I find the quiet resting in my chair to be an oasis for me. Spiritually, I find these early morning times with the Lord to be times of refreshing in my life. We all need "Elims" in our lives to remind us of the goodness and the graciousness of our God. God bless you and have a great day!

April 8

As I think about the deliverance of the Israelites from Egypt and their journey to the promised land, I am reminded of the words of Heb. 11:6. *"But without faith it is impossible to please him: for he that cometh to God must believe that he is, and that he is a rewarder of them that diligently seek him."* As I look at the events in the life of the nation of Israel, I can see how God was teaching His people to trust Him— first for deliverance from the Egyptians as they walked through the Red Sea, and then after one month of traveling, they were to trust God for their daily food. In Exodus 16 God promised to provide "manna" from heaven each morning. It is worth noting that the manna was only good for the day, so they had to trust God for their "daily" bread. The Bible says in Ex. 16:4, *"Then said the Lord unto Moses, Behold, I will rain bread from heaven for you; and the people shall go out and gather a certain rate every day, that I may prove them, whether they will walk in my law, or no."* God often allows **need** to come to our life to teach us to trust Him. How could I ever know that He was the God of all supply if I never had a need greater than my ability? My life has been a walk of faith. From having to trust God to meet the medical expenses for our son, Paul, to trusting God for churches to speak at, to believing God for strength to continue in ministry in my later years. However, I do not complain! Every morning, there has been manna sufficient for the day. Look beyond your need today and see God's provision for your daily need. He still sends manna to His children daily. It may not come in the form of a wafer that tastes like honey, but it is still from the hand of God — who, according to Phil. 4:19, *"shall supply all your need according to His riches in glory by Christ Jesus."* God bless and have a great day!

God designed our bodies to need a time of rest. Even as the Israelites made their journey to the promised land, God instructed them to gather enough manna on the sixth day of the week for two days that they might rest on the Sabbath. Read Ex. 16:23. *"And he said unto them, This is that which the Lord hath said, To morrow is the rest of the holy sabbath unto the Lord: bake that which ye will bake to day, and seethe that ye will seethe; and that which remaineth over lay up for you to be kept until the morning."* I believe the **principle** of the Sabbath still applies for us today — that we are to set aside a portion of our time to worship the Lord, and that we need to have a time of rest for our bodies. The day we set aside to worship is Sunday, the first day of the week. We worship on Sunday because Jesus rose from the grave on the first day of the week (Luke 24:1-6). It would seem obvious that the early church met on the first day of the week from Paul's instruction to the church in Corinth in I Cor. 6:2. *"Upon the first day of the week let every one of you lay by him in store, as God hath prospered him, that there be no gathering when I come."* We need to spend intentional time worshipping the Lord. We also need to have some down time from the pressures of the week. My challenge for us today is that we honor God with our time. We do that when we set aside time to worship Him. All of us need a time to rest and meditate upon the things of God. May God help each of us this Sunday to dedicate the day to the Lord. It would be good if we could rest and reflect on the goodness of our God. God bless and have a great day.

April 10

God's blessings come from a variety of places and in many ways. As I was reading Exodus 17 and the account of God providing water for Israel from a rock, I was reminded how God had turned bitter water sweet in Exodus 15. I also recounted Israel journeying to Elim where there were 12 wells of water. Every time there was a need, God provided — always on time, but not always from the same place. I have found this to be true in my life. God's provision often comes in the most unexpected ways and from the most unexpected places. My thought for today is that we continuously look for God's hand of provision in our lives. As I travel and speak in churches, I have seen God's hand of provision in my life and for our ministry. This often comes from unusual and unexpected places. God has provided for our ministry through generous offerings sent from various people, such as a member of the military, a retired couple and their daughter, or a Godly lady who is battling cancer. I could go on and on. God can still bring water from the rock and provide for our every need. Maybe He supplies through employment or through investments. But we should remember that **all** we have comes from God. Our health and our wealth come from Him. When God meets a need in an unexpected way, He does so to build our faith. God wants us to trust Him — to look beyond our needs and see His awesome power to turn bitter water sweet, to lead us to twelve wells of water, or to send water from a rock. Oh, thank God for His ample provisions of life and ministry! God bless and have a great day!

Sometimes our words do not convey what we really mean. I recall some years after my father died, as my mother and I were driving along, I asked her, "How long did it take you to get over the death of Dad?" Her response was eye-opening: "I don't know. He hasn't been gone that long." It was Good Friday — April 9, 2004 — when our son, Paul, went home to be with the Lord. It was the day after Easter when we laid his body to rest. More than a decade has passed, but he is still missed. I learned that that you never get over the death of a child; you just get through it! Easter is always a bittersweet time of the year for our family. We recall the death of our son, but also recognize the hope of the Resurrection. As the Son of God rose from the dead the third day, we live with a certain hope that one day those who have gone before us and knew Christ as Savior, will be raised from the dead, and we will be with them throughout eternity. We see in I Thess. 4:13-18 a threefold hope: **The hope of the Resurrection.** Verse 16 ends with the phrase, *"and the dead in Christ shall rise first."* **The hope of the Rapture.** Verse 17 begins, *"Then we which are alive and remain shall be caught up together with them in the clouds, to meet the Lord in the air ..."* The word "rapture" is not mentioned, that is promised in this verse. **The hope of a reunion.** That's what the phrase *"caught up together with them"* promises us, and it's a hope we can cling to. Note also verse 18: *"Wherefore comfort one another with these words."* The bodily resurrection of Jesus is the foundation of our salvation and also provides all of us with a hope of a reunion with those who have gone before us. Thank God we can get through the suffering of the loss of a loved one because of the hope of the Resurrection! God bless and have a blessed day!

April 12

God's work must be done God's way and with God's power. Those who endeavor to serve must recognize their limitations. There are times when assistance from others is a must if the servant is to succeed. God's plan often involves a variety of people doing various things. The first conflict of the Israelites with another group of people is recorded in Ex. 17:8-16. The Amalekites came up against them and Joshua led an army to defend the people. Verse 9: *"And Moses said unto Joshua, Choose us out men, and go out, fight with Amalek: to morrow I will stand on the top of the hill with the rod of God in mine hand."* In verse 11 we are told that as long as Moses held up his hand the army of Israel prevailed. When his hand fell, they were overcome by the enemy. Along with Moses on the hill were Aaron and Hur, who help up his hands when he grew weary so that the army of Israel might prevail (v. 12-13). There is work for all of us to do. Some can lead an army; some can fight in the army; some can hold their hands up (in prayer); and some hold up the hands of another. The challenge for us is to find our place in the work of God. It takes all of us doing our part for us to win the battle against our adversary, the Devil. We cannot and must not try to go it alone! We need each other! We need the Joshuas, we need the soldiers, we need Godly leaders like Moses, and we need those who will hold up the hands of others, as Aaron and Hur, so that victory may come in our lives. God bless you today and have a great day.

He is alive! Yes, Jesus is alive! His resurrection was a literal bodily resurrection! To deny the bodily resurrection of Jesus is to deny the veracity of the Scriptures and bring into question if there is salvation for any sinner. The Apostle Paul, under the inspiration of the Holy Spirit wrote clearly in I Cor. 15:17, *"And if Christ be not raised, your faith is vain; ye are yet in your sins."* As a matter of fact, that entire chapter is devoted to the defense of the bodily resurrection of Jesus. I challenge you to read this chapter today. It will encourage you and reassure you that our Savior lives. Because He is alive, I can talk to Him today. I know He hears me and is able to help me through every problem of life. The Christian faith is not a religion; it is a relationship with a living, loving Savior who died for my sins, but was raised from the dead and is alive today, to not only be my Savior, but to be a friend that will stick closer than a brother. This Easter season may we not just sing about the resurrected Christ and just listen to the Biblical account of the empty tomb, but may we truly acknowledge that He is alive! Speak to Him today; this we call prayer. Allow Him to speak to you; He does not speak with an audible voice, but through His Word, the Bible! What a joy to have and know a living Savior! God bless and have a great day!

April 14

For many people, Easter is just another holiday. Many do not know the significance of Good Friday. There are differing views as to the day that Jesus died, Wednesday or Friday, but there is no debate that He was raised from the dead on Sunday. The Gospel is clear that it was on the first day of the week that the tomb was empty (Matt. 28:1; Luke 24:1-5). The first day of the week is Sunday. Every Sunday is a reminder of the resurrection of our Savior. We worship on Sunday because it was the day Jesus rose from the dead. My thought for today is that we should celebrate the Resurrection every week, every Sunday. The significance of the Resurrection can never be over emphasized. It is the foundation of our salvation — the hope we have to live beyond this life. Our son, Paul, died 13 years ago on Good Friday. I recall placing my arms around my wife and daughter and through my tears I uttered to them, "It is Friday, but Sunday is coming." Those words are the title of a sermon that I had heard preached, and truer words have never been spoken. Because Jesus conquered death, hell, and the grave, we have hope for the resurrection of those that have gone before us. Yes, Jesus died, but He arose from the dead and ever lives to give us an eternal salvation and the blessed hope of resurrection. God bless you today.

April 15

As I think about this Easter season, my mind goes to that Saturday more than 2,000 years ago. Jesus has been crucified, His body is in the tomb, and His death had become a reality in the hearts and minds of His followers. I can only imagine the sadness and gloom in their lives at that hour. Yes, Jesus had told them of His resurrection, but How, When, Will it really happen? These must have been the questions in their minds and hearts. But in the words of the gospel song, "then came the morning." As Ps. 30:5 states, *"Weeping may endure for a night, but joy cometh in the morning."* Yes, on that third day (Sunday), their darkness was turned to day! Jesus rose from the dead and was, and **is,** alive! My thought for us today is twofold; first, Jesus is alive today! Secondly, there are times in our lives when the darkest hour is just before the dawn. We must not lose hope; joy comes in the morning of our lives. What seems hopeless today can become a blessing tomorrow. Jesus lives to be our Savior, but also is to be our strength for the night times of our lives. He brings hope; He brings help; and ultimately, He brings Heaven! So, you see, joy does come in the morning! Easter surely declares we have a Savior. He is described in Rom. 4:25, *"Who was delivered for our offences, and was raised again for our justification."* We also have One who goes along beside us to help us through the dark hours of our life. He has promised that joy comes in the morning! God bless and have a great day!

April 16

Each year at Easter, I try to emphasize the fact that Jesus was **bodily** raised from the dead. There have been those who proposed that His resurrection was only a "spiritual awakening" in the minds of His followers. I read a study by Charles Pope (whom I do not know) where he listed 12 appearances of the resurrected Christ recorded in the Word of God. To deny the bodily resurrection of Christ is to deny the veracity or truth of the scriptures. Upon the authority of the Word of God, I declare our Savior, Jesus, **is alive!** The Apostle Paul gives a sample statement of those who saw the resurrected Christ in I Cor. 15:4-7. *"And that he was buried, and that he rose again the third day according to the scriptures: And that he was seen of Cephas, then of the twelve: After that, he was seen of above five hundred brethren at once ... After that, he was seen of James; then of all the apostles."* There were several appearances of the resurrected Christ to Mary and other women recorded in the Gospels — enough to say He is risen from the dead. (By the way, I know He lives today, because I just talked to Him this morning.) As you make your way to church this week, please remember that **He is alive.** He is truly **risen from the dead.** The significance of His bodily resurrection is not only to prove the accuracy of Scripture, but to give us hope of our own resurrection and the resurrection of those who have gone before us. Beyond all of this, the resurrection of Christ ensures us of a living Savior to guide and provide for us in this life. Raise your voice and your hands today in praise! We have a living Savior that died for our sins, was buried, but was raised from the dead and is alive today. God bless you and have a blessed Easter!

April 17

It is important that our testimony is known. The first five verses of Exodus 18 describe how Jethro brought his daughter Zipporah (Moses' wife) and their two children to Moses after he had sent them to stay with Jethro for a while. Verse 1: *"When Jethro, the priest of Midian, Moses' father in law, heard of all that God had done for Moses, and for Israel his people, and that the Lord had brought Israel out of Egypt ..."* Word of the blessings of God had reached Jethro in Midian. I am afraid that too often our lives do not reflect God's blessing to others. Either we are not living for the Lord, so we have no testimony, or we have not shared God's blessing in our lives with others. The Bible says in Ps. 107:2, *"Let the redeemed of the Lord say so, whom He hath redeemed from the land of the enemy."* Recently after I spoke in a church service, the pastor asked if there were any praises from the people before we dismissed. There were several who shared the blessings they had received from the Lord. As I listened to how God had blessed those who spoke, I found myself encouraged and blessed. My challenge to all of us is that we live in the will of God, allow His blessings to speak for themselves and be willing to share the news of those blessings in our lives, when given the opportunity. The one thing doubters and unbelievers cannot refute is what God has done in our lives. There should be no stronger witness for the Lord than our testimonies of the goodness and greatness of the Lord. If you are redeemed today, then, say so! God bless and have a great day!

April 18

Know your limits! Don't try to do everything yourself. I have always disliked the term "burnout." However, we all need to recognize we cannot do but so much before we begin to wear out. Consider Jethro's advice in Exodus 18 to Moses, who was trying to give counsel to all of the people. Verse 14: *"And when Moses' father in law saw all that he did to the people, he said, What is this thing that thou doest to the people? why sittest thou thyself alone, and all the people stand by thee from morning unto even?"* Verse 18: *"Thou wilt surely wear away, both thou, and this people that is with thee: for this thing is too heavy for thee; thou art not able to perform it thyself alone."* The subsequent verses show how Moses heeded Jethro's advice and delegated numerous duties to other men. The work of God requires a human leader and many servants. I have been in the place of leadership and I can testify that the burden of being a pastor requires the assistance of others. I have also been in the position of a servant and had a portion of responsibility delegated to me by a leader of a ministry. Both positions are necessary for the work of God to go forward. If you are in a place of leadership, delegate to others some of your responsibilities. If possible, maybe some of us can be available to lift the load from our leader, our pastor. Remember, your pastor is but one man. He can only do so much. You could be a helping hand to him to lighten his load and prolong his ministry. God bless you and have a blessed day.

April 19

God has a plan for your life. You are where you are in life to fulfill God's purpose. It had been three months since Israel left Egypt. They had experienced deliverance from slavery and from the armies of the pharaoh at the parting of the Red Sea. God was feeding them with manna from heaven and had given them a great military victory over the Amalakites. The people had seen God turn a bitter water source sweet and create another water source from a rock. All of this happened for God to bring them to Mt. Sinai, where He would give them His law to direct their lives. It is interesting to note that, according to one commentator, there are 57 chapters in the Bible dedicated to this Sinai experience of Israel. Surely we can conclude that God is interested in how we live. According to Ex. 19:1, *"In the third month, when the children of Israel were gone forth out of the land of Egypt, the same day came they into their wilderness of Sinai."* It was here that God gave His law to Moses to give to the people. Though we be under grace and not the law, God still has a plan for our lives and we are to fulfill His purpose. God's character has not changed. As Christians we are to live according to God's standards and for His glory. Our desires must be His desires. Our responses to the world and all of its glitter must be His response. The Ten Commandments are still just that — commandments, not suggestions that change with the culture. May God help each of us to live according to His plan and His purpose for our lives! God bless you and have a great day!

April 20

There are so many preachers with differing messages. How do you know which one to believe? God is not the author of confusion. When He led Moses and the Israelites in the wilderness, there was no question that the people heard Him when He spoke. According to Ex. 19:9, *"And the Lord said unto Moses, Lo, I come unto thee in a thick cloud, that the people may hear when I speak with thee, and believe thee for ever. And Moses told the words of the people unto the Lord."* Today, we have no cloud and we cannot audibly hear the voice of God. So how do we know the messages we hear are from God? In Exodus God was establishing His covenant with His people concerning worship, sacrifice and their obedience to Him. Today in His Word we have the written instructions as to how we are to worship, how to receive the **one and only** sacrifice for our sins, and instructions on how to live. Though we certainly respect and appreciate those God has called to teach and preach the Bible, we must judge their words from the Book ourselves. The test of the message is not the messenger; it is the Bible, God's Holy Word. As certain as the cloud was on those days at Sinai, and as clear as God's voice was that day, so is the Word of God for us today. All believers should be students of the Bible, reading and studying it for their own edification and knowledge. Then, as we hear those who are called to teach and preach, we will know if their message comes from God. I am not suggesting we become every preacher's critic, but we need to guard ourselves from false doctrine. Thank God for those who teach the Word. Surely we appreciate those preachers who are true to the Scriptures, but we must listen carefully to the Holy Spirit and know the Scriptures so we aren't drawn into false teachings. God bless you and have a great day!

April 21

Should we spend time studying the Old Testament? Is there any merit in the law for us today? Are these devotions from Exodus relevant for this age of grace? I would remind us of the words of the Apostle Paul in II Tim. 3:16-17 to his preacher boy, Timothy: *"All scripture is given by inspiration of God, and is profitable for doctoring, for reproof, for correction, for instruction in righteousness: That the man of God may be perfect, throughly furnished unto all good works."* Now I believe "all" means **all.** However, to challenge us to be students of the entire Bible, I will share with you the exhortations from the New Testament as to why we should study the Old Testament. First, we are told that Old Testament things are useful for our learning. I Cor. 10:11 says, *"Now all these things happened unto them for examples: and they are written for our admonition, upon whom the ends of the world are come."* Lessons of spiritual living and the character of God can be gleaned from the Old Testament. Though the Law has no saving power, it is said in Gal. 3:24 by the Apostle Paul, *"Wherefore the law was our schoolmaster to bring us unto Christ, that we might be justified by faith."* The character of God, His holiness, His grace, and His power to provide for His people serve as an encouragement to me, for God has not changed. Rom. 15:4 declares, *"For whatsoever things were written aforetime were written for our learning, that we through patience and comfort of the scriptures might have hope."* Today we are free from the law. We are saved by grace, live by grace, and will be given dying grace. However, there is much to learn about God and His working in the life of Old testament characters. God's principles have not changed. Let us be students of the entire Bible! God bless you and have a blessed day!

April 22

As I traveled to Virginia a few months ago for a four-day revival, I was reminded that there are not many churches having extended meetings these days. When I recall the one and two-week revivals of the past, I miss the excitement and blessing of seeing God work in the lives of the saints and the altars filled with sinners coming to receive Christ as Savior. As a matter of fact, just a few miles from the recent meetings is a church where I held a revival in the late 1970s which God blessed with many coming to know the Savior. I would like to ask you to pray for the Lord to save souls in the meetings where I am privileged to speak in the coming weeks and months. Pray also that God would speak to the hearts of the believers who attend. My cry to the Lord today is from Ps. 85:6. *"Wilt thou not revive us again: that thy people may rejoice in thee?"* We need to pray for revival across our land! We need the people of God to experience a spiritual awakening. We need a return to the God of the Bible. We need for God to revive our hearts with a passion for the souls of men. We occasionally see a moving of God that reminds us of His desire to bless His people and that He still saves those that will come to Him with repentance and by faith. Oh, that we could see a great moving of God again in our churches across our land! God bless you today, and I covet your prayers for our ministry.

April 23

My God is my **defender** and **protector!** We all seek safety and security. We all should be grateful for law enforcement and our military that seek to protect us and provide safety and security for us. But the ultimate Provider for our protection is the God of Heaven. Yes, He uses the men and women in the military and law enforcement, but there are many dangers that go beyond the scope of these that threaten us. There is disease, there are the attacks on our character, there are accidents, and there are many other evils that threaten us — not the least of which is the attack of Satan in our lives. There are a host of verses in the Bible that remind us that God is our protector. One good example is Ps. 34:19. *"Many are the afflictions of the righteous: but the Lord delivereth him out of them all."* Then, there is my favorite, Ps. 46:1. *"God is our refuge and strength, a very present help in trouble."* These are but a sample of the many promises in the Bible of the protection that God promises for His people. I was reminded again of the protection of God as I read Ex. 19:4, in which God said to Moses, *"Ye have seen what I did unto the Egyptians, and how I bare you on eagles' wings, and brought you unto myself."* An eagle will carry its young on its back, not in its claws or beak. It is reported by some commentators that this practice of the eagle is a picture of a place of safety for the young eagles. My God has carried me through many tough situations on His back. As that old hymn says:

> *Through many dangers, toils, and snares,*
> *I have already come.*
> *'Tis grace that brought me safe thus far,*
> *And grace will lead me home.*

Thus, I can face today and tomorrow free from fear. My God is with me and will protect me! God bless you and rest safely in the hands of Jesus today.

April 24

The late evangelist Lester Roloff said, "Tell me what you most often think about, what dominates your conversation, and I will tell you who or what is your God." This maybe a simplistic statement, but there is some truth to be gleaned from it. One summer Sunday I heard a pastor say, "Well, as I was coming to church this morning, I met several people headed for the lake with their God hitched to their vehicle." Again, this may be a bit judgmental, but many of us have "things" we place in priority before the things of God. The Ten Commandments are recorded in Exodus 20. The first two of those commandments are instructions concerning the Israelites' worship of their God. Verse 3: *"Thou shalt have no other gods before me."* Verse 4: *"Thou shalt not make unto thee any graven image, or any likeness of any thing that is in heaven above, or that is in the earth beneath, or that is in the water under the earth."* Does God have **first** place in our lives? Does our private and public worship of God really take priority in our lives? Do we spend time daily with the Lord? Do we place a priority on attending church to **worship?** God has not changed; He still desires the worship of His people. My challenge for us today is that we do not cease from spending time with the Lord. Take time to read His Word, to pray, and to give Him praise for all that He has done and all He is doing in our lives. God bless you and have a great day!

April 25

The third of the Ten Commandments, found in Ex. 20:7, says, *"Thou shalt not take the name of the Lord thy God in vain; for the Lord will not hold him guiltless that taketh his name in vain."* This commandment goes beyond using God's name as a swear word. It means that we are not to dishonor His name. We often dishonor the name of our God by the way we live. We profess to know Jesus as Savior but live in such a way as to bring reproach upon His name. We call ourselves Christians but do not live up to our name. We are taking the name of the Lord in vain. Thank God for His grace that covers my failures and stays the hand of judgment of a holy God. As a Christian, I want to be like the Jesus that the name "Christian" implies. I do not want to dishonor His name. My challenge for today is simply that we not only call ourselves Christian, but we live, we respond, and we love like the name Christian suggests. We need to live like Jesus, love like Jesus, and look like Jesus. Looking like Jesus is not about how you dress, but your countenance. There are people whose facial expressions alone announce that they are Christians. Their conversation announces their love for the Savior. If I am to call myself "Christian," I do not want to take that name in vain. My prayer today is that others may see Jesus in you and in me. God bless and have a great day.

April 26

The words of the Apostle Paul in II Thess. 3:10 are rarely spoken from the pulpits of today. *"For even when we were with you, this we commanded you, that if any would not work, neither should he eat."* God has always put a premium on **work.** I hasten to add that if there are those who cannot work, we that are able are to take care of them. The problem today is there are many who choose not to work. They have an attitude of entitlement. The emphasis placed upon the fourth commandment in Ex. 20:8 is that we are to set aside a day to **worship.** *"Remember the sabbath day, to keep it holy."* For those under the law, this day was Saturday. For the church I believe it is Sunday, as a reminder of the resurrection of the Savior. However, this commandment goes beyond worship. Read the next verse. *"Six days shalt thou labour, and do all thy work ..."* I remember hearing my dad and my grandparents say, "Work never killed anyone." I would suggest that living with purpose and a healthy attitude toward work, will extend a person's life. Yes, we must set aside time to worship, but we also need to be busy the other six days of the week working to provide for our living and for our families. The one thing we cannot create for ourselves is time. Remember the words of Jesus in John 9:4. *"I must work the works of him that sent me, while it is day: the night cometh, when no man can work."* If Jesus was concerned about doing the work that He had been given to do by the Father, should we not be concerned that we also be found busy about our Father's business? God bless you and have a great day!

It has been said in the past, "If you want to see what's wrong with the youth of today, maybe we who are parents should look in the mirror." There was a day when this statement was really true, but today social media and the entertainment world have replaced so much of that influence in the lives of our youth. Many young people are choosing lifestyles contrary to the teaching of their parents. This is not to say that many parents haven't forsaken Biblical methods of raising their children. Family devotions are neglected, church attendance is optional, modest dress is viewed as old-fashioned, and parental examples of Godly living has given way to career seeking or personal ambitions. I was blessed to have parents that instilled in me such virtues as a good work ethic, a love for God, and faithfulness to His church. In recent years I have often visited my mom in a memory facility. She would not remember that I was there, but I remember that I was there. She was the one who prayed that I would be a preacher as she rocked me as baby. She never told me of her prayers until the night I called and told her I felt God was calling me into the ministry. It was my dad who imparted wisdom to me about work and family and just how to deal with the ups and downs of life. Today I devote this space to my parents. I am grateful to them for loving and teaching me. I thank the Lord for them. I seek to obey the fifth commandment as expressed in Ex. 20:12. *"Honour thy father and thy mother: that thy days may be long upon the land which the Lord thy God giveth thee."* My challenge to all of us is that we do not neglect our parents. Visit them, pray for them, be sure they are well taken care of, and recognize their investment in your life. Parents, be the parent that influences your children to live for Jesus. God bless you and have a great day!

April 28

As I prepare to participate in a National Center for Life and Liberty seminar, as I do several times each year, I am reminded that Christians are being persecuted around the world and that the Lord's church is under attack even in the United States of America. There are those who think we should keep our message within the walls of our church buildings. Biblical principles of morality are perceived as being a threat to the rights of others. We must be diligent to stand for our faith and the First Amendment of our Constitution that protects our right of religious liberty. I am proud to be a part of NCLL and help defend religious liberty. My challenge for today is that ALL believers might join together in **prayer** and **participation** in defending our religious liberties. Our verse for today is II Chr. 7:14. *"If my people, which are called by my name, shall humble themselves, and pray, and seek my face, and turn from their wicked ways; then will I hear from heaven, and will forgive their sin, and will heal their land."* God bless you today and please pray for us as we lead these seminars throughout the year. Thank you and have a great day!

April 29

"Times have changed." This is the theme of much of what attorney David Gibbs III addresses in his seminars to pastors and Christian leaders. We certainly live in a different America than I grew up in. One of the major changes has been our view of life. We hear much today about the quality of life. It has been this argument that has fueled people's attitudes about abortion and euthanasia. Recently as I listened to Gibbs speak in a church in Kentucky, my eye caught a mother and father with their special-needs son in the service. The son was physically and mentally challenged. As I watched this family, I thought about how in the minds of the world, this child has no quality of life. Since my wife and I had a special-needs son, the sight of this family struck a note of compassion in my heart. I was reminded how much we loved our son and how precious his life was to us. You see, as Gibbs presented the argument so eloquently, it is not the quality of life; it is the sanctity of life. God is the giver of life, and He alone should be the taker of life. My thought for today is a reminder that God commanded us in Ex. 20:13, *"Thou shalt not kill."* Thou shall not kill the elderly! Thou shall not kill in the womb! Thou shall not kill the physically and mentally challenged! Thou shall not kill because you have determined there is no quality of life! Life is holy in the eyes of the God who created life. The created has no right to tell the Creator that the life He created should end. Sad to say, this is not the philosophy of many today. Yes, times have changed, but God has not changed, and He says, *"Thou shalt not kill."* God bless and have a great day!

April 30

"Marriage is to be between one man and one woman as they were at birth." This is the recommended language for churches' constitutions and bylaws. God has much to say about the sanctity of marriage. Wedding vows are holy before the Lord. Quoting from the Associated Press, according to the Journal of Marital and Family Therapy, 41 percent of spouses admit to infidelity, either physical or emotional. That statistic was taken from an article written by Lisa Haisha in the Huffington Post. The accuracy of the article could be debated, but the reality of the problem of marital fidelity is certainly prevalent in today's society. Some suggest that maybe we should change the mores or moral values of today to fit this seeming epidemic of adultery. I would suggest and declare that the commandments of the Lord have **not** changed. *"Thou shalt not commit adultery"* (Ex. 20:14) is still the law of God. Guard your relationships with your spouse. Spending time together, remaining friends, and continuing to build your relationship with your spouse are necessary steps in protecting your marriage. Remaining in love demands effort. The marriage that is strong with both parties faithful is a marriage that has been built with intention. The one important foundation stone of a good marriage is to keep God in the center of your marriage. Pray together, worship together, and acknowledge His presence in your relationship. Satan desires to destroy marriages, and he uses adultery as his tool to breakup God-sanctified homes. Build a hedge around your marriage today and guard yourself from the temptations of the flesh. God bless and have a great day.

We have had our home broken into on two occasions. The feeling of having our goods taken from us by a thief is a horrible feeling. You work hard to get the things you have and then someone comes along and takes them from you. The eighth commandment in Ex. 20:15 simply states, *"Thou shall not steal."* This commandment implies the right of ownership of property and the sin of taking from others what is not yours. It is my opinion that many times we are guilty of breaking this commandment and do not realize we have stolen from others. For instance, when publishing this book, I was always careful not to steal another person's intellectual property and present it as my own. In other words, I cannot use information that is not my own without giving credit to my source. We often steal another's good name by slander. The good name someone has worked to obtain can be stolen away with the accusations of others. Yes, the most obvious theft is the taking of physical properties that belong to another, but let us be careful of taking the character or the efforts of others from them. We should labor for what we have and respect the properties, the person, and the products produced by others. Sometimes we are guilty of minimizing some of the Ten Commandments. However, all of them carry equal value and importance in the eyes of the Lord. They are all to be obeyed and honored. May our lives be lived to reflect an attitude of obedience and the character of our Savior. God bless and have a great day!

May 2

I am reminded every week that I am on the road in churches around the country of how much God has blessed me. I am humbled by the opportunities granted me to preach His Word. A great responsibility has been granted me to present the Gospel and the need for all of us to be diligent to defend our religious liberties. There are those in our society today who would lead others to believe that Christians are the purveyors of hate and intolerance. The truth is, Christians are the proclaimers of truth, and though we may hate sin, we love the sinner. If we are truly to be like Jesus, we must love people where they are and seek to help them become better. The lie of the world is that Christians reject those that do not agree with them. We may reject their actions or teachings, but we value every person. We must be careful with regard to what we say about people. It is so easy to communicate wrong information about others. The ninth commandment in Ex. 20:16 warns us, *"Thou shalt not bear false witness against thy neighbour."* This verse is certainly a warning against lying, but it also is a warning against leading others to believe something about someone that is not true. Insinuations are are sin; passing along gossip is sin; and outright falsehoods are sin. Christians are the victims of being falsely represented by many in our society today, but I fear many believers are guilty of doing the same against others as well. May we remember, "Be careful little mouth what you say." God bless you and have a great day!

Ralph Waldo Emerson wrote, "Sow a thought and you reap an action; sow an act and you reap a habit; sow a habit and you reap a character; sow a character and you reap a destiny." It all begins with a thought. The Bible says in Prov. 23:7, *"For as he thinketh in his heart, so is he."* The last of the Ten Commandments, found in Ex. 20:17, has to do with how we think. *"Thou shalt not covet thy neighbour's house, thou shalt not covet thy neighbour's wife, nor his manservant, nor his maidservant, nor his ox, nor his ass, nor any thing that is thy neighbour's."* The other commandments deal with our relationship to God and how we are to treat our fellow man. This last commandment warns of a covetous thought life. Before there is a murder or a theft, there is an inner attitude or a thought that paves the way for the action. Therefore, we must guard our thoughts, and the best way to do that is to fill our minds with the Word of God. Phil. 4:8 exhorts us, *"Finally, brethren, whatsoever things are true, whatsoever things are honest, whatsoever things are just, whatsoever things are pure, whatsoever things are lovely, whatsoever things are of good report; if there be any virtue, and if there be any praise, think on these things."* My challenge for us today is that we guard our thoughts and fill our minds with the Word of God so that it will filter our thoughts. If we **think** right, we will **act** right. God is interested in our thought life as well as our actions. If you look back at Phil. 4:8 and study the description of things we are to *"think on,"* you will find a good description of the Bible. May we fill our minds with the Word of God and allow the Bible to govern our thoughts. God bless and have a great day.

May 4

In my opinion, many people do not have a reverential fear of God. His holiness is not respected. He is "The Man Upstairs" and we take Him casually with no thought of His holiness. This was not the case with the Israelites after they had received the Ten Commandments. Ex. 20:18-21 describes the response of the people to the awesome display of the presence of God. *"And all the people saw the thunderings, and the lightnings, and the noise of the trumpet, and the mountain smoking: and when the people saw it, they removed, and stood afar off. And they said unto Moses, Speak thou with us, and we will hear: but let not God speak with us, lest we die. And Moses said unto the people, Fear not: for God is come to prove you, and that his fear may be before your faces, that ye sin not. And the people stood afar off, and Moses drew near unto the thick darkness where God was."* There are times when we should worship God with a spirit of reverence. God is holy and we who are so sinful need to approach Him humbly and reverently. His power is seen in His creation. His grace is seen in His provision of our salvation through the death of Jesus on the cross. His compassion is manifested to us daily. He truly is an awesome God. Let us bow down today and praise Him for His greatness. Let us reverently approach Him in all His holiness and power. Truly, He is God of all Gods and Lord of all. God bless and have a great day!

May 5

A slave for life. That is how the Apostle Paul identified himself in Rom. 1:1. *"Paul, a servant* [bond slave] *of Jesus Christ ..."* A bond slave was a servant who chose to be the slave of his master for life. We read of this practice being established in Ex. 21:6. *"Then his master shall bring him unto the judges; he shall also bring him to the door, or unto the door post; and his master shall bore his ear through with an aul; and he shall serve him for ever."* I once developed a message from this passage titled "Pierced Ears." Every believer is to have spiritual pierced ears! God desires that we be His bond slaves — His servants for life. Each of us needs to make an intentional declaration of our commitment to be God's bond slave. I recall the day and the hour I trusted the Lord as my Savior. I also recall the day and the hour I committed my life to be His servant for life. Some make the decisions of salvation and service at the same time. Others, like me, make a conscious decision to serve the Lord to be a lifelong endeavor. In other words, I have pierced ears (spiritually speaking; I do not have my physical ears pierced). Who is the master of your life? Who do you serve? Do you serve **self** and not the **Savior?** Do you live for the things of **creation** rather than for the **Creator?** Do you have spiritually pierced ears as a declaration of your commitment to the Lord? Is Jesus the master of your life? Only you can answer these questions. I can tell you from experience that Jesus is a kind, forgiving, and gracious Master. I choose to serve no other. God bless you and have a great day!

May 6

The pains and sufferings of this life seem to never end. I remember hearing my pastor say, "For every mountaintop experience, there are two valleys." Nothing seems to hurt more or be any greater burden than watching the suffering of your child or grandchild. For 26 years, Doris and I watched the suffering of our son, Paul. He had a brain tumor that left him physically and mentally challenged. Now we are called to witness the suffering of our granddaughter with auto immune disorders that are raging in her body at this time. The feeling of helplessness is almost unbearable for the parents and, yes, the grandparents. Where do you go in these moments? Is there help? Is there hope? I praise my God that there is help and hope in His promises given to us in His Word. The words of I Pet. 5:7 encourage me in these times. *"Casting all your care upon Him; for He careth for you."* The night I trusted the Lord to save me, He gave me a verse that has been my anchor through the storms of my life. That verse is I Cor. 10:13. *"There hath no temptation taken you but such as is common to man: but God is faithful, who will not suffer you to be tempted above that ye are able; but will with the temptation also make a way to escape, that ye may be able to bear it."* Never in a million years would I have realized just how much this verse would define my need through my life. This verse reminds us that troubles are common to all men. You may be sitting beside the bed of a dying spouse or loved one. Some may be facing what seem to be impossible financial challenges. The truth is that all of us experience troubles in this life. God is aware of every test in our lives! He is faithful and never leaves us without help and hope. We can trust Him in the midst of our suffering and sorrow. God will make a way through every trial and storm of life. God bless and have a blessed day.

Where is that special place of worship for you? I am not talking about a church, but a place for personal worship — where you meet God and fellowship with Him. I would call this place your altar. It is interesting to note how often God asked His people to construct an altar. So it is in Ex. 20:24 after the Ten Commandments were given that God speaks to Moses and tells the people. *"An altar of earth thou shalt make unto me, and shalt sacrifice thereon thy burnt offerings, and thy peace offerings, thy sheep, and thine oxen: in all places where I record my name I will come unto thee, and I will bless thee."* Now I know the cross was the altar upon which God sacrificed His Son for the sins of the world. There need be no other payment for sin — in fact, there can be no other payment. However, in the Old Testament the altar was more than the place of sacrifice. It was also a place of worship. All of us need a special place to worship our Lord. Each morning I go to my chair and it becomes my altar. It is in that chair I worship the Lord. It is my place of prayer. It is my place of fellowship with the Lord. You may have more than one "altar" that you visit to spend time with the Lord. I want to challenge each of us to build an altar. The place is not important, but the worship and fellowship are a necessity for spiritual health. The quiet moments spent with God prepares us for the trials of the day. Today find that special place for you and God to spend some time together.

May 8

Everyone needs rules and laws to govern their lives. God presented the Ten Commandments in Exodus 20, then in Ex. 21:1 said, *"Now these are the judgments which thou shalt set before them."* In Exodus 21-24, God gave the laws that were to govern the people. Some are not applicable for today but were set in place for the nation of Israel. However, the principle of setting laws to govern is still very much needed. A nation without laws is a nation that lives in chaos. As Christians, we must obey and respect the laws of the land. The only exception is when the law of the land violates the law of God. An example of this civil disobedience is the occasion when the apostles were forbidden to teach and preach in the name of Jesus. According to Acts 5:29, *"Then Peter and the other apostles answered and said, We ought to obey God rather than men."* We could be living in a time when, as Christians, we will be called upon do the same thing. I would suggest that we must first exhaust every means to live peaceably within the laws of the land. Secondly, we must guard our spirits; humility and graciousness toward those in authority should be our testimony. God established government. He commands us in Rom. 13:1, *"Let every soul be subject unto the higher powers. For there is no power but of God: the powers that be are ordained of God."* In verse 4 government is called *"the minister of God to thee for good."* My challenge is that we obey and respect the laws of our land, and that we honor those in authority and pray for them. God bless you today and have a great day.

May 9

Christians are to be "in the world" but not "of the world." This is a challenge for every believer. Just how much should we separate ourselves from the world? Should our dress be so different that we seem to challenge the fashions of the day? Should we refuse to participate in activities accepted by society to the point we are perceived to be isolationists? In Ex. 23:20-33 God gave detailed instruction to Israel about being influenced by pagan nations. His warning in verse 33 could not be clearer: *"They shall not dwell in thy land, lest they make thee sin against me: for if thou serve their gods, it will surely be a snare unto thee."* My fear for the church and for Christians today is that we have been so influenced by the world that there is no difference in the two. The admonition of II Cor. 6:16-17 still stands as God's standard: *"And what agreement hath the temple of God with idols? for ye are the temple of the living God; as God hath said, I will dwell in them, and walk in them; and I will be their God, and they shall be my people. Wherefore come out from among them, and be ye separate, saith the Lord, and touch not the unclean thing; and I will receive you."* We cannot unduly compromise our values and our lifestyles to conform to this world. We do not need to look weird nor be antisocial, but we do need to reflect the character of the holy God we serve. We can graciously say no to activities that violate God's standards. We can have appearances of modesty and not appear to be unusual or weird. We must guard against the influences of evil and the world. In John 17:15 Jesus prayed for His disciples, *"I pray **not** that thou shouldest take them out of the world, but that thou shouldest keep them from the evil."* (emphasis mine) I believe this is the Lord's prayer for you and me today. God bless you and have a blessed day.

May 10

Every religion except Christianity has a god totally removed from the presence of its people. Christianity has a God always seeking to be in the midst of His people. Some of the last words spoken by Jesus in Matt. 28:20 were, *"... and, lo, I am with you always, even unto the end of the world."* In Exodus 24-31 God gave Moses the instructions to build the Tabernacle and how the priests were to take care of it. He said in Ex. 25:8, *"And let them make me a sanctuary; that I may dwell among them."* God is omnipresent, but He desires to dwell **personally** with us. Paul asked in I Cor. 6:19, *"What? know ye not that your body is the temple of the Holy Ghost which is in you, which ye have of God, and ye are not your own?"* God dwells **with** us and lives **in** us! What a blessing today that we can acknowledge His presence with us and in us — to guide us, to comfort us, and to empower us. The Tabernacle built in Exodus became the dwelling place of God in the midst of the people. As the people moved, so the Tabernacle moved. It was always in the center of the camp of the people. Today, God dwells in the bodies of His children in the person of the Holy Spirit. We must allow Him to direct and control our lives. We can depend upon the Lord for the power to live in the midst of the trials of life. I give my God praise that He is with me and He is in me. God bless you today, and remember whatever you are facing today, you do not face it alone. God is with you. Have a great day!

I recently heard a young man say, "I thank God for my mother. If were not for her I would not be here." He was referring to his position in life, not to the fact his mother gave birth to him. Many of us can express the same sentiments. A mother's influence can be one of the greatest influences in a person's life. *"Her children arise up, and call her blessed,"* according to Prov. 31:28. There are no perfect mothers, but there are mothers who can be called "blessed," due to their devotion to their God and their children. Allow me to describe, in my opinion, what makes up the "blessed" mother. She leads her children by **example**. The best example to follow would be the description of *"a virtuous woman"* as seen in Prov. 31:10-31. This Mother's Day weekend, take the time to read these verses and meditate upon them. She is given to **exhortation.** According to verse 26, *"She openeth her mouth with wisdom; and in her tongue is the law of kindness."* She is one who *exalts* the Lord God of Heaven. Verse 30: *"... but a woman that feareth the Lord, she shall be praised."* My thought for today is that those of us who have a "blessed" mother give recognition to her on this Mother's Day weekend. We also must give God praise for giving us godly mothers. All of us need to show our appreciation to our mothers. Remember, "If were not for them, we would not be here!" God bless you and have great day.

May 12

this time of year our minds turn towards Mother's Day. That is the day set aside each year to honor mothers. As I think about the day and my mother, and the mother of my children, and the mother of my grandchildren, I praise the Lord for the godly influence of each of them in the lives of their children. Let us not forget our responsibility to honor our mothers. Our great example is our Lord. While hanging on the cross, Jesus remembered His mother. According to John 19:26-27, *"When Jesus therefore saw his mother, and the disciple standing by, whom he loved, he saith unto his mother, Woman, behold thy son! Then saith he to the disciple, Behold thy mother! And from that hour that disciple took her unto his own home."* Some of us will not be able to be with our mothers, but we can make every effort to contact them and express our love and appreciation for them. My thought for today is a reminder to all of us of the sacrifices made by our mothers for us. Many of us can say that the prayers of our mothers have been the motivating thing that has influenced our lives. All of us can agree that the sacrifices of mothers for their children is surpassed only by the sacrifice of Jesus for our sins. Let's not forget Mom. May all of us express our love and appreciation for our mothers, not only this week, but all the time. God bless and have a great day!

May 13

In an article written in Slate, a commentary on business and finance, Jordan Weismann wrote, "Among women under 30, more than half of all births happen outside of marriage." This statistic brings up two questions. Why do these women desire to have children? Why have we, as a society, lost our moral compass to direct us? Surely there are multiple causes for such a decline in moral values, but on this Mother's Day I would like for us to consider one. Could it be that we have forgotten the divine purpose for mothers? As I read through the Word of God, I find the roll call of mothers had one common trait: they all desired that their children be servants of the Lord. The one example I choose to use today is Hannah, the mother of Samuel. I challenge every mother to read I Samuel 1 to her daughters. Hannah was a mother who **prayed** for a child (v. 11). The Psalmist reminds us in Ps. 127:3, *"Lo, children are an heritage of the Lord: and the fruit of the womb is his reward."* Children are literally a loan from God, and mothers should raise them for Him. Hannah **presented** her child to the Lord in I Sam. 1:27-28. *"For this child I prayed; and the Lord hath given me my petition which I asked of him: Therefore also I have lent him to the Lord; as long as he liveth he shall be lent to the Lord."* I challenge every mother to acknowledge that her children are a gift from God and are to be raised to love and serve the Lord. I thank God for a mother who prayed that God would make me a preacher as she rocked me as a baby. She presented me to the Lord as an infant, and now I am a fulfillment of her prayers. I realize there are many brokenhearted mothers whose children have made decisions contrary to their prayers. May I encourage you to keep on praying. God can change the heart of your child. He is still in control. God bless every mother on her special day!

May 14

All of this world's goods and wealth come from the Lord. God gives to each of us so that we may give back to Him. When Israel left Egypt according to Ex. 12:35, *"And the children of Israel did according to the word of Moses; and they borrowed of the Egyptians jewels of silver, and jewels of gold, and raiment..."* Exodus 25 details God's desire that a sanctuary be built for Him. Verse 2: *"Speak unto the children of Israel, that they bring me an offering: of every man that giveth it willingly with his heart ye shall take my offering."* Verses 3-7 contain a list of the specific items that God asked the people to bring. These items coincided with the very things that the people took from Egypt. God gives to us so that we may give to Him. Each day, most of you go into Egypt, a picture of the world, and on payday you take from Egypt for your labor. God asks that each of us return a portion of that which we have to Him. We will never be faithful to give to the Lord until we acknowledge that **all** we have comes from the Lord. Our giving is not just an act of obedience, but an acknowledgement of His ownership of our lives. Giving is also an expression of love and desire for the presence of God. Perhaps it was best said by the old preacher, Uncle Buddy Robison: "You must have three books to worship the Lord — the Good Book, the hymnbook, and the pocketbook." I fear too many of us fail to bring our pocketbooks to the Lord. God bless and have a great day.

Looking again at the instructions given to Moses for the building of the Tabernacle in Exodus 25-27, I wish to emphasize how particular God was in giving every detail regarding its construction. I would suggest that God is a God of order and detail. I fear that today God is taken much too casually, and our lives are not given to spiritual detail. God is interested in every part of your life. Remember what Paul said in I Cor. 6:19 about us. *"What? know ye not that your body is the temple of the Holy Ghost which is in you, which ye have of God, and ye are not your own?"* We need to acknowledge and include God in every aspect of our lives. Our bodies are His dwelling place, and He has particular plans for the building of our lives. Each challenge, each opportunity, and each trial are materials used by God to build our lives to be just what He wants us to be. His plans are better than our plans; His place for our life is better than our desired place; and His purpose for our lives is better than our desired purpose. My challenge for today is that we listen to Him for the building of our lives. We must follow His leadership. He guides us by His Holy Spirit that lives in us and by the instructions of the Word of God. Oh, that we might be sensitive to the details of our lives, so we become *"holy, acceptable unto God, which is your reasonable service"* (Rom. 12:1). God bless and have a great day!

May 16

There are two types of agreements made between God and man. There is the **conditional covenant** and the **unconditional covenant.** God made some of both with Israel. In Gen. 12:1-3, God made an unconditional covenant with Abraham and his descendants. That agreement still stands today! In Gen. 15:18-21 the land that was given to to Israel by God is described. The nation of Israel is promised the provisions of the Abrahamic Covenant without conditions. In Exodus, the Lord made certain promises to bless Israel **if** the people kept certain commands. The Mosaic Covenant, recorded in Ex. 20:1-31:8, is a conditional covenant. For God to bless Israel they were expected to keep approximately 600 specific commands divided into three categories: commandments (Ex. 20:1-26), judgments (Ex. 21:1-24:11), and ordinances (Ex. 24:12-31:18). In the New Testament, there is a new covenant that is unconditional, made between God the Father and His Son Jesus whose sacrifice on the cross would be the total payment for the sins of **all** men. There is nothing man can do to earn God's salvation. It is a gift received by faith, not earned by works. Praise God for His gift of salvation to all who will receive it. All the laws of the Old Testament serve as a *"schoolmaster to bring us unto Christ"* (Gal. 3:24). The Israelites had to continually offer sacrifices to atone for their sins. We have a Sacrifice for our sin that was offered once and atones for our sin continually (Heb. 9:1110:18). The Bible says in Heb. 10:12, *"But this man, after he had offered one sacrifice for sins for ever, sat down on the right hand of God."* Take a few minutes today and give God praise for the salvation freely given to you (Eph. 2:8-9). God bless and have a great day!

May 17

Wednesday is still prayer meeting night for many churches. As a child, I remember going to church on Wednesday night where there was a time of prayer and then a Bible study. Today many churches no longer have Wednesday night services, and many no longer have a Sunday night service. These services have been replaced with "small group" or some other gathering of the church in various groups. My thought today is not the **time** nor the **place** for the gathering for prayer, but rather that we intentionally **pray.** Jesus said in Matt. 21:13 of the temple, *"My house shall be called the house of prayer."* I would suggest that our churches today should be houses of prayer. Even the "prayer meetings" in most churches are not really times of prayer. I recall times when the church I pastored held all night prayer meetings. Others have had "cottage" prayer meetings held in members' homes. Prayer rooms in the church before the services are a thing of the past for many churches. Dr. Jerry Falwell said, "Nothing of eternal value is ever accomplished apart from prayer." We need a daily time of **personal** prayer — a time before the Lord praising Him and presenting our petitions to Him. We also need times of **public** prayer, when the church gathers to pray together. We need to pray for one another; we need to pray for the leaders in our communities and country. We need to pray for revival to come to our churches and country. Remember the call of God in I Thess. 5:17 for us to *"pray without ceasing."* This verse literally means we are to be in a constant attitude of prayer. May God give each of us a renewed passion to pray! God bless and have a great day!

May 18

Problems and trials are part of life. Sometimes they are physical, at other times financial — and occasionally several things at once. The troubles seem to continue to mount. In the midst of all this, God gives us hope! According to Ps. 34:17, *"The righteous cry, and the Lord heareth, and delivereth them out of all their troubles."* As I write this, I am reminded of the closing words of Dr. Bill Pennell's devotions: "Remember to be good to everybody. Everybody is having a hard time." That thought echoes the word of Job 14:1. *"Man that is born of a woman is of few days, and full of trouble."* My thought for today is that each of us consider the hardships of others and pray for each other. I read daily of the hurts and heartaches of others, and I have committed to whisper a prayer for them. I may not know them, but I can pray for them. Whenever possible, we should encourage those who may be going through difficult times. Just a word of concern often brightens the moment for those that are hurting. What trauma are you facing today? Cry unto the Lord, and listen for the words of encouragement coming from others. God has not forsaken you, and He will send just the right people into your life to bless you. May each of us be the voice of encouragement to some hurting soul today. Today, it is someone else who may need our prayers and encouragement; tomorrow, it could be us! The Bible says in Gal. 6:2, *"Bear ye one another's burdens, and so fulfil the law of Christ."* God bless you and have a blessed day.

May 19

Like many of you, I have occasionally found myself unable to sleep at night. Years ago, someone came up with the idea of "counting sheep" when you cannot sleep. I've never tried that method, but I have found that talking to the Shepherd relieves the anxiety and concerns of life. The Bible says in Ps. 127:1-2, *"Except the Lord build the house, they labour in vain that build it: except the Lord keep the city, the watchman waketh but in vain. It is vain for you to rise up early, to sit up late, to eat the bread of sorrows: for so he giveth his beloved sleep."* As I read these verses, God reminds me that the ultimate solutions to the problems of life are in His hands. My attempts to solve my problems or those of my friends and family without the Lord never bring the desired result or God's perfect plan. Once again, we are reminded that we need God to be involved in every aspect of our lives. Whether we *"build the house"* or *"keep the city,"* we need to allow God to direct our way. He has a **plan**, a **purpose,** and the **power** to see us through every challenge of life. This passage also illustrates the necessity of resting in the Lord. In other words, I can trust God in the midst of the storms of life *"for so he giveth his beloved sleep."* As humans we need sleep, but according to Ps. 121:4, *"Behold, he that keepeth Israel shall neither slumber nor sleep."* If the God of the universe is going to stay awake and watch over me, then I think I will rest in Him. And the Psalmist reminds us in the next verse, *"The Lord is thy keeper: the Lord is thy shade upon thy right hand."* Be sure to involve God in the concerns and challenges in your life. Trust Him and rest in His promises. Sleepless nights never bring solutions, only weariness and anxiety. God is bigger than our troubles! God bless and sleep tight. Have a blessed day!

May 20

Life is a series of seasons. We begin as infants and progress into our childhood years, then adolescence and on to adulthood. Our adult lives are also a series of seasons. Young adults mature into middle age before moving to their "golden years" as we often refer to our elderly citizens. Every season of life brings new challenges as well as new opportunities. Ecclesiastes 3 addresses the various seasons of life. The chapter begins, *"To every thing there is a season, and a time to every purpose under the heaven."* Each of us is where we are in life for a divine purpose. I am now in the age group that is considered elderly, but God is not finished with me. I still am healthy and able to serve Him. Some are young and still learning or preparing for some special callings from God. There are others who, due to physical limitations, may need to seek God's purpose knowing the limits of their abilities. No matter your situation, God is not finished with you. You are but in a particular season that affords new challenges and opportunities. Enjoy the season of life or service God has given you. I can't do what I used to do, but I can do something! That "something" defines my purpose for this season of my life. There may be some who have been given a ministry of prayer or have been blessed financially and now have a ministry of giving. Others have ministries of evangelism or of teaching the Word of God. If you are young, seek to find God's purpose for your life. The prosperous and happy life is lived in the will of God. He has a plan for your life right where you are today! As one contemporary Bible teacher said, "Find out what God is up to in your life, and join Him." God bless you and have great day.

May 21

On a recent trip to Colorado for some speaking engagements, I drove from the Denver airport through the Rocky Mountains to Gunnison. There had been a snow storm a few days before, and the snow was still on the mountains. The roads were clear, and the sun was shining brightly. I must tell you, I have never beheld such beauty — the snow glistening on the mountains, the green trees holding bits of the snow and the quiet serene feeling of God's creation with few signs, towns, or other man-made facilities. There were times when I fought emotions of being overwhelmed with the awesome power of our Creator. My thoughts turned to Ps. 19:1. *"The heavens declare the glory of God; and the firmament sheweth his handywork."* Today I challenge you to take a walk or a drive to some secluded area of God's creation and behold His majesty and His mighty power. As for what I saw that day in Colorado, the mere thought that it could have happened without a Master Planner and the power of a sovereign God is absurd. It is as ridiculous as the thought that I could remove every working piece of my watch, throw them into the air and see them reassemble as a working watch before hitting the ground. The beauty and majesty of God's creation defies the "logic" of evolutionary theory. This same Creator is the giver of life. He also created the master plan for our salvation and has designed an eternal abode in Heaven for all who receive His Son Jesus as Savior. Right now, we can only imagine the beauty of that place. God bless you today and have a great day.

May 22

Often when trying to give instruction and encouragement we use terms that we think people understand, but while there may be general understanding, the true meaning is not conveyed. One example: "Well, I know your situation is difficult, but just trust the Lord." What does it mean to trust the Lord? I would like to suggest three explanations as to the meaning of the word **trust.** First, it means to rest upon, as one would **rest upon** a crutch. When the circumstances of life have crippled us, we can rest upon the Lord to help us through the difficult times. Second, to trust means to **rely on.** Through any and all of life's twists and turns we can have confidence in our God. Thirdly, to trust means to **roll off.** We do not need to carry the burdens of life. We can roll them off and onto the Lord. In Psalm 11, one of my favorite psalms, we see in verse 1, David's response to his friends who advised him to *"flee as a bird to your mountain"* to escape from Saul's attempts to kill him. In that same verse is David's answer: *"In the Lord put I my trust."* Let me challenge you today, whatever your situation, to do as David did and put your trust in the Lord. We can rest upon Him, rely on Him, and roll our burdens onto Him. I do not know about you, but I think I will live my life trusting God. He is worthy of my trust. God bless you today and have a blessed day!

May 23

News of terror attacks around the world have become, sadly, more common than we would like. From Paris to Manchester and even in our own nation, the horror of each event and the unnecessary death of innocent people is a reminder to all of us of the evil in our world. Each time our president or another key official is in Israel, I am reminded that we are to pray for the peace of Jerusalem. Indeed, I would challenge all of us to pray for peace around the world. I know there will be no lasting peace until the Prince of Peace (Jesus) returns. However, we can seek the grace and the goodness of God for a reprieve from the violence that seems to be escalating daily. The real hope of peace is the Gospel. We must "love like Jesus" those who would despitefully use us. This is not to say that the perpetrators of evil should not be dealt with, but we must guard our spirits. We cannot become vessels of bitterness toward any people. I have read the definition of bitterness as "resentful cynicism that results in intense antagonism or hostility towards others." We are instructed in Eph. 4:31-32, *"Let all bitterness, and wrath, and anger, and clamour, and evil speaking, be put away from you, with all malice: And be ye kind one to another, tenderhearted, forgiving one another, even as God for Christ's sake hath forgiven you."* I believe we must seek to remove those from our world who seek to harm us, but we must also seek to reconcile our differences without becoming bitter. May God help each of us to define what is right; stand for the right; but to be sure and stand with a right spirit. Pray for the victims, but also may we pray for those that seek to bring such hurt and devastation upon us. God bless and have a blessed day!

May 24

The instructions for the building of the Tabernacle (Ex. 25:9-27:21) began with the specifications of a box to be constructed 2.5 cubits long, 1.5 cubits wide and 1.5 cubits high. It would be overlaid with gold. The most significant part of this box was the top, called the mercy seat. That name comes from a Hebrew word meaning "to cover, to appease, cleanse, cancel, or make atonement for." It was here that the high priest offered the blood of animals, usually a lamb, for his sins and the sins of the people (Leviticus 16). The box was called the Ark of the Covenant because it contained the commandments given to Moses, as He commanded in Ex. 25:16. *"And thou shalt put into the ark the testimony which I shall give thee."* Let's focus for a moment on the mercy seat. This was the only place where the sacrifice, commanded by the Lord in Leviticus 16, could be offered. It had to be offered yearly. When Jesus died for the sins of the world, He became the atonement for our sin. No other sacrifice was needed; He is the perfect and eternal sacrifice for sin. This is covered in detail in Heb. 10:1-18, but note two verses in particular. Verse 12: *"But this man, after he had offered one sacrifice for sins for ever, sat down on the right hand of God."* Verse 17: *"And their sins and iniquities will I remember no more."* Oh how I praise God that my sins are forgiven, covered by the blood of the Lamb of God. Let us give Him praise today for His death on the cross for our sin. Jesus is our Mercy Seat! His death is the payment, the atonement for our sin! Praise His name for His unspeakable gift! God bless and have a blessed day!

God blesses us in spite of our bad decisions. This statement may be challenged, but I have witnessed this truth in the pages of the Word of God and have experienced it in my own life. In I Samuel 8 we see the people of Israel demanding a king to reign over them. God's plan was that He alone would be their King, but in chapter 9 He chose a man to be king. Verses 15-16: *"Now the Lord had told Samuel in his ear a day before Saul came, saying, To morrow about this time I will send thee a man out of the land of Benjamin, and thou shalt anoint him to be captain over my people Israel, that he may save my people out of the hand of the Philistines: for I have looked upon my people, because their cry is come unto me."* It is true that Israel suffered the consequences of having Saul as their king, but they also were blessed to have a God-chosen leader to deliver them from their enemies. Don't allow your bad choices to keep you from serving God. There may be consequences for our decisions, but God has neither forsaken nor forgotten us. We only have to cry out to Him and He will *"abundantly pardon"* (Isa. 55:7) and will bless us again. You are not defeated until you quit, and you need never quit because God does not quit on us. God is bigger than my mistakes. He is greater than my failures, and He loves us! Oh, the words of that chorus:

> **He loves me when I am sad;**
> **He loves me when I am bad;**
> **Jesus loves, loves me!"**

God has a plan for your life in spite of your blunders and failures. God blesses in spite of us, not always because of us. What a wonderful Savior! God bless you today!

May 26

"If there is a God, where is He?" I have heard this question posed by unbelievers and thought how foolish it is. However, it is interesting to note as God gave the instructions for the building of the Tabernacle, He declared **one** place that He would meet with His people. This is not to suggest that God was not omnipresent; He is in all places, at all times. This was a particular place for the people of God to have a special encounter with Him. This place was between the cherubim located on the Mercy Seat, which was the top of the Ark of the Covenant. The Lord commanded in Ex. 25:21-22, *"And thou shalt put the mercy seat above upon the ark; and in the ark thou shalt put the testimony that I shall give thee. And there I will meet with thee, and I will commune with thee from above the mercy seat, from between the two cherubims which are upon the ark of the testimony, of all things which I will give thee in commandment unto the children of Israel."* Our Mercy Seat, our place to meet God, is in the Bible. Our bodies are the Temple, the Tabernacle, of the living God. As I Cor. 6:19 says, *"What? know ye not that your body is the temple of the Holy Ghost which is in you, which ye have of God, and ye are not your own?"* The only way the people of Israel could come into the presence of God was if the high priest offered a sacrifice, and if he entered the Holy of Holies to offer the blood upon the Mercy Seat as an atonement for the sins of the people. Jesus offered His blood as an atonement for our sin, and we have access to God through Him. Where is God? He is everywhere; He is in Heaven; He is in the Bible; but He is also living in me. The Christian faith is all about a relationship with a living Savior. Today, I challenge you to meet with this loving, forgiving God through the pages of His Word and in conversation with Him in prayer. God bless and have a great day!

I can still hear the melody of Charles Widmeyer's gospel song "Come and Dine" being sung by Lester Roloff. While preaching Bro. Roloff would often break into a song, and it was often this one. The chorus says:

> **Come and dine, the Master calleth, Come and dine;**
> **You may feast at Jesus' table all the time;**
> **He Who fed the multitude, turned the water into wine,**
> **To the hungry calleth now, Come and dine.**

God has always desired the fellowship of His people. As God gave the instructions for the building of the Tabernacle, He ordered a three-foot table, made of acacia wood and overlaid with gold, to be built. This table was to set on the right side of the Holy Place across from the lamp stand and was to have 12 loaves of bread on it at all times. The bread, called shewbread, was baked by the priest and could only be eaten by the priest in the Holy Place. In Ex. 25:30 we have the instruction from God, *"And thou shalt set upon the table shewbread before me alway."* One commentator wrote, "The table and the bread were a picture of God's willingness to fellowship and communion with man." Surely our God desires to fellowship with us. In the New Testament we see Jesus, "the bread of life," coming to dwell among men that we might have fellowship with God. We note all through the earthly ministry of Jesus that He fellowshipped with people. In Rev. 3:20 we read, *"Behold, I stand at the door, and knock: if any man hear my voice, and open the door, I will come in to him, and will sup with him, and he with me."* We should all enjoy fellowship with the Lord Jesus. We can invite Him into our lives today and commune with Him. Meet Jesus in the pages of His Word, in prayer, and in the spirit of worship. As you walk through this day, walk hand in hand with the Savior. He desires to fellowship with you! God bless and have a great day!

May 28

Memorial Day is the day that we Americans remember and honor the men and women who have died while serving in the U.S. military. To every family of a fallen solder, we offer our gratitude for your sacrifice. To every soldier who gave his or her life, we owe a debt of thanks for our "life, liberty, and the pursuit of happiness." We are a free people and we live in freedom because of the sacrifice of these brave men and women. I am reminded of John 15:13 in which Jesus said, *"Greater love hath no man than this, that a man lay down his life for his friends."* For the love of country and *"friends,"* we celebrate the lives and the sacrifice of those who paid the supreme price for our liberty. God bless the families and friends of those who have given all for our freedom. God bless you today and may you ever know that your departed family member or friend is not and will never be forgotten. God bless and have a wonderful day.

In Exodus 25:31, we have the instructions given for the making of the golden candlestick, which was to be placed in the Holy Place with the table of shewbread. It was to be hammered out of a single piece of gold and was to have six branches. Each of the branches and the top of the shaft were to have bowls shaped as the bud of the almond tree. These bowls were to be filled with oil and provide light in the Holy Place continually. There were no windows in the Tabernacle, so the only light came from the candlestick. The symbolism contained in the materials and the function of the candlestick are numerous. It was a reminder to the Israelites. It was a reminder that they were to be "*a light to the Gentiles*" as stated in Isa. 49:6. For us it should stand as a symbol of Jesus being *"the Light"* for the entire world (John 1:4-9). It should also remind us that we, as Christians, are to be "*the light of the world*" as stated in Matt. 5:14. The **only** light that shines in the darkness of this sin cursed world is Jesus. We who know Jesus as Savior are the only bearers of this light. Our challenge is in Matt. 5:16. *"Let your light so shine before men, that they may see your good works, and glorify your Father which is in heaven."* How brightly does our light shine for Jesus? It is my prayer that each of us will examine our lives to be certain we are being a light in this dark world of sin. God bless and have a great day.

May 30

"I like to go to a church where the Bible is preached." I have heard many people make this statement — some honestly desiring to hear the Word of God, and others not so much. It has been my observation that there is a falling away of preachers who will preach on the judgment of God. Think about it. When was the last time you heard a message on Hell (Luke 16:19-31) or the chastening of God in the lives of believer for sin (Heb. 12:5-11)? A church that preaches the whole council of the Word of God must be a church that preaches the love of God, the forgiveness of God , the mercy and the grace of God, but also must declare the judgment of God. As the Tabernacle was constructed, there were 10 curtains made to cover or separate the areas in the Tabernacle. The Lord commanded in Ex. 26:1, *"Moreover thou shalt make the tabernacle with ten curtains of fine twined linen, and blue, and purple, and scarlet: with cherubims of cunning work shalt thou make them."* Note the inclusion of the cherubim in the making of the curtains. These embroidered cherubims could be seen by the priests as they ministered in the Holy Place, and were also seen in the Holy of Holies. They were visual reminders of the holiness of God. One commentator stated of the cherubim: "They represent the righteous government of God, and are the executors of God's righteous judgment." God has not changed. He is still a God of judgment. Thank God our sins were judged on the cross! The Bible says in II Cor. 5:21, *"For he hath made him to be sin for us, who knew no sin; that we might be made the righteousness of God in him."* God does not excuse sin; praise Him for his mercy and forgiveness! According to I John 1:9, *"If we confess our sins, He is faithful and just to forgive our sins, and cleanse us from all unrighteousness."* Yes, I want to go to church where all of the Bible is preached. God bless and have a great day!

Everybody needs encouragement. Everyone faces problems and trials in their lives. As I travel and come in contact with people, I am reminded of the truth found in Job 14:1. *"Man that is born of a woman is of few days and full of trouble."* With that in mind, allow me to exhort each of us to be sensitive to the needs of others. Where I live we have an enormous number of homeless people. On a recent day I was approached by three at different places asking for help. Now I know some are homeless by choice, but the majority of those I meet are victims of mental illness or have been overwhelmed by circumstances of life. My thought as I met these folks was, "But for Calvary, there go I." Yes, that could be me and it could be you! Only by God's grace are we physically and mentally well. Only by His goodness do we have a roof over our heads and food in our cabinets. That is why we should reach out to someone in need today and be a blessing, while giving God praise for the blessings He has bestowed upon us. Today, you may be blessed with good health and your needs are supplied. You can be a blessing to someone in need. Tomorrow, you may be the afflicted one or the one struggling to make ends meet. Extend the same mercy and grace to others that you would hope for, if you were in need. Remember, "Be good to everybody. Everybody is having a hard time." God bless and have a blessed day.

I recall hearing that there were some critics of Christianity who referred to our faith as a "slaughter-house religion." They called it that due to the thousands of animals that were offered as sacrifices at the Tabernacle and Temple. They also knew that the Christian faith required the shedding of blood for the payment for sin. What does the Bible say? Look at Heb. 9:22. *"And almost all things are by the law purged with blood; and without shedding of blood is no remission."* We are reminded in Rom. 5:9, *"Much more then, being now justified by his blood, we shall be saved from wrath through him."* Then there is 1 John 1:7. *"... and the blood of Jesus Christ his Son cleanseth us from all sin."* Yes, Mr. Critic, it is the blood of the Lamb of God that purchased our redemption! The sacrifice of those lambs and other animal sacrifices that preceded the Cross were all temporary offerings until the **perfect** sacrifice could be offered upon the Cross! In Ex. 27: 1-9 God gave Moses the details regarding how the brazen altar was to be built. This altar was outside the Holy Place and was one of the first things seen as you entered the Tabernacle. Before one could go into the Holy Place or the presence of God, there had to be a blood sacrifice offered. Our entrance into the presence of God is based upon the sacrifice of Jesus on the cross. May we **never** be ashamed of the blood. It is His blood that purchased us out of the slave market of sin. It is His blood that assures us that our sins are forgiven. Oh, the precious blood that wrought salvation to all who will believe! God bless and have a great day!

June 2

There is no higher honor than to be called of God to a particular place of service. It does not elevate the called above other believers, but it does require dedication to the calling, and there is honor to be given to the position. The Bible says much about honoring those who teach or preach the Word. According to Heb. 13:17, *"... for they watch for your souls, as they that must give account, that they may do it with joy, and not with grief: for that is unprofitable for you."* The Apostle Paul admonishes us in I Tim. 5:17, *"Let the elders that rule well be counted worthy of double honour, especially they who labour in the word and doctrine."* He also identifies several areas of specific service in Eph. 4:11-12. *"And he gave some, apostles; and some, prophets; and some, evangelists; and some, pastors and teachers; For the perfecting of the saints, for the work of the ministry, for the edifying of the body of Christ."* In Exodus 28-29 God told Moses to separate Aaron and his sons to be the priests in charge of caring for the Tabernacle and offering the sacrifices on behalf of the people. God has always had his chosen servants for particular places of service. Today, I believe God calls some to pastor, some to be missionaries, some to teach, some to be evangelists, but He calls **all** who know Him as Savior to a place of service for Him. Our task may vary, but our responsibility to our Savior is the same. By the way, there are **no** little positions in the service of the Lord. You may not be called to preach or teach, but God's calling in your life is worthy of honor in the eyes of God. Seek God's calling for your life and serve well. God will bless you and your life will be lived with joy and self-fulfillment. God bless and have a great day!

June 3

Tragedy strikes when least expected. I remember the day I received word of a 17-year-old losing his life in an auto accident. I had known this young man from his childhood. His father and mother and other family members had been members of the church where I had pastored. He was a fine young man with his life before him. In a moment, he was with the Lord. Family and friends were heartbroken. It was a stark reminder of the brevity of life. As James 4:13-14 states so well, *"Go to now, ye that say, To day or to morrow we will go into such a city, and continue there a year, and buy and sell, and get gain: Whereas ye know not what shall be on the morrow. For what is your life? It is even a vapour, that appeareth for a little time, and then vanisheth away."* Whether 17 years or 70-plus years, life is but a vapor and appears but what seems to be a moment. In light of the brevity of life, may I exhort you to be sure to enjoy each day. We are reminded in Ps. 118:24, *"This is the day which the Lord hath made; we will rejoice and be glad in it."* Days of sorrow come, but we must live even those days anticipating the goodness and the grace of our God. The days we have to live in this life are numbered; may we not waste them. May we enjoy the moments. Hug your children today; call your family members and express your love for them; enjoy friendships and praise God for his blessings of the day. Being ready to meet the Lord is the most important preparation for all of us to face the day. May each of us be able to say with the Apostle Paul in II Cor. 5:8, *"We are confident, I say, and willing rather to be absent from the body, and to be present with the Lord."* Yes, life is short, but I am going to enjoy every day the Lord gives me, and I am going to live as if this day may be my last. I want to be ready when He calls me home! God bless and have a great day!

June 4

Prayer is more than just getting things from God. It is **praise, petition,** and **personal conversation** with the Savior. God desires a relationship with His people, and there is no relationship without communication. Prayer is communication with God. In the Tabernacle was placed an altar of incense. This was a small altar, 18 inches square and three feet tall, placed between the Holy Place and the Holy of Holies. God gave instructions in Ex. 30:1. *"And thou shalt make an altar to burn incense upon: of shittim wood shalt thou make it."* Incense was to be offered by the priest in the morning and evening. It was continual and representative of the prayers of the people. As I think of the altar of incense, I am reminded of I Thess. 5:17 and its exhortation: *"Pray without ceasing."* We are to be continually in a state of mind of prayer. I recall, as a young minister, asking my pastor how he prayed over the multitude of decisions he had to make each day. His answer was, "You must always be in communication with the Lord. His Holy Spirit can direct your thoughts and actions if you are totally surrendered to him." In other words, *"Pray without ceasing."* My challenge for us today is that we begin and end each day with the offering of the incense of prayer, but also keep the sweet fragrance of prayer ever flowing in our lives. God bless you today and have a great day.

June 5

The beginning of another week — that is the reality of the day. Yes, it is Monday and we begin another week. Only God knows the events that will unfold in our lives this week. However, each of knows there will be trials and opportunities set before us. As we enter this week, and every week, let us claim Prov. 3:5-6 as our promise for the week ahead, *"Trust in the Lord with all thine heart; and lean not unto thine own understanding. In all thy ways acknowledge him, and he shall direct thy paths."* God is the GPS that directs us to the appropriate place for our lives. I recall singing that little chorus, "My Lord knows the way through the wilderness; All I have to do is follow." These lyrics simply define our responsibility as a Christian. Place your trust in the Lord to guide you through the day. Take no thought of your own inabilities, but rather rest in the strength and wisdom of the Lord for your every need. The statement, *"he shall direct thy paths,"* means He will make your path smooth and straight. I do not know what the future holds, but thank God, I know **Who** holds the future. I do not know why I felt led to remind us today of the promise of Prov. 3:5-6, but I am encouraged to know my God has every detail of my life in His Hands. I can and will trust and acknowledge Him in all my ways. God bless and have a great week.

June 6

The work of God is every Christian's business. If every Christian gave of his or her finances, if every Christian was a witness, and if every Christian served in some capacity, the work of the Lord would flourish. The problem today is, it is reported that 20 percent of the people do 90 percent of the work and 20 percent of the people give 90 percent of the money needed in the work of God. Though we do not live under the law as given to the Israelites, we certainly can learn of the character of God and His principles from God's instructions to them. As God gave instruction for the building of the Tabernacle, He also directed how it was to be maintained. In Ex. 30:11-16 this included an order Moses to number the children of Israel. Verse 12: *"When thou takest the sum of the children of Israel after their number, then shall they give every man a ransom for his soul unto the Lord, when thou numberest them."* Verse 14: *"Every one that passeth among them that are numbered, from twenty years old and above, shall give an offering unto the Lord."* In verse 16, we note that this annual offering, equaling about two days' pay, was to be used *"for the service of the tabernacle."* **ALL** of us are responsible for the work of the Lord and the ministry of our church. God has given each of us the responsibility to give of our treasures, our time, and our talents for the work of the Lord. May God help us be faithful in our service to Him. God bless and have a great day.

I once heard a preacher say, "The Bible is God's detergent!" He made the statement in a sermon from John 15:3 where Jesus said, *"Now ye are clean through the word which I have spoken unto you."* It has also been said, "This Book (the Bible) will keep you from sin, or sin will keep you from this Book." In Ex. 30:18, God instructed Moses to place *"a laver of brass and his foot also of brass, to wash withal: and thou shalt put it between the tabernacle of the congregation and the altar, and thou shalt put water therein."* The next three verses instruct the priests to wash their hands and feet before they approached the altar to minister. We are not prepared to minister to others until we have applied the Word of God to our own lives. It is the Word of God that reveals our sin. The blood of Jesus cleanses from all sin (I John 1:7), but the Word of God convicts us of our sin. This is one reason why we should spend time in the Word of God daily. Surely the Bible encourages us, it instructs us, but it also cleanses us as we see our sin revealed. The Word of God is a *"mirror"* (James 1:23) and our *"schoolmaster"* (Gal. 3:24) to teach us. May we all pass by the *"laver of brass"* today as we prepare to serve the Lord. May we spend time in the Word of God so we may be ready to be used of God. God bless and have a great day!

June 8

God has always had a **place** and a **time** for His people to worship. The place for the nation of Israel was the Tabernacle and later the Temple. Today, for the Jewish people, it is the synagogue, as they await the rebuilding of the Temple. The time of their worship has been and still is the Sabbath, or from sundown Friday until sundown Saturday. The command to worship on the Sabbath is given to Moses in Ex. 31:12-17. In verse 16, the Lord said, *"Wherefore the children of Israel shall keep the sabbath, to observe the sabbath throughout their generations, for a perpetual covenant."* When Jesus died and was raised from the dead on the first day of the week, the church began meeting for Sunday worship. The word "Sunday" does not appear anywhere in the Bible, but the first day of the week is referred to several times to define the time of the gathering of the believers. In Matt. 28:1, we have the account of Jesus being raised from the dead, and the other Gospels also record His resurrection on *"the first day of the week."* Acts 20:7 says, *"And upon the first day of the week, when the disciples came together to break bread, Paul preached unto them ..."* There are other passages such as I Cor. 16:2 and John 20:19 that define the *"first day of the week"* as the time for the church to worship. Surely the church can worship any time, but God has set aside the *"first day of the week"* to be the time and the church to be the place. The church is not the building, as was the Tabernacle, but rather the people who gather. My thought for today is that we forget not the time and the place to worship each week. No, we are not Israel, but we serve the same God and He still desires to meet with His people. Going to church does not make you a Christian, but if you are a Christian, you should desire to go to the place of worship. God bless and have a great day!

June 9

God is a jealous God! Moses had been on Mount Sinai for 40 days. The children of Israel became restless, as seen in Ex. 32:1. *"And when the people saw that Moses delayed to come down out of the mount, the people gathered themselves together unto Aaron, and said unto him, Up, make us gods, which shall go before us; for as for this Moses, the man that brought us up out of the land of Egypt, we wot not what is become of him."* The next verses record Aaron leading the people to construct a golden calf from their jewelry and worship it. God's response as spoken to Moses is in verse 10: *"Now therefore let me alone, that my wrath may wax hot against them, and that I may consume them: and I will make of thee a great nation."* I heard evangelist Lester Roloff say, "Tell me what you talk about most often, tell me what you think of most often, and I will tell you who or what is your God." I fear many of us have golden calves in our lives that we worship instead of the God of Heaven. I will not attempt to define your God, but I will remind you that God is a jealous God. His warning in Ex. 20:3 — *"Thou shalt have no other gods before me"* — is still relevant today. There is a further warning in Ex. 20:4-5 about the worship of idols. Today I want to challenge you to tear down any and all idols in your life. God alone is worthy of our worship! Your idol may be your money or pleasure, or some other person. God seeks to be the **only** object of our worship. God bless you and have a great day!

June 10

One of the most neglected ministries is the ministry of intercessory prayer — of praying for others and interceding on their behalf before a holy God. He has so graciously placed several intercessors in my life and ministry. They pray for me when I have failed or in times that that I have special needs. I long to be an intercessor for others. All of us should have a ministry of intercession for others. Exodus 32 describes the sin of the people of Israel when they built a golden calf for idol worship. This was a direct violation of the commandments given them by God and received by Moses on Mount Sinai. Aaron was a weak leader and succumbed to the desires of the people. Verses 7-10 illustrate God's anger with the people and His desire to destroy them. But in verses 11-15, we see Moses interceding on behalf of the people. The result, as recorded in verse 14: *"And the Lord repented of the evil which he thought to do unto his people."* I confess that prayer is one of the mysteries of our relationship with God that I do not fully understand. We pray and God answers, even to seemingly change His mind and His direction. Then there are times we pray and nothing seems to change. Someone said, "Prayer is not getting our will done in heaven, but getting God's will done on earth." However, there is a real sense that prayer changes things, as seen in the intercessory prayer of Moses. I want to challenge each of us to enter into a ministry of intercessory prayer for one another. A few days ago, I received a phone call concerning one who has been diagnosed with a tumor behind his eye. I was solicited to pray for this individual, and I must do that. It is my my privilege and my duty to intercede for the needs of my family, my friends, and for my country. It is an awesome experience and a wonderful privilege to pray and watch God work. God bless and have a great day!

Nearly every Sunday I am privileged to stand in a pulpit somewhere in the United States with a message God has given me for that day, and I look forward to delivering His message to His people. How blessed I am to be given the opportunity to be used of God to deliver His message. Reading through Exodus 32 recently, I was moved with the thought of the great blessing Moses experienced in the presence of God on Mount Sinai. Yet, he also faced a great challenge as he descended from the mountain to find the people dancing around naked as they worshipped a golden calf. The initial response of Moses upon seeing the people around the calf was, according to verse 19, that his *"anger waxed hot, and he cast the tables out of his hands, and brake them beneath the mount."* Emotions such as anger, sadness, happiness, and all the rest are normal. However, upon facing the burdens of life, we must seek the face of God. In verse 31, we note that Moses *"returned unto the Lord."* In verse 34, the Lord said to Moses, *"Therefore now go, lead the people unto the place of which I have spoken: behold mine Angel shall go before thee."* Rejoice today in the blessings of the Lord! Cast your burdens upon Him and move forward trusting God to direct your path. The emotions of the moment may bring sorrow or anger, but we have the promise of God in Ps. 30:5. *"For His anger endure the but a moment: in His favour is life: weeping may endure for a night, but joy cometh in the morning."* God bless you and have a great day!

June 12

"Sin will take you further than you want to go, cost you more than you want it pay, and keep you longer than you want to stay." This phrase, which has been quoted by many and is the basis for a famous gospel song, contains a message that never gets old. It is so true. Never a day goes past that I do not hear of someone whose life has been ravished by the consequences of sin. We read in Ex. 32:35 of the consequences of the sin of the nation of Israel and their worshipping the golden calf: *"And the Lord plagued the people, because they made the calf, which Aaron made."* It is not my intent to dwell on that event but rather to remind us that our actions — yes, our sins — have consequences. Thank God for the promise of Isa. 55:7. *"Let the wicked forsake his way, and the unrighteousness man his thoughts: and let him return unto the Lord, and He will have mercy upon him; and to our God, for He will abundantly pardon."* Forgiveness, or pardon, does not always remove the consequences of our sins. The alcoholic can be delivered from his addiction but often is left with a broken life that cannot be repaired, or a deceased body that goes with him the rest of his life. Sin has consequences. We must guard our lives from sin. I know that *"all have sinned and come short of the glory of God"* (Rom. 3;23), but may we flee the very appearance of evil, knowing that with every sin, there is a consequence. When we sin, may we **immediately** seek forgiveness. According to I John 1:9, *"If we confess our sins, He is faithful and just to forgive us our sins, and to cleanse us from all unrighteousness."* Thank God for His mercy and His forgiveness. May we live our lives surrendered to Him and seek to live in obedience, knowing our sin has consequences. God bless and have a blessed day!

June 13

While a student in college, I became very discouraged. I was a freshman, had no money, and could not find a job. (Yes, I worked and paid my way through college. No grants, no loans, no help from home for tuition.) I recall going to chapel and hearing a pastor from Atlanta, Dr. Ray Hancock, preach a message entitled, "I Think I'll Just Go on Anyway." It was a message on not quitting. It was then that I decided I would not quit. As I read through the events of the Exodus and all the murmuring and "stiffneckness" of the Israelites, I am sure Moses wanted to quit. In Exodus 33, we see God giving Moses a special visitation and words of instruction. It is in the midst of trouble or in the aftermath of a trial we need to **see God** — not a visible manifestation of God but a reality check that God is with us and has a plan for our lives. The Lord told Moses in Ex. 33:22-23, *"And it shall come to pass, while my glory passeth by, that I will put thee in a clift of the rock, and I will cover thee with my hand while I pass by: And I will take away mine hand, and thou shalt see my back parts: but my face shall not be seen."* Moses did not see the face of God but was allowed to see His back. My thought for today is that we seek to see God in the midst of our troubles. In my discouragement as a college student, I saw God in the message that day at chapel. I have seen Him so many times in the hours of discouragement and defeat. Look closely today; God may be passing by you. He still has a plan for your life. He wants us to **see** Him in the midst of our troubles. God bless and have a great day!

June 14

Have you ever been around someone on whose countenance you could actually see the presence of God? I recall an old man that radiated the presence of God. He was a great prayer warrior and tremendous soul winner named R.C. Worley. Children loved him. Great men like Dr. Jerry Falwell called upon him to pray for them. I was privileged to be one that he prayed for regularly. I can still hear his raspy voice saying to me, when I would see him, "I prayed for you this morning about 6:15." There was always a smile on his face and a testimony for the Lord on his lips. To be a glowing example of Jesus, we must spend time with Him. In Exodus 34, we read of Moses going up on Mount Sinai to meet with God, and verse 30 describes what happened when he came back down. *"And when Aaron and all the children of Israel saw Moses, behold, the skin of his face shone; and they were afraid to come nigh him."* After being in the presence of God for 40 days and as he returned to the camp with the Ten Commandments written upon two tablets of stone, his face shone with the glory of God. Being in the presence of God will change our attitudes and our appearance. Moses had been with the Lord 40 days without food or drink (Ex. 34:28). This reminds me that becoming a reflection of God takes time and sacrifice. My challenge for each of us today is that we make that sacrifice. May our actions reflect His heart. May our very appearance show that we have been with Him. You are the only Jesus some people will ever see or know. In the words of that old hymn by Thomas Chisholm:

> *O to be like Thee! O to be like Thee,*
> *Blessed Redeemer, pure as Thou art;*
> *Come in Thy sweetness, come in Thy fullness;*
> *Stamp Thine own image deep on my heart.*

God bless you today!

June 15

Live like Jesus, love like Jesus, and look like Jesus in a world that needs to know Him! God never asks of us what He does not give us the ability to accomplish. Beginning in Exodus 25 we see that God instructed Moses to have the people build a tabernacle. These were a people on a journey to a land that had been given them by God. There was no building supply store for them to acquire the needed materials to build the tabernacle. Where would they get what they needed? In Exodus, we find the answer to that question. Moses told the people in Ex. 35:5, *"Take ye from among you an offering unto the Lord: whosoever is of a willing heart, let him bring it, an offering of the Lord."* It is interesting to look ahead to the very next chapter. According to Ex. 36:5, *"And they spake unto Moses, saying, The people bring much more than enough for the service of the work, which the Lord commanded to make."* The children of Israel illustrated a very important principle: God gives to us that we might give back to Him. God had provided the people with the gold, silver, and fine linens from the spoils of Egypt (Ex. 12:35-36). Then He asked that they *"willingly"* bring an offering for the building of the tabernacle. God provides for us through various avenues in the world. We work, but it is God that gives the abilities to work. We invest, but it is God that blesses our investments. All we have comes from the hand of God. The Bible tells us in Mark 16:15, *"Go ye into all the world, and preach the gospel to every creature."* The financial need for the task is to come from the wealth that God has given us. We give back willingly of that which God has given us, that the work of God can be accomplished. My challenge this morning is that we willingly be the conduits of supply for the work of the Lord. God bless and have a great day!

June 16

Did you ever want something so bad but when you finally got it you wished you hadn't? I remember my father warning me not to buy a certain car, but I thought I had to have it. I bought it and had nothing but trouble. In three months, the motor blew and I sold it for a fraction of what I paid for it. I Samuel 8 introduces us to a similar situation: **The prophet Samuel grows old.** He served the people well and pleased God. His sons who were to take his place *"walked not in his ways, but turned aside after lucre, and took bribes, and perverted judgment"* (v. 3). **The people desire a king.** The people said in verse 5, *"Now make us a king to judge us like all the nations."* God had been their ruling authority, their King, but the people desired to be like their wicked neighbors. **The perception of God is rejection.** Verse 7: *"And the Lord said unto Samuel, Hearken unto the voice of the people in all that they say unto thee: for they have not rejected thee, but they have rejected me, that I should not reign over them."* God often permits us our request, but we sacrifice the perfect and best for fleshly desires. **The problems of having a king.** Samuel warned the people to no avail. Verse 19: *"Nevertheless the people refused to obey the voice of Samuel; and they said, Nay; but we will have a king over us."* **The position is granted**. Verse 22: "And the Lord said to Samuel, Hearken unto their voice, and make them a king." Here are some things to ponder from this episode. Be careful what you pray for; you may just get it. This is why it is so important that our prayer requests include the phrase "if it be Your will." **Consider God's will over the desires of the flesh.** Don't compare your circumstance to those around you. There is no better place to be than in the center of God's will for your life. Remember Phil. 4:11. *"Not that I speak in respect of want: for I have learned, in whatsoever state I am, therewith to be content."* God bless you today.

June 17

Every third Sunday of June we celebrate Father's Day across the country. I am so thankful for a godly father. He is in heaven, but his influence lives on in my life. My desire is to heed the admonition of Prov. 4:1. *"Hear, ye children, the instruction of a father, and attend to know understanding."* My father taught me many things. He taught me to have a good work ethic, to love and cherish my family, to serve the Lord through my local church, and to be loyal to my pastor. He taught all these things not only in word, but by example. As I think of my dad, there is one characteristic that sticks in my mind that I so desire to process. My dad was a man of strong convictions, but I never heard him raise his voice at my mother or to us children. When he spoke, we all knew he meant what he said and there were no idle threats. If he said he was going to spank me, I could count on getting a spanking. His gentle yet firm spirit provided a sense of security for the family. He certainly lived according to the words of Eph. 6:4. *"And ye fathers, provoke not your children to wrath: but bring them up in the nurture and admonition of the Lord."* Be sure and give your dad a call this week. There is no greater responsibility and no greater joy than be a father. God bless and have a great day!

June 18

Today's thought is from Ex. 36:4-7. God had conveyed to Moses that the people were to bring *"willingly"* their silver, their gold and their brass, as well as other materials for the construction of the tabernacle. In our text is recorded the dream of every pastor or Christian worker. The people had brought **more** than enough to build the tabernacle. The workers had requested that no more be brought. It has been my experience that there is **never** enough money to do all that the Lord's work requires. Could it be that we consider our giving to be to the church rather than understanding that we give to the Lord? Would it not be a glorious experience for the pastor to have to say as is recorded in Ex. 36:6-7 *"And Moses gave commandment, and they caused it to be proclaimed throughout the camp saying, Let neither man nor woman make any more work for their offering of the sanctuary. So the people were restrained from bringing. For the stuff they had was sufficient for all the work to make it and too much."* There is **more** than enough wealth and workers in the church to do all that God requires. The problem is that the people do not have willing hearts to give. May each of us remember today that our giving is not to an institution and it is not to an individual. Our giving is unto the Lord! God bless you and have a blessed day!

I cannot do everything, but I can do something — and that which I can do, I must do. This should be the attitude of each of us regarding the work of the Lord. I am reminded of Rom. 12:4-5. *"For as we have many members in one body, and all members have not the same office: So we, being many, are one body in Christ, and every one members one of another."* As you read the last five chapters of Exodus, you will see how different men with different skill sets were used to construct the tabernacle and its furnishings. These men used their talents and abilities to do the work and will of God. It starts with Ex. 36:1. *"Then wrought Bezaleel and Aholiab, and every wise hearted man, in whom the Lord put wisdom and understanding to know how to work all manner of work for the service of the sanctuary, according to all that the Lord had commanded."* My thought for today is that God does not expect us to do what we cannot do, but He does expect us to do what we **can** do in His service. I have always wanted to sing, but I am no singer. However, I can preach — maybe not as well as some others, but I know God has enabled me to preach. I am not mechanically inclined, but I do have some people skills that God can use. Whatever God has gifted you to do, **do it**. Whether it is to teach, to preach, to sing, or to clean the building, the reward will be the same if we just do what we can, what we have been gifted to do in the work of the Lord. God bless you today and remember God has a work for you today. Be busy doing what you can for Jesus, and He will bless you. Have a great day!

June 20

From time to time, I attend various conferences with several hundred pastors. It is interesting to be with pastors from across the country. There are a variety of personalities and some minor differences in practices and doctrines but usually there is agreement on the fundamental doctrines of the Bible and the traditional beliefs of that particular association. As I walked the halls and the meeting rooms at a recent event, meeting and greeting these servants of God, my mind went to Ps. 133:1. *"Behold, how good and how pleasant it is for brethren to dwell together in unity."* It is our unity that sets us apart from the world. Verse 2 states, *"It is like the precious ointment upon the head, that ran down upon the beard, even Aaron's beard: that went down to the skirts of his garments."* The anointing oil referred to in this verse was the anointing oil that sanctified (set apart) the priest for service. Our unity sanctifies us for a greater service for our Savior. Our unity allows us to be more productive in our service for the Lord. *"As the dew of Hermon, and as the dew that descends upon the mountains of Zion: for there the Lord commanded the blessing, even life for evermore."* (Ps. 133:3) My thought for today is that we who know the Lord should look for the things we agree upon and live and serve the Lord in unity. Satan and all his forces are seeking to destroy us. We need the strength and the encouragement of each other in the work of the Savior! Today, may we join hands and hearts with those in our church and in our community for the cause of the Lord. Unity is necessary for victory. God bless and have a great day!

June 21

Motel rooms are a part of my life at this stage of my ministry. I am thankful for the accommodations and a place to rest after a long day. However, after a while of staying in motels, they are all the same — a room with a bed, usually a table or desk, maybe a chair or a couch, and a bathroom. Being alone gives me time to pray, to think on the things of the Lord, and to study the Word of God. I am so thankful for the blessings of God in my life and ministry, and I have spent much time lately thinking about various milestones and important days in my life. I also spend a lot of my time thinking and anticipating the next great day in my life — the day I see my Savior! I may go to Him through the door of death, or He may come for me in the rapture. This reminds me of the words of Rev. 22:20. *"He which testifieth these things saith, Surely I come quickly. Amen. Even so, come, Lord Jesus."* No, I am not sad nor depressed. As a matter of fact, I feel just the opposite. I am excited and rejoice to live every day for my Savior. My heart leaps with joy with the reality that Jesus could come today. The Bible says in I Thess. 5:2, *"For yourselves know perfectly that the day of the Lord so cometh as a thief in the night."* The anticipation of the coming of the Lord is a reality, just as certain as any other day on the calendar. Spend some time today just **thinking** about the coming of the Lord. Today could be the day we see Jesus! God bless and have a great day!

June 22

A short time ago, I attended a conference with this theme: "Jesus ... Oh, What a Savior." Every song and every sermon exalted Jesus! As I prepared to leave my hotel and drive home at the conclusion of the conference, I thought of how I should be exalting the name of Jesus every day with my conversation and with my actions. He, and He alone, is worthy of all praise and glory. He is worthy because of **who** He is. He is the Creator; He is the Savior; and He is our Sustainer. He is worthy because of **what** He has done for us! He was our substitute. The Bible says in II Cor. 5:21, *"For He hath made Him to be sin for us, who knew no sin; that we might be made the righteousness of God in Him."* We need to be reminded continually of the goodness and the grace of our God. One of my favorite portions of Scripture is Phil. 2:5-11. Take a few minutes today and read and meditate upon these verses. They describe the person and the work of Jesus. He died for you and me. He has a name *"above every name."* One day, *"at the name of Jesus every knee should bow"* and *"every tongue should confess that Jesus is Lord."* Yes! "Jesus ... Oh, What a Savior." Give Him glory and praise today! God bless and have a great day!

June 23

In 2017 my wife Doris and I celebrated our 50th wedding anniversary. At that time she said, "You know, honey, we are so fortunate and blessed to be able to celebrate our 50th. So many of our friends no longer have their mates." Thank you, Jesus, for giving us these years together! As I think back over the years, the words of the third stanza of the hymn "Amazing Grace" pulse through my mind:

> *Through many dangers, toils, and snares,*
> *I (we)* *have already come;*
> *'Tis grace hath brought me (us)* *safe thus far,*
> *And grace will lead me (us)* *home.*

We began our lives **together** when I was still a college student, and she had just finished her secretarial degree. Two years later, we planted a church in Roanoke and started our family. We began with **no** money, **no** supporting churches or organizations, and **no** people. Just us and the Lord. That church is viable and active today, praise the Lord. With the birth of our second child, Paul, came our greatest trials. At the age of six, he was diagnosed with a brain tumor and became mentally and physically challenged, having multiple seizures every day. **Together** we took care of him until his death in 2004. **Together** we pastored three other churches and have seen many come to know Jesus as Savior. Today, though I say I am retired, we still serve our Savior **together,** and I preach in a different church every Sunday. Thank you, Sweetheart, for standing with me through our struggles, our victories, our sufferings and my bad choices. You have always been there and are still there. I'm looking forward to many more years to live with and love you! Surely Prov. 18:22 applies to me. *"Whoso findeth a wife findeth a good thing, and obtaineth favour of the Lord."* God bless and have a great day!

June 24

As my wife and I reached and surpassed the 50th anniversary of our wedding, those days served to remind me how blessed I have been the past 50 years. We have lived through some good times and some bad times together, and I am certainly thankful that I have had a companion to share the joys and sorrows of life. When I did weddings as a pastor, I would often incorporate in the ceremony the following statement to the bride and groom: "When you share a joy, the joy is doubled, and when you share a sorrow, the sorrow is halved." Marriage was established by God to be between one man and one woman for life. It is a sacred relationship and should be honored in society. The Bible says in Prov. 18:22, *"Whoso findeth a wife findeth a good thing, and obtaineth favour of the Lord."* Several commentators have pointed out that the text implies that the wife has been found through the providence of God. In other words, the wife is a gift from God to the man, which would seem to be in agreement with the creation of the first woman as recorded in Gen. 2:18. *"And the Lord God said, It is not good that the man should be alone; I will make him an help meet for him."* We should never take our spouses for granted. They are a gift from God to bless us and help us through the good times and the bad times along life's journey. Seems like just yesterday I was anxiously waiting for 6 p.m. to finally arrive on that special day, so I could marry the love of my life. I could never have imagined the road we would travel the next 50 years. I am so thankful God gave me a loving and supportive mate to make the journey with me. God bless you today and give your spouse an extra hug today and let them know you love and appreciate them.

June 25

Recently, I had lunch with a young (compared to me) pastor who is very successful and has a large church. He has studied the culture of the day and focused his ministry to reach the younger generation. By all standards of the religious community he is a successful pastor. He told me, "I preach the same message of my father (who was a good pastor) and the message of the Gospel. We have reached many people with the Gospel. However, there seems to be something missing from the days of my youth when I went with my father to conferences and heard the old fundamental preachers preach." I pondered his words and finally asked him, "Do you want to know what I think is missing in a lot of preaching today?" He quickly said yes. I told him, "I believe the missing element in a lot of preaching and ministry is passion — a passion to see people saved, a passion to preach the Word of God, and a passion to personally be a blessing to people." This young pastor thought for a moment and then with tears in his eyes exclaimed, "That is it — passion. Not just a professional production that reaches people, but a Holy Spirit-filled ministry evidenced by passion." Passion is defined as "a strong and barely controllable emotion." We see this expressed by the Apostle Paul in Rom. 9:3. *"For I could wish that myself were accursed from Christ for my brethren, my kinsmen, according to the flesh."* Again, we see Paul's passion for the salvation of his people in Rom. 10:1. *"Brethren, my heart's desire and prayer to God for Israel, is that they might be saved."* My prayer for today is that God would give me a passion for souls, a passion to serve others, and a passion to speak the Word of God in the power of the Holy Spirit. May God renew in each of us a passion to be used of God to make a difference in a sin-cursed world. God bless and have a great day!

June 26

In his book "The Treasure Principle," Randy Alcorn credited Mathew Henry with saying, "It ought to be the business of every day to prepare for the last day." As I read these words, I was reminded how quickly the years pass. Another very familiar passage from a poem by C.T. Studd expresses this so well:

> **Only one life, 'twill soon be past.**
> **Only what is done for Christ will last.**

With age comes the reality of our mortality, and the words of James 4:14 convey this truth. *"Whereas ye know not what shall be on the morrow. For what is your life? It is even a vapour, that appeareth for a little time, and then vanisheth away."* The brevity of life behooves each of us to make the most of every day for the Savior. We must live every day as it is our last. If Jesus does not return, one day **will** be your last day. As I begin another day and another week, I pause to think: What is it my Lord would have me to do today and this week? The value of my life is summed up in doing His will. Time is short, and I must be about the Master's business. Yes, I must make time for family and personal time for myself. However, my priority must be to seek the will of God for my life daily. My thought for today is that each of us live daily for the Savior. Take seriously your service for the Lord. On that last day of life, only what has been done for Jesus will matter! God bless you and have a great day!

June 27

The words of an old hymn just rang in my ears on a recent morning and seemed to be the cry of my soul. The hymn is "I Need Thee Every Hour" and the chorus includes these words:

I need Thee every hour,
Most gracious Lord.
No tender voice like thine
Can peace afford.

We live in times of trouble. Many are facing financial difficulties; others are going through physical problems; still others are in hurtful relationships with spouses, children, or friends. The **one** constant in life is the faithfulness of our God. The promise of Jesus in Matt. 28:20 is this: *"Lo, I am with you alway, even unto the end of the world."* Those words are still true. The word "alway" suggests that Jesus is with us "the whole of the day." There is nothing that we will face today that we will face alone. Our God is with us! The thought for today is that we recognize our need for Him every day and every hour of the day. The Lord tells us in Jer. 33:3, *"Call unto me, and I will answer thee, and shew thee great and mighty things, which thou knowest not."* My prayer to God this morning is simply, "Lord, I need you today. I need you every hour. I call upon you to lift my burdens and bless me today." I challenge you to join me in this prayer and let's watch God work!

June 28

Not all advice is good advice! The wise man wrote in Prov. 11:14, *"Where no counsel is, the people fall: but in a multitude of counsellors there is safety."* Again in Prov. 15:22 we are exhorted to seek counsel: *"Without counsel purposes are disappointed: but in the multitude of counsellors they are established."* Then why would I say not all advice is good advice? There are times when the will of God defies the wisdom and understanding of men, even those who would want the best for you. One such illustration is found in Psalm 11. Here David's friends, knowing Saul was seeking to kill David, advised him in verse 1 to *"flee as a bird to your mountain."* In other words, just quit and go hide in the mountains. Give up the fight with Saul. This seemed like good advice considering that David's army was outnumbered and, humanly speaking, no match against the army of Saul. But it was not good advice for David. God had David's back, so his response was: *"In the Lord put I my trust."* My thought for today is that we seek the counsel of others in times of decision, but God's plan and purpose must always take precedent over the advice of others. Seek God's will for your life. Often the advice of others will confirm His will, but there are times when our answer to the advice of others is: "In the Lord put I my trust." When you **know** what God desires of you, do it. Trust Him for the provisions and the power to do what He calls you to do. God is our **ultimate** counselor. His way is always the **right** way. God bless today and remember to seek the counsel of others, but never forsake God's advice or leading in your life. Have a great day!

June 29

"There is more persecution of Christians today than any time in history." I heard this quote recently in a prayer meeting, as the church was called upon to pray for "persecuted Christians around the world who are standing and dying for Jesus today, this hour." All you need to do is tune in to the world news and hear of the slaughter of Christians around the world to know that persecution of believers is a common practice. Here in the United States, we are spared physical persecution but are often the target of slander, ridicule, and other verbal abused because of our faith. I fear it is only a matter of time before Christians will suffer greater persecution here in America. This should not surprise us, seeing the Apostle Paul warned us in II Tim. 3:12, *"Yea, and all that will live godly in Christ Jesus shall suffer persecution."* Jesus gave us instructions in Matt. 5:44 as to how we are to deal with our persecutors: *"But I say unto you, Love your enemies, bless them that curse you, do good to them that hate you, and pray for them which despitefully use you, and persecute you."* The only thing that will stem the tide of persecution is the spreading of the Gospel to the uttermost parts of the world. The hope of staying the tide of persecution here in America is the evangelistic outreach of the church. Every time a new Gospel-preaching church is planted, and men and women are won to Christ, we slow the tide of persecution. The answer to persecution around the world is missionary endeavors to spread the Gospel. Yes, the Great Commission is not only the command of our Lord for the salvation of the souls of men, but is also the command that is the answer to the persecution of believers. May each of us determine to share the Gospel with as many people as possible. May we renew our commitment to "preach the Gospel to every creature." God bless and have a great day!

June 30

   I heard a preacher answer the question of evolution with this: "I may have had some relatives to hang by their necks, but I never had relatives hang by their tails." The theory of evolution is taught as scientific fact. However, it is but a **theory,** and a false theory at that. The fact that evolution denies the Biblical account of creation exposes its error. Though I am neither scientist nor apologist for creation, I believe the Bible to to be the inspired, infallible, inerrant Word of God. So for me the matter is settled in Gen. 1:1. *"In the beginning God created the heaven and the earth."* God is the Creator of all things, and His creation declares His power and majesty. According to Ps. 19:1, *"The heavens declare the glory of God; and the firmament sheweth his handywork."* It is my opinion that our society has become a jungle of raving human animals largely because we have been taught that we are a higher form of an animal, instead of a creation in the image of God. Gen. 1:26 says, *"And God said, Let us make man in our image, after our likeness: and let them have dominion over the fish of the sea, and over the fowl of the air, and over the cattle, and over all the earth, and over every creeping thing that creepeth upon the earth."* We must remember who made us. We belong to God by creation, and we are to honor our Creator. We are to reject the notion that we are a product of an evolutionary process coming from a lower form of life. May I also remind us that we who have received Jesus as Savior belong to God through salvation. Note I Cor. 6:20. "For ye are bought with a price: therefore glorify God in your body, and in your spirit, which are God's." If we were created by God, if we have been purchased out of the slave market of sin by the blood of the Son of God, surely we should live in a way that reflects the character and the grace of our Creator. May others see Jesus in each of us today. God bless and have a great day.

Once I had the opportunity to speak at a "God, family and country" rally in Dayton, Tenn. At that time, there was some controversy about the proposed erection of a statue of Clarence Darrow in the town square with the existing statue of William Jennings Bryan. You may recall that a famous trial known as the Scopes Monkey Trial took place there in 1925. John Scopes, a substitute teacher, violated state law when he attempted to teach evolution in a public school. Darrow, an atheist, defended Scopes' right to teach evolution. They lost the case, and the state of Tennessee did not repeal the law prohibiting the teaching of evolution in public schools until 1967. Bryan successfully defended the state's creationist position. Reflecting on this makes me think about how there needs to be a resurgence of Christians taking a stand for Judeo-Christian principles in our society. Whether we lose or win, we must let our convictions be known. Attorney David Gibbs III often says, "We must stand for what is right; we must stand in the right way; and we must stand with a right spirit." My fear is that the church and Christians today cave to the pressures of the world. Compromise marks the character of the church and Christians. It is time that we again *earnestly contend for the faith which was once delivered unto the saints"* (Jude 3). God bless you and have a great day!

July 2

One morning while speaking in another city, I was driving to breakfast and heard a statement on the radio that caught my attention. It was a statement by President John F. Kennedy, "We choose to go to the moon ..." (The entire speech, given at Rice University in Houston in 1962, is now known by that phrase and can be seen on YouTube.) The commentator noted that Kennedy spoke the most powerful words of his presidency when he said, "We choose." He did not say the task was impossible. He did not say we would try. He said, "We choose." As I heard these words, my mind went immediately to a phrase in Jos. 24:15. *"... choose you this day whom ye will serve."* Every evil act begins with a **bad** choice and every noble endeavor begins with a **good** choice. Just as President Kennedy did regarding travel to the moon, so we must look beyond the impossible and see the possibilities in our lives. For us who know Jesus as Savior, we have the power of God within us to accomplish all that God has for us to do. As the angel said in Luke 1:37, *"For with God nothing shall be impossible."* My challenge for us today is that we choose to do something great for our God. May we look beyond our abilities, our resources, and the expectations of others, and step out by faith and believe God for the impossible. I remember the nay-sayers who doubted that we would ever put a man on the moon, but the president's choice was accomplished. Our choices as believers must always be accordance with the will of God, but our responsibility is to choose to do His will. Let me encourage you again to *"choose you this day whom you will serve."* Miracles begin with a choice. God bless and have a great day.

July 3

America is still the greatest country on planet Earth! Tomorrow, our country will celebrate another year of freedom. America is not perfect and seems to more divided today than any other time in my lifetime. However, we are still the most blessed nation in the world. There are many arguments that will be presented tomorrow as to why America has remained free and the most prosperous nation on earth over these two-plus centuries. One speaker I heard recently addressed that question by examining Prov. 14:34. *"Righteousness exalteth a nation: but sin is a reproach to any people."* He emphasized how our Founding Fathers acknowledged the need for God for our nation to survive. They included a recognition and need for the blessing of God in every document of governance adopted for the establishment of our country. The Bible and the principles of the Word of God were the foundation of our laws. This speaker pointed out that the word *"exalteth"* in Prov. 14:24 literately means to "rise above." America has risen above the nations of the world because America was founded upon Biblical principles. Sad to say, we are reaping the blessing of God upon our nation due to the *"righteousness"* of our forefathers. If America is to continue to be blessed by God, America must again become a righteous nation. We must not allow the secular humanists to push God out of our national discourse. Though we are a pluralistic society and welcome all religions, we must seek to be a nation that honors the God of the Bible. The foundation of our greatness is our Judeo-Christian heritage. If we are to continue to rise above the other nations of the world, we must retain our righteousness. God bless you and have a great day.

July 4

Happy Fourth of July to all! Today, we celebrate the adoption of the Declaration of Independence on this date in 1776. It is fitting that we consider the preamble of that document today: "We hold these truths to be self-evident, that all men are created equal, that they are endowed by their Creator with certain unalienable Rights, that among these are Life, Liberty, and the pursuit of Happiness." Please note that these rights come from God, not government. God provides these rights and government is to protect these rights for their constituents. As we mentioned yesterday, America has been blessed by God because America was founded on the principles and precepts of the Bible, God's Holy Word. Whereas *"exalteth"* in Prov. 14:34 means "rise above," we must also note that *"reproach"* means "to bring low." America has lost its standing in the world because we have departed from the God-given rights and principles of the Bible. James Madison said, "The future and success of America is not this Constitution, but in the Law of God upon which this Constitution is founded." America is being "brought low" and made a reproach due to our sin! One educational survey ranked us 14th in the world out of 40 nations, while another placed the U.S. 24th in literacy and 17th in educational performance. An economic study ranked America 17th in the world. When we sought to be righteous and live according to the principles of the Word of God, He blessed America. Now that we have embraced secular humanism and sought to remove God from our schools and halls of government, while legalizing practices and lifestyles that are contradictory to Biblical principles, the God that raised us up as the leader of all nations is now allowing us to be lowered in our standings before men because of our sin. Join me in prayer that God will send a revival to our country. Yes, we are still the greatest country on the earth, but we are losing ground due to our sin. God bless you today and God bless America.

July 5

The older I get, the more I enjoy the simple things of life. I enjoy conversation with a friend, being home in my chair, being with my wife at dinner, and going for a walk. Though God is a complex and an all-knowing God, He also seems to be a God of the simple. Case in point: a very popular tract titled, "God's Simple Plan of Salvation." Think about the simplicity of God's plan for our salvation. It cost the Father His Son; it cost the Son His life; it cost us nothing but a repentant heart and the faith to receive Jesus' finished work on the cross for our sin. Consider these Biblical statements. *"For whosoever shall call upon the name of the Lord shall be saved."* (Rom. 10:13) *"Believe on the Lord Jesus Christ, and thou shalt be saved, and thy house."* (Acts 16:31) *"But as many as received him, to them gave he power to become the sons of God, even to them that believe on his name."* (John 1:12) These are but a few of many that illustrate that God has made the way of salvation simple so that men might be able to be saved. We, who know Jesus as Savior, need to to be sharing God's simple plan of salvation with others. Its simplicity does not remove its value or the awesomeness of Christ's sacrifice on the cross for our sins. As II Cor. 5:21 states, *"For he hath made him to be sin for us, who knew no sin; that we might be made the righteousness of God in him."* This simple message needs to be shared. You and I have a God-given responsibility to do that. May we be found faithful today in telling others about this wonderful salvation. God bless and have a great day!

July 6

I have heard it said, "We may get weary in the work of the Lord, but never weary of the Lord of the work." God is not finished with you or me. As long as we live, He has a work for us to do. Our faithfulness depends on our personal relationship with the Lord. Lam. 3:22-23 reminds us, *"It is of the Lord's mercies that we are not consumed, because his compassions fail not. They are new every morning: great is thy faithfulness."* The closer I draw to Jesus, the more I desire to serve Him. The passage of time changes my ability to serve, but with every season of life are new opportunities to be used of God in His service. The preacher may become the teacher, while the Sunday School teacher may become the prayer warrior, interceding on behalf of others. God reveals His place of service to us as we stay in fellowship with Him. It has been my experience that the older I get and the longer I serve Him, the more I must have time with Him. Don't neglect your personal time with the Lord. It is in those times that God reveals His will for our lives. No, God is not finished with you. He has a work for you to do, and you will know His place and purpose for your life as you stay in His presence. I close with the words of the Apostle Paul in Phil. 1:6. *"Being confident of this very thing, that he which hath begun a good work in you will perform it until the day of Jesus Christ."*

July 7

I can still hear that raspy old voice over the phone at about 4 or 5 a.m. from evangelist Lester Roloff, quoting II Tim. 4:1-2. *"I charge thee therefore before God, and the Lord Jesus Christ, who shall judge the quick and the dead at his appearing and his kingdom; Preach the word; be instant in season, out of season; reprove, rebuke, exhort with all long suffering and doctrine."* I was saved in a revival meeting where Bro. Roloff was preaching. We developed a friendship, and he was an encouragement to me during the early days of my ministry. His early morning phone calls would always be followed with the question, "You weren't asleep, were you?" Of course, I was asleep, but I remember responding on one occasion, "No, Bro. Roloff, I was not asleep. I had to wake up to answer the phone," to which he chuckled. There are times when the memory of those calls and the many expressions of encouragement from others still motivate me to keep on keeping on for the Lord. I heard a TV commentator say a few days ago, "Words matter." My thought for today is that you and I speak words of encouragement to someone. I would suggest a word of encouragement to your pastor. The work of the ministry can be lonely and often discouraging. Just a word from you may brighten the day for a struggling servant of the Lord. It may be that there is a friend or loved one who needs a word of comfort. I challenge you to provide that to them. You do not need call them in the early hours of the morning, but as God gives opportunity, seek to be a blessing to someone today. As I grow older, it is amazing how many words of help and encouragement come to my mind from those in my past. You see, our words never die. They live on in the hearts and minds of those that hear them. Let's be sure our words are worth remembering. God bless and have a great day.

July 8

Continuing our thought from yesterday about how "words matter," I have recalled other words that have influenced my life — words spoken by friends, fellow ministers, and professional acquaintances. I have written some of them down and would like to share them with you over the next few days. I was a young pastor facing my first real opposition in my ministry. People I thought would stay with me through thick or thin were leaving the church and causing me great anxiety. Not a large number, but folks I loved and had known for a while. One day, I was out of the office when a friend stopped by. Seeing I was not in, he asked my secretary if he could leave a note on my desk. She invited him into my office where he left these words: "Hang in there, it is lonely at the top." It was signed by Locklan Downs. Leadership has its price because decision makers are always going to be questioned. Every person is given a place of leadership at some point in life. It may be in the home, or at a business, or in the ministry. No matter the position, at times we all feel alone, forsaken, and discouraged. God promised in Deut. 31:6, *"Be strong and of a good courage, fear not, nor be afraid of them: for the Lord thy God, he it is that doth go with thee; he will not fail thee, nor forsake thee."* Many times of discouragement and disappointments in life have come to me due to my own bad choices. Other times, they have come due to circumstances beyond my control, and then there have been times when being the leader has caused conflict. Through all the times of feeling alone, I have recalled those words written on a 3-by-5 card, "Hang in there, it is lonely at the top." Thank God I have *"a friend that sticketh closer than a brother"* (Prov. 18:24) to go with me through the lonely times in life — who strengthens me, gives encouragement and promises that He will never forsake me. If you are going through a tough time, hang in there. You are not forsaken. God bless and have a great day!

July 9

I recall seeking God's will for my life as I approached graduation from college. My pastor, Dr. Jerry Falwell, had asked me to pray about going to Roanoke, Va., to plant a church. I had only been to Roanoke once in my life, and I was only 23 years old with very little experience in ministry. I was considering doing some post-graduate studies, or maybe taking a staff position that had been offered at a church. I recall making an appointment with Dr. Lee Roberson to seek advice for my decision. As I shared with him my desire to do the will of God, he said, "If it is the will of God for you to continue your education, **do it.** If God wants you to start a church, **do it.** Just do the will of God." To some, these words may not be a definitive answer, but they are the words that God used to direct my decision. What really got my attention were the two words, **"do it."** I am reminded of the words of Jesus in John 7:17. *"If any man will do his will, he shall know of the doctrine, whether it be of God, or whether I speak of myself."* Jesus was answering the Jews who questioned how He could be so knowledgeable. In this verse, I see plainly three things about knowing the will of God. First, you must **desire** to know the will of God. The word "will" is translated "willeth" in some translations. Do you really want to know God's plan for your life? Second, you must **do** what you know to do. It has been said that 98 percent of all God wants you to do is recorded in His Word. Knowing the will of God is determined by our doing what we know to do. Third, you must **discern** His teachings, not only the doctrines of the Bible, but the place and purpose for our life. My prayer today is that each of us seek to do His will. God bless and have a great day.

July 10

"Keep the main thing the main thing." As I continue to reflect on how "words matter," this phrase has had a definite impact on my life. Though I do not know if it was original with Dr. Raymond Hancock, it was from him that I first heard it. He spoke directly to me when I was a guest speaker at his church. I recall asking myself, "What is the **main thing**?" I heard Len Curtis deliver a message exhorting us to stay focused on that which the Lord has given or called us to do. His text was from Nehemiah, whose adversaries told him in Neh. 6:2, *"Come let us meet together."* It was their way to get him to leave his work. Note Nehemiah's response in verse 3: *"I am doing a great work, so that I cannot come down."* The **main thing** for every Christian and every church is to get the Gospel message to every person. Our Savior's last command to us in Mark 16:15 was, *"Go ye into all the world, and preach the gospel to every creature."* This is called The Great Commission, not The Great Suggestion. Bible Study is important, but is not the main thing. Worship is necessary, but it is not the main thing. Fellowship is greatly to be desired, but it is not the main thing. The main thing is presenting the Gospel message to a sin cursed and lost world!! May God help each of us to "keep the main thing the main thing". God bless and have a great day!

"Words that matter" fall upon our ears every day. It was just an ordinary day, and I was visiting my home church, Thomas Road Baptist in Lynchburg, Va. As I walked across the parking lot, I heard a deep robust voice call out to me, "Hey Brother, I prayed for you this morning about 6:15. Pray for you every morning." I turned to see an old gentleman named R.C. Whorley, a great soul winner, who did visitation for the church. He had no formal education to prepare him to serve as a staff member of the church, but he was filled with the Holy Spirit of God and a vital member of the church's leadership. Over the years, I heard him say to me more than once, "Hey, Brother, I prayed for you this morning." Thinking of this reminds me of our responsibility to pray for others, and also how much I need the prayers of others. It is interesting to note how often the Apostle Paul requested others to pray for him. You can find in I Thess. 5:25 and II Thess. 3:1 the phrase, *"Brethren, pray for us."* He also prayed for others. As noted in Phil. 1:3-4, "I thank my God upon every remembrance of you, Always in every prayer of mine for you all making request with joy." I wonder how often we say, "I'm praying for you," but we have not prayed? I must pray for others with the same urgency that I feel to have them pray for me. Hearing someone say, "I am praying for you," is the greatest encouragement when you know that person prays. I want to challenge each of us today to pray for others, and I also ask you to pray for me. May we covet together to pray one for another! The day my mother called to tell me of Bro. Whorley's death, my eyes filled with tears and I thought, "Who is going to pray for me now?" How sweet to hear from a sincere heart that someone is praying for me. God bless and have a great day!

July 12

Ever felt like just quitting? Maybe it's to join the 1,500 pastors who quit the ministry each month, or the nearly 50 percent of marriages that end up in divorce. Maybe it's just giving up on some calling in your life. Quitting can become habit forming. It always seems easier to quit than to stay the course or stick to the calling or the position in which you find yourself. As a student in college I heard a speaker say, "The test of a man's character is what it takes to stop him." In later years, I heard some preachers say the same thing. These words became "words that matter" in my life. I wrote them in the cover of my Bible and I often read them. My challenge for us today can be summarized from the words of the Apostle Paul in Gal. 6:9. *"And let us not be weary in well doing: for in due season we shall reap, if we faint not."* We all get weary in the work of the Lord or in other endeavors of life, but beyond the **problem** of weariness is the **promise** of reaping. The **prerequisite** is that we do not faint. Claim the promise of II Chr. 15:7. *"Be ye strong therefore, and let not your hands be weak: for your work shall be rewarded."* If you are where God wants you to be, and you are doing what God wants you to do - take heart. Stay faithful. God is greater than all your problems. As you face the trials and tribulations of the day, remember that the test of your character is what it takes to stop you. God bless you today.

July 13

I was in a church service as a young man when the pastor called upon a visiting businessman to lead in prayer. That gentleman declined, and the church member who invited him immediately began to pray. I recall feeling sorry for the gentleman who, no doubt, was embarrassed. As I began my ministry, I discovered there were some people who were not comfortable praying out loud in the presence of others. I have also heard many young believers express that they did not know **how** to pray. There was a time when Jesus was asked by one of his disciples in John 11:1, *"Lord, teach us to pray."* Note the request was not **how to** pray, but rather *"teach us **to** pray."* Pretty words do not make a prayer. The place or posture does not define the significance of the prayer. The important thing is that we pray. Dr. Harold Wilmington defined prayer as "a child of God in communication with his Heavenly Father on the merits of the blood of Jesus." Being unable to pray in public is not terrible, but not to pray at all, is unacceptable. Among the "words that matter" in my life are the words I heard as a teenager from Dr. Jerry Falwell. This statement still challenges me today. "Nothing of eternal value is ever accomplished apart from prayer." No, your prayer does not need to be a public utterance, but it must be a communication with the Heavenly Father. How long has it been since you communicated with the God of Heaven? Do you pray daily? When and where do you meet the Lord for a time of prayer? These are pertinent questions to assure our relationship with God. Your prayer needs be heard only by the one to whom you pray. I heard once of a children's Sunday School teacher who asked little Johnny to pray. He bowed his head and began to silently move his lips. The teacher leaned over and said, "Johnny, we can't hear you." Johnny responded, "I am not talking to you." Remember to whom you are speaking when you pray. God bless and have a great day.

July 14

Last words spoken are often "words that matter." I have many fond memories of my grandparents. I lived with them in the summer months for several of my teen years, working on the farm to earn money to buy my school clothes. My paternal grandfather was a devout Christian with his own ideas about preachers. When I told him that I was going to college to study for the ministry, he replied, "If God has called you to preach, then God will give you the messages to preach. You do not need to go to college to learn to preach." My grandfather believed that the problem with many churches was "college-made preachers." I have to admit, though I believe in academic preparation for the ministry, I have seen college and seminary ruin many a young man's faith. I recall the last words spoken to me by my grandfather. As I left his home to return to college after our discussion, Pa Holland (as I called him) called to me as I walked toward the door. "Son, just preach this Book. If you must go to college, OK, but never stop preaching this Book." He held his Bible — a red-letter King James Version — in his hand as he spoke. Several years later as I stood by his casket, looking at his lifeless body, I looked up to the heavens and said out loud, "Pa, I have been faithful to preach the Bible, and I promise to never cease preaching the Word of God!" May we never allow the philosophies of this world to detract us from preaching, teaching, and sharing the Gospel of Christ. May our hearts be filled with the sentiments of the Apostle Paul as he wrote in I Cor. 9:16, "For though I preach the gospel, I have nothing to glory of: for necessity is laid upon me; yea, woe is unto me, if I preach not the gospel!" The hope of every soul is the message of the Gospel of Christ. We must not cease from declaring that message. God bless you and if you're a preacher, preach the Word!

The church was doing great! People were attending, and the church was experiencing growth. The church congregation consisted mostly of hard-working, middle-class American families. I invited Dr. Jack Hyles to speak at the church for a couple of services. At the last service, I asked him if he had any suggestions or criticisms that would help me be a better pastor or otherwise help the church. "Your church needs more poor people," he said. "Poor people give your people an opportunity to serve others — not to mention Jesus' ministry was primarily to the poor." These became "words that matter" in my life. From that night forward, as a pastor, I always sought to involve our church in ministering to the poor. We fed the poor, we helped the needy with the necessities of life, and we welcomed the poor with open arms to our church. We, as individual Christians and church congregations, need to bless the poor. I John 3:17 says, *"But whoso hath this world's good, and seeth his brother have need, and shutteth up his bowels of compassion from him, how dwelleth the love of God in him?"* I found that the poor are often more receptive to the Gospel. I believe this is because they seek help and hope. The comfortable or wealthy often feel they have need for nothing nor no one, not even God. Surely we must seek to reach all people, the up-and-outer as well as the down-and-outers. But let us not forget to reach out to the poor. God bless and have a great day!

July 16

"Everything rises or falls on leadership." I can still hear Dr. Lee Roberson saying these words. They certainly have been "words that matter" in the lives of many. As I have travelled around the country and even abroad, I have heard former students of Tennessee Temple University, where Dr. Roberson was founder and president, and others repeat these words. I am not sure they originated with him, but they certainly are true. Nations experience change under new leadership; families are shaped by the leadership of parents; and churches are a reflection of their leadership. All of us are leaders of someone. Our influence may not affect a nation, but it may affect a family or even a friend who looks up to you as an example to follow. I am reminded of the words of James 3:1. *"My brethren, be not many masters, knowing that we shall receive the greater condemnation."* This verse is a warning that God will judge more strictly those that are leaders or teachers. It is important that we seek to follow the right kind of leadership. There are some circumstances where we cannot choose our leader because he or she has been chosen for us. If a leader violates the principles of our ultimate leader, the Lord Jesus Christ, then we are to follow Jesus. We can choose our leadership in many cases, such as the church we attend, the authors of the books we read, and the sermons we listen to on TV or social media. Rest assured that these leaders are having an influence on the way you live your life. Also, beware of the leadership you give to those that would be influenced by you. My prayer is that others might see Jesus in me! I desire to lead others to follow Jesus, not to follow me. Great leaders are followers of Christ. God bless and have a great day.

I never cease to be amazed at the goodness of the Lord. The Bible says in Ps. 27:13, *"I had fainted, unless I had believed to see the goodness of the Lord in the land of the living."* It is easy to only look at the negative things around us and lose sight of the goodness of God in our lives. Let's count our blessings today rather than focusing on our burdens. Look around you and rejoice for the good things in your life, rather than bemoaning all the negative things around you. To truly see the goodness of God, we need to follow the exhortation of the following: Ps. 27:14. *"Wait on the Lord: be of good courage, and he shall strengthen thine heart: wait, I say, on the Lord."* Take a moment to think about just how good the Lord has been to you. He has provided us with salvation. The hope of Heaven is a good thing! Most of us can rejoice that God has supplied our physical needs. Through times of hardships and sorrow, God has been good to provide strength for every trial. Do not allow Satan to rob you of the joy of knowing Jesus today. Look beyond the burdens, look beyond the negatives in your life and see the goodness of God. Yes, God is good all the time, and all the time God is good. One writer wrote, "God not only **does** good things; God **is** good." God bless you today and have a great day!

July 18

As I conclude my series of thoughts about "words that matter" in my life, I wish to share with you some of the words spoken that matter to all people. They are familiar words to most of you, but they are the words that have made a difference in our lives. They are the words spoken by Jesus in John 3:16. *"For God so loved the world, that he gave his only begotten Son, that whosoever believeth in him should not perish, but have everlasting life."* Several years ago, I preached a series of messages from this verse. I do not recall the exact number of messages, but I remember that I took each phrase and examined it and explained it. My thought for today centers around this question: Who loves? Who is it that loves *"the world"* as described in this verse? Jesus declared that it was God. That *"world"* includes you and me. We often feel alone and maybe forsaken by friends and family. We feel no one cares about us, but I am glad to report to every person reading this that God loves you — just as you are, wherever you are. His love was and is manifested (made known) by Him sending His Son to die on a cross for your sin and my sin. His love is unconditional; it is unbelievable; and it is always available. Praise God for the words, "For God so loved." I can say, "For God so loved Rudy." You can insert your name at the end of that phrase. God still loves us and will always love us. There is no greater need in our lives than to be loved. Thank God for loving us. God bless and have a great day.

"I am not looking for the **undertaker**; I am looking for the **upper taker!"** I can't tell you how many times I have heard preachers and others say those words. The truth is that each of us who knows Jesus as Savior should live every day expecting Him to return to catch us away to be with Him. We are reminded in Titus 2:13 that we are to be *"Looking for that blessed hope, and the glorious appearing of the great God and our Saviour Jesus Christ."* Jesus said in John 14:3, *"And if I go and prepare a place for you, I will come again, and receive you unto myself; that where I am, there ye may be also."* These are but two of many verses in the Word of God that tell us of the promise of Jesus to return for His own. Each of us should live as if this were the day the Lord would return. This **could be** that day. Let me ask you a question. If you knew today was the day of His coming, what would you do? How would you live? What changes would you make in your life? My friend, one day will be the day of His return. This could be that day. May God help each of us to live looking for the upper taker, the Lord Jesus, today! For those who do not know Jesus as Savior, do not delay; trust Him to be your Savior today, for this could be the day Jesus returns. God bless you and have a great day looking for His return.

July 20

Our lives are the sum of the decisions we have made. As a young pastor, I heard a message concerning how to make good decisions. I do not remember the speaker, but I wrote the scripture references in my Bible. These principles have served to guide me in my decision making, especially to determine if a particular act or practice is right or wrong. Let me share these verses and principles with you today. First, consider if the act or practice could **control** you. I Cor. 6:12 says, *"All things are lawful unto me, but all things are not expedient: all things are lawful for me, but I will not be brought under the power of any."* Second, consider if it will **glorify** God. According to I Cor. 6:20, *"For ye are bought with a price: therefore glorify God in your body, and in your spirit, which are God's."* Third, consider if it will **offend** your brother. Paul wrote in I Cor. 8:13, *"Wherefore, if meat make my brother to offend, I will eat no flesh while the world standeth, lest I make my brother to offend."* Fourth, consider if it will **edify** you (make you better). Note I Cor. 10:23. *"All things are lawful for me, but all things are not expedient: all things are lawful for me, but all things edify not."* My prayer today is that these guiding principles will help each of us make good decisions. Remember that decisions are the hinges upon which the doors of our future swing. God bless and have a great day.

Living with Heaven in mind! This is what I believe the Apostle Paul was speaking about as he wrote in Col. 3:1-2, *"If ye then be risen with Christ, seek those things which are above, where Christ sitteth on the right hand of God. Set your affection on things above, not on things on the earth."* This goes beyond just thinking about the afterlife and the place called Heaven. It refers to seeking things in this life that are of a heavenly or godly quality. With the media so filled with vulgar language and lewd content, and the philosophies of our society so removed from Biblical morality, it is difficult for even Christians to focus on godly things rather than the things of this world. Consider focusing on what is described in Phil. 4:8. *"Finally, brethren, whatsoever things are true, whatsoever things are honest, whatsoever things are just, whatsoever things are pure, whatsoever things are lovely, whatsoever things are of good report; if there be any virtue, and if there be any praise, think on these things."* With all the negatives in our society, let's strive to guard our minds. The challenge of the day is for each of us to focus on the **good** and the **godly** things around us. Each of us need to fill our minds with the Word of God. We must view every aspect of our lives with Heaven in view and on our minds. This life will soon be over, after which comes an eternity to live in the joy and bliss of Heaven. Even in the midst of sufferings in this life, we must remember the words of Rom. 8:18. *"For I reckon that the sufferings of this present time are not worthy to be compared with the glory which shall be revealed in us."* Live today with Heaven in mind. God bless and have a great day!

July 22

We are bombarded in the media today with political arguments. For virtually every issue, you can find each major party going on and on about how awful the other party is and what should really be done. It is especially intense during election season, when each candidate will rehearse all of the evils in our country and the proposed solutions for each. When I watch this kind of political discourse on TV, I cannot help but recall a quote from attorney David Gibbs III: "The hope of America is not in the state house, or in the courthouse, or even in the White House. Our hope is in the **church house**." Yes, I believe we should actively seek to elect leaders that will protect our freedoms and uphold our laws. But the ultimate answer to our national or personal problems is a life or a nation that honors the God of creation — the God of the Bible. In Matt. 5:13-16 the Lord called His church and each of us who know Him to be *"the salt of the earth"* and *"the light of the world."* Salt is used as a preservative. We are to preserve the doctrines and practices declared in the Bible. A light illuminates in darkness. We are to be beacons of light directing men and societies to righteousness. Through the Bible, the blessings of God have come to the masses due to the faithfulness of the few. Let's not be discouraged with the condition of our world. Resolve to be salt and light for the glory of our Lord. God bless you and God bless America!

July 23

Each day is a day of opportunity. Each day we face some kind of opposition or obstacle in our lives. The opportunities must be seized upon, and the obstacles or opposition must be dealt with. The opportunities that come your way today may only present themselves once. Do not procrastinate and miss God's open door of possibilities for you. The Apostle Paul faced opportunity and opposition as expressed in I Cor. 16:9. *"For a great door and effectual is opened unto me, and there are many adversaries."* As I listen to the news of the day and travel around the country, I am aware of the opposition to the cause of Christ in our culture. I see and hear of the opposition to our religious freedom, and I am made aware of the obstacles that Christians and churches face in carrying out their mission or living out their faith. It is my opinion that the spiritual darkness of the hour gives opportunity for the light of the Gospel to shine brighter. My challenge for the day is to all Christians — that we ask God for a positive attitude and a fresh enduement of Holy Ghost power to reach our communities with the Gospel of Christ. Instead of complaining about the opposition and obstacles, may we see them as rocks along the hillside of life for us to climb on. They are opportunities for our light to shine and our testimonies to be heard. Remember the exhortation of I John 4:4. *"Ye are of God, little children, and have overcome them*: **because greater is he that is in you, than he that is in the world."** God bless and have a great day!

July 24

"What we know is not always what we do." I recently heard a Sunday school teacher say that, and it reminded me of one definition of sin I had been taught: "To know to do good and not do it." That principle is taken directly from James 4:17. *"Therefore to him that knoweth to do good, and doeth it not, to him it is sin."* A worthy goal for us, as stated in James 1:22, is to be *"doers of the word, and not hearers only, deceiving your own selves."* What we **believe** should determine how we **behave.** However, I think God is much more interested in our behavior than He is with our knowledge. For instance, I read much debate on the details of particular doctrines, such as the sovereignty of God, but witness very little obedience to sharing the Gospel with others. I often hear much discussion of the need for more Bible studies, but little emphasizes on taking the message of the Gospel to a lost and dying world. I sometimes hear criticism of entitlement programs to those who will not work, but very little effort to feed the homeless or help those who could work find meaningful employment. It is obvious that what we know to do is not always what we do. We just love to show off our knowledge without providing the effort to help correct the problem. We often are well informed about the doctrines but not so keen on fulfilling our duty. May God help us today to be *"doers of the word."* God bless and have a great day!

July 25

"The two additional commandments added to the Old Testament commandments, found in the New Testament, are to preach the Gospel to every creature and to love one another." Recently I heard this statement for the first time in my life. I do not know how I missed it, but it sure sparked some thoughts. My first thought was a question: Where and when were these commandments given? The first commandment was given by Jesus in the Gospels as well as Acts 1:8. It is often referred to as the Great Commission and is recorded, among other places, in Matt. 28:19. *"Go ye therefore, and teach all nations, baptizing them in the name of the Father, and of the Son, and of the Holy Ghost."* The second was also given by Jesus in John 13:34. *"A new commandment I give unto you, That ye love one another; as I have loved you, that ye also love one another."* We need to embrace these two commandments and obey them. They are not suggestions for the Christian; they are commandments, and failing to obey them is disobedience. Both commandments demand action and involve touching the lives of others. When obeyed, both will bring great joy to others and to the one that obeys them. Today, I challenge you show some love to someone and share the Gospel with some soul today. God bless and have a great day.

July 26

My wife tells the story of attending an old-fashioned tent meeting as a teenager. It was her first experience in a meeting with so much excitement. There were those who shouted and praised the Lord during the service. A lady holding a baby evidently got caught up in the spirit of the service and asked my wife, "Honey, would you hold my baby? I think I am going to shout." As I pondered that thought, I was reminded of how the Lord desires our **praise**. The psalms are filled with admonitions for us to praise the Lord. The Bible says in Ps. 113:1-3, *"Praise ye the Lord. Praise, O ye servants of the Lord, praise the name of the Lord. Blessed be the name of the Lord from this time forth and for evermore. From the rising of the sun unto the going down of the same the Lord's name is to be praised."* Each of us should take a few moments and just praise the Lord. You may need to set aside a time or make preparation for that special time to give praise to your God. Find someone to "hold your baby" if need be, but do not fail to praise Him today. Praise Him for **who** He is — the sovereign God who is in control. He is our Savior! Praise His name! Praise Him for **what** He has done. He has saved us from our sins. Thank you Lord for our salvation! He has supplied our needs. I give Him praise for His provisions for my every need! My mind is filled with thoughts of all the blessings that are mine because of God's blessings on me. Hey, friend, "Would you hold my baby? I think I am going to shout!" God bless and have a great day!

July 27

I recall attending a pastors' conference with the theme, "Write The Vision." It was taken from Hab. 2:2. *"And the Lord answered me, and said, Write the vision, and make it plain upon tables, that he may run that readeth it."* Habakkuk was a prophet during a time of unrest in Judah. An evil nation, the Babylonians, was on the move and Judah was living in disobedience to their God. As the prophet sought to know the will of God for the people, God instructed him to *"write the vision."* For many years I set aside a time at the end of each year, usually in the month of November, to get alone and seek God's direction for my life and ministry for the coming year. At that time, I wrote the vision. There is something about putting one's thoughts on paper and reviewing them as time goes by. We must first **have** a vision from God before we can write it. A vision is simply a direction from God for your life or the ministry God has given you. Your vision may be for your family, your vocation, or some other aspect of life. Whatever you feel God leading you to accomplish, write it. Be sure you make your vision **plain.** You must be able to understand it, obviously, and others who need to be involved in your plans must be able to understand your vision. You should **share** your vision with others. The last phrase of verse 2, *"that he may run that readeth it,"* implies that someone would communicate the message to others. Sharing the vision not only gets others involved in fulfilling and accomplishing it, but it also is an opportunity for accountability for you to fulfill your responsibility to carry out your vision. Take a few moments today and write the vision that God gives you. Make it plain and then share it with those who will be involved in its fulfillment. God bless and have a great day.

July 28

Change is inevitable. We are reminded in Eccl. 3:1-8 of the changing times and circumstances of our lives. Verse 1 sums it up: *"To every thing there is a season, and a time to every purpose under the heaven."* I have been blessed with 70 years of health, and as far as I know, I am still healthy. I praise God for good health. I do have some problems with my knees (torn meniscus and arthritis), but I know failing health is an inevitable change that will overtake me in time. How should we face the changing times in our lives? It's not just changes in our health, but of all kinds — our vocations, financial positions, social status and other areas of life. I suggest we accept the changes and view them as *"a season ... and a time"* with a particular God-ordained purpose. Wherever you are today, whatever your circumstances, God has a purpose for your life. I recall the story of a dear lady who had suffered a stroke and was left totally disabled. Each day as her caregiver came to care for her, she would cry, "I just want to die! I am good for nothing, and can do nothing for myself." One day the caregiver said, "Please don't say that you want to die! You are very important to me." "How could I be of value to you or anyone else? I can do nothing for myself." "You are valuable to me," the caregiver replied. "A few years ago my husband died suddenly of a heart attack and left me with two children. I had never worked outside the home. This job provides me with the money I need to care for my family. You see, you are very important to me." Remember: *"To every thing there is a season, and a time to every purpose under the heaven."* God bless and have a great day!

Conflicts with others are a part of life. We are human and sinful, so we often fail to meet the expectations of others. As you read through the Bible, there are conflicts recorded between some of the most spiritual characters. The conflict between Paul and Peter recorded in Gal. 2:11-21 should serve as an example that even servants of God can have differences. The question is not whether we will have conflicts, but how we should resolve them when they come. Our answer is found in the words of Jesus in Matt. 18:15-17. *"Moreover if thy brother shall trespass against thee, go and tell him his fault between thee and him alone: if he shall hear thee, thou hast gained thy brother. But if he will not hear thee, then take with thee one or two more, that in the mouth of two or three witnesses every word may be established. And if he shall neglect to hear them, tell it unto the church: but if he neglect to hear the church, let him be unto thee as an heathen man and a publican."* Resolution of conflict between believers is a threefold process. First, go to the one who has offended you and attempt to settle your differences privately. If the matter is not settled, take a witness and go to the individual again and attempt to resolve the issue. Third, and as a last resort, take the matter to the church for resolution. It is my opinion that the vast majority of differences can be resolved between those offended if they will but talk and hear each other out. Backbiting and gossip will only divide and destroy relationships. Remember that our testimony before the unsaved and the weaker brethren should be that we love one another. God bless you today and have a great day.

July 30

I was sitting at my desk when a junior high student came into my office to address the fact that he did not desire to be a student in our Christian school. He was a good student, obedient (for the most part) and from a good Christian home. I asked why he did not desire to be in the school and his reply was, "Well, I am just not happy." I once read a survey that out of the ten greatest desires of people, the first was to be happy. May I say to you, as I said to that student, happiness is a choice. Each of us can choose to be happy, or we can allow the circumstances of life to dictate the level of joy or happiness in our lives. I have traveled to the poorest countries and found a happy, joyous people who had very little of this world's wealth. I have stood by the bedside of the sick and afflicted and sensed an inner joy and contentment in their lives, despite their illness. Then, I have met people who had plenty of money and were healthy but were without happiness. Happiness is a choice. I often need to read Phil. 4:11-13. *"Not that I speak in respect of want: for I have learned, in whatsoever state I am, therewith to be content. I know both how to be abased, and I know how to abound: every where and in all things I am instructed both to be full and to be hungry, both to abound and to suffer need. I can do all things through Christ which strengtheneth me."* Keep in mind that Paul wrote these words while in a Roman prison. I surmise that Paul made a choice to be happy regardless of his circumstances. The Bible says in Phil. 4:4, *"Rejoice in the Lord always: and again I say, Rejoice."* That exhortation is mentioned throughout the book. My challenge for today is that each of us choose to be happy. God bless and have a joy-filled day!

July 31

It has been said, "Our disappointments are often His appointments for our lives." As a traveling speaker, I often experience cancellations or changes in my schedule. They are often unexpected and sometimes disappointing, but I have learned that God often has particular plans for me beyond my own knowledge. I am reminded of the words of Jer. 29:11. *"For I know the thoughts that I think toward you, saith the Lord, thoughts of peace, and not of evil, to give you an expected end."* Some translations translate the word *"thoughts"* to *"plans."* The message to Jeremiah was that God had a plan for his life. He also has a plan for our lives and it is a plan that includes *"peace"* and an *"unexpected end."* I recently heard Dr. Bill Pennell say, "God always wants us to do something else." He was referring to the changing places and often-changing types of ministry God gives to each of us. I have pastored in four different places. I have traveled as as evangelist and now, I travel speaking in various capacities, including representing the National Center for Life and Liberty. God's plans are perfect. He has a plan for your life. Each of us needs to be flexible to do the will of God in our lives. As Henry Blackaby said, we only need to "find out what God is up to in our lives and join Him." Don't fret over disappointments; they could well be God's appointments for something great in your life. Have a great day and stay faithful to the Master.

August 1

Declining attendance is a challenge for every church. How do we reach people with the Gospel in these days? There are some churches that seem to be increasing in attendance, but for the most part there are increasing empty pews or chairs in the churches across the land. In Luke 14, Jesus told a parable of a man who made ready a banquet and invited guests to attend. The invited guests made excuses as to why they could not come to the banquet (v. 16-20), so in verse 21, the master commanded his servant to, *"Go out quickly into the streets and lanes of the city, and bring in hither the poor, and the maimed, and the halt, and the blind."* When that didn't fill the house, he gave another order in verse 23. *"And the lord said unto the servant, Go out into the highways and hedges, and compel them to come in, that my house may be filled."* I live in a southern city that has an unusual number of homeless or street people. I have often wondered why our local churches are not reaching these people. I recall the day when many Bible-believing churches ran buses to pick up people, often in poor neighborhoods, to bring them to church. It is my conviction that whether poor, homeless, middle class, or wealthy, **all** need the Gospel. The only house the Lord has on earth is the local church. The banquet for today is the Bread of Life. We are His servants, and I believe there are more than enough people who will come to the banquet and fill the houses of worship, if the servants will go into the *"highways and hedges"* and *"compel"* or entice them to come in. We may need to entice them to come with food or shelter, but the goal is to get them to the banquet and introduce them to the Savior. May God give us a passion for the souls of all men today. God bless and have a great day.

August 2

In Gordon Livingston's book "Too Soon Old, Too Late Smart," the first chapter is titled, "If the map doesn't agree with the ground, the map is wrong." The premise of the chapter is that circumstances in life necessitate that we change the course of our lives. Though this may be true of our daily lives, God has given us a map for us to follow that is never wrong and will always lead us to our desired end. That map is the Bible, God's unchanging Word. The Bible says in Ps. 119:89, *"For ever, O Lord, thy word is settled in heaven."* Jesus said in Matt. 24:35, *"Heaven and earth shall pass away, but my words shall not pass away."* Though society or circumstances may change, God's Word is still true and is still the guiding beam from Heaven to direct our lives. Though man may attempt to change the message of the Bible, its message is still true. We do not need to alter it to accommodate today's culture; we need only follow the instructions as given. The Bible is the map that leads to **salvation**, to **satisfaction** in life, and to emotional and spiritual **security**. Though I applaud intellectual pursuits into the study of the original languages of the Bible and appreciate those who spend their lives seeking the deep meaning of the Scriptures, we are not to seek to change the map to accommodate the terrain of the moment! An altered course from Biblical truth will lead to error and an undesired destiny. Today I give thanks to God for an unchanging message to be my guide to Heaven and a map to follow in this life. "The B-I-B-L-E; yes, that's the Book for me. I stand alone on Word of God, the B-I-B-L-E." God bless and have a great day!

August 3

It was in a revival meeting, and the evangelist had been preaching some straight and pointed sermons against sin. The offering plates were passed and there was a note in the plate addressed to the evangelist. The usher brought the note to the evangelist, who opened it as he approached the pulpit and read it to the congregation. The note read, "You go to Hell!" The quick-witted evangelist responded, "I'm not going to do it!" He then delivered another Bible message. There is a message for all of us in this little story. There is a devil who desires for the souls of men to burn in Hell. Yet those who receive Jesus as Savior can join that old evangelist and say, "I'm not going to do it!" There is a story told by Jesus in Luke 16:19-31 of two men, one wealthy and the other a beggar. Both men died. In verse 22 the beggar *"was carried by the angels into Abraham's bosom."* Verse 23 says of the rich man, *"in hell he lift up his eyes, being in torments."* This should be a reminder to each of us of a place called Hell. You don't hear much about it from the pulpits of today, but that does not remove the reality of a literal Hell where sinners who die without Jesus will spend eternity. May all of us who know Jesus as Savior pause and thank Him that we are not going to this horrible place. To those who read this and have never received Christ as Savior, I plead with you to do so today. Evangelist Robert Sumner wrote a book of sermons entitled, "Hell Is No Joke." It is a literal place! This truth should motivate every believer to share the Gospel with someone today. It should move any unbeliever to faith in Christ that they may escape this place of torment. Hell is not a popular subject to discuss or think about, but my prayer is that all of us will consider the reality of hell today. God bless and have a blessed day.

August 4

"Everybody Is Going Somewhere" was the title of a message I delivered several years ago. The point was that there is life after death, and every one of us will spend eternity in either Heaven or Hell. The longer I live the more the reality of Heaven grips my soul. It is a literal place. Jesus said in John 14:2, *"In my Father's house are many mansions: if it were not so, I would have told you. I go to prepare a place for you."* I did an online search and found that there were 35 verses in the Bible with references to Heaven. There could be many more; I have never counted. Heaven is the hope of every one of us. Just think of all that we will see in Heaven. We will see our loved ones who have gone before us. Dr. B.R. Lakin was once asked, "Will we know each other in Heaven?" He responded, "Surely I will be as knowledgeable in Heaven as I am on earth." To that I say amen! We will see awesome beauty. To get a word picture of Heaven, one but needs to read Revelation 21-22. It is a beautiful place where there will be no more dying nor pain. Rev. 21:4 tells us, *"And God shall wipe away all tears from their eyes; and there shall be no more death, neither sorrow, nor crying, neither shall there be any more pain: for the former things are passed away."* The greatest sight to behold in Heaven will be Jesus. The Apostle Paul said in II Cor. 5:8, *"We are confident, I say, and willing rather to be absent from the body, and to be present with the Lord."* What a day, what an experience, what a joy to see our Savior! Each of us should live our lives with Heaven in view. That is, we live with hope — a steadfast hope that is sure and promised by God Himself, that we have a home for eternity in Heaven with our Savior. God bless you today and may these thoughts comfort those who have lost loved ones or friends in death. God bless you and remember that everybody is going somewhere. Have a great day!

August 5

Hundreds of ministers and pastors quit every month. Several thousand missionaries come home from the field each year and never return. Every week there are those who drop out of church after years of faithful attendance and service. The statistics are staggering as we see a falling away of Christians and Christian leaders from the things of God. Allow me to challenge you not to quit. Jesus offered some stern words to those who do not finish well, to those who quit. In Luke 9:57-62 He spoke about people who made excuses not to follow Him. The chapter concludes with this: *"No man, having put his hand to the plough, and looking back, is fit for the kingdom of God."* Paul wrote in II Cor. 4:1, *"Therefore seeing we have this ministry, as we have received mercy, we faint not."* The Lord has called each of us to serve — some as pastors or missionaries, some as laborers in His church, but every Christian has a place of service. There are diverse opportunities but equal responsibilities. Paul's testimony in I Tim. 1:12-13, in which he thanks Christ for *"putting me into the ministry"* and acknowledged that it was only possible because *"I obtained mercy,"* could be the testimony of any of us. Therefore, because to serve the Lord is a God-given opportunity, and He has chosen to use me even though I am unworthy to be used, I *"faint not."* I cannot, I must not forsake my responsibility to serve my Lord. Our call is from God and the cause is to great for us to quit. May we be reminded of the words of Romans 8:18. *"For I reckon that the sufferings of this present time are not worthy to be compared with the glory which shall be revealed in us."* Stay faithful; it will be worth it all. God bless and have blessed a day.

August 6

"If a person does not have enough religion to get them to church, it is doubtful they'd have enough to get them to Heaven." This statement made by an old uneducated believer may not be theologically correct, but it does cause us to think about our responsibility of *"not forsaking the assembling of ourselves together, as the manner of some is; but exhorting one another: and so much the more, as ye see the day approaching"* (Heb. 10:25). Allow me to suggest why the gathering together as a church is so important. These are not theological but practical reasons for going to church. Corporate worship strengthens the individual in his or her faith. When we worship together, we draw from the experiences of others and are strengthened in our faith. Carrying out the Great Commission can be best fulfilled by the church. As individuals, we are to obey the command to share the Gospel, but taking the message around the world can best be accomplished through the New Testament church. Caring for the poor and the needy can best be done through a local church. Together, a body of believers can best provide for the needs of a community. Communion and baptism are ordinances given by our Lord to be administered by the local church. Though this statement is doctrinal in nature, as a practical matter it is the church that observes the Lord's Supper, and it is the church that provides the opportunity for believers to be baptized. These are but a few suggestions for why we should be faithful to attend church. Going to church will not and cannot keep anyone out of Hell nor assure you of Heaven. However, it is vital part of our Christian experience. Determine today that you will not forsake assembling with other believers at the church. We need that fellowship. We need the instruction from the Word of God. We need to **be the church**. God bless and have a great day!

August 7

When I was a child, our family attended a Baptist church that practiced foot washing as a church ordinance. As a child, I never understood the practice. After leaving that church due to our family relocating, we joined a Baptist church that did not practice foot washing. The theological training I received did not teach foot washing as an ordinance, and as a pastor I never practiced it. I once heard a Sunday School teacher say that Jesus was teaching discipleship in John 13 as He washed the disciples' feet. It taught them humility and that they were to be the servants of others. If we are to be His disciples, we certainly must have humility and be servants of others. It is interesting to note the words of Jesus in John 13:14. *"If I then, your Lord and Master, have washed your feet; ye also ought to wash one another's feet."* Though as a Pastor I did not practice foot washing, I certainly do not have a problem with those that do. I recall a humbling experience when a member of my church, a former pastor who practiced foot washing, came to my office and ask if he could wash my feet. I agreed and in the privacy of my office, this humble servant of the Lord read from John 13, washed my feet, and then prayed for me. God broke my heart and the tears flowed as I experienced this act of humility and servitude. Each of us needs to learn to live as humble servants of others. The character of a follower of Jesus is a humble spirit and a servant's heart. May our prayer be today, "O to be like Thee, blessed Redeemer." God bless you today and have a great day!

August 8

The Bible says in Job 14:1, *"Man that is born of a woman is of few days and full of trouble."* I have been blessed with good health for my 70-plus years of life. A few months ago, I had to have knee surgery to repair a meniscus tear. I recovered nicely and thought all was good. Then the other knee had a meniscus tear, and I had surgery to repair it. Yes, it is frustrating to have to go through the surgery, the rehab, and the inability to be about the ministry. However, as my wife and I were driving home from dinner last night and were discussing the situation, my wife said, "Aren't we grateful that the surgery is not for cancer?" Though troubles come our way, we need to realize that, as Dr. Bill Pennell has often said, "Everybody is having a hard time." I recall hearing the little cliché, "I complained that I had no shoes, until I met a man with no feet." My challenge for us today is to accept the reality that our days are *"full of trouble."* The pains and problems of life are designed to mold our lives. In my message, "Five Lessons I have Learned from Tragedy," I point out that often our troubles in life are designed to **confirm our faith.** How could I ever know that God could meet my needs if I never had a need greater than my ability to supply, and how could I ever know the God of all comfort if I never suffered the sorrows of life? I also point out in the message that the trials of life also are God's tools to **conform us to the image of Christ.** As I face each problem, I will trust the Lord and seek to learn more of Him during this time. It could be that you are facing a far greater trial than I, but the God we serve knows no limits to ability nor power. Look beyond your trouble today and see the goodness of God. God bless and have a blessed day!

August 9

Bitterness is the cancer of the soul! According to Prov. 14:10, *"The heart knoweth his own bitterness."* Bitterness is defined as "anger and disappointment at being treated unfairly; resentment." The truth is that all of us are treated unfairly from time to time. Disappointments are common to all people. Our response to unfair treatment or disappointments in life will reflect our relationship with the Lord and will also determine the joy and peace in our own lives. I heard a preacher say, "Never allow others to determine your happiness." I would also say that you should never allow the circumstances of your life be the thief of your happiness. Then how do we guard ourselves from bitterness? I would suggest three practical steps. **Read the Word of God.** This may seem elementary, but Jesus said in John 15:3, *"Now ye are clean through the word which I have spoken unto you."* The Bible has much to say about bitterness and you will be surprised at the healing effect of the Word of God in your life during times of anger or disappointments. **Release your anger and verbalize your disappointments through prayer.** The words of that hymn come to mind: "I must tell Jesus all of my trials." Do not be afraid to tell Jesus how you really feel about your circumstances; after all, He already knows your heart. **Reconcile yourself to your circumstances.** Realize that God is in control of every circumstance in your life. Live by faith in the promise of Rom. 8:28. *"And we know that all things work together for good to them that love God, to them who are the called according to his purpose."* Remember, bitterness is the cancer of the soul. It will rob you of your joy and replace it with a life of resentment and defeat. There is victory over bitterness in a forgiving spirit and faith in a God that is bigger than all our trials. God bless you today!

August 10

Do you ever allow your mind to dwell on difficulties or trouble? That is the definition of worry. As Christians we have an important exhortation from Phil. 4:6. *"Be careful for nothing* [don't be anxious or worry]; *but in every thing by prayer and supplication with thanksgiving let your requests be made known unto God."* I recall the little chorus, "Why worry, worry, when you can pray?" I remember, as a young pastor, getting some advice from a man in the church who knew I was worried about a situation. "Most people worry about things **three** times. First, they worry about them **before** they happen. Most things worried about never happen. Secondly, we worry about things after they happen, and there is nothing we can do to change the past. Thirdly, we worry **as** they are happening. It is only then that we can do anything about our situation." I have learned that even when circumstances are difficult and trouble comes, prayer is the great escape from worry. All of us seek relief from the worries of life, which is why the promise of Phil. 4:7 is important. *"And the peace of God, which passeth all understanding, shall keep your hearts and minds through Christ Jesus."* My challenge for today is that we enter into worry-free lives by committing our difficulties and troubles to the Lord. It is God who changes things, and we have access to Him through prayer. Your burden may seem too heavy to bear. Your circumstances may be beyond your control and your problems may be many, but God will ease the anxiety, remove the fear, and calm the worried soul, if we will just commit our difficulties and troubles to Him in prayer. All of us need to take our burdens to the Lord and leave them there. God bless you today, and remember — don't worry, just pray.

August 11

There are days when praising The Lord is just not natural. The circumstances of the day are negative, and life is not good. It is during those days that we must step back and take a look at the big picture of our life. Today may be filled with problems, but we must not lose sight of the blessings of yesterday and the anticipated blessings of tomorrow. The first step to rejoicing in the Lord is to **give thanks** for His blessings. The first verse of Psalm 188 proclaims, *"O give thanks unto the Lord; for he is good: because his mercy endureth for ever."* Thank Him for your salvation, for His supply of your needs, and for the promise of His soon return. Look around you and see the blessing of family and friends. There are times when we must live by faith in the **promises** of our Lord. Today, we may not be having a good day, but God has promised to give us strength for the journey. He has promised in Matt. 28:20, *"and, lo, I am with you always, even unto the end of the world. Amen."* I can give Him praise that I do not face the trials of life alone. God is with me, and He is with you today. I can praise Him that he will **provide** grace, unmerited favor, for every trial of life. In II Cor. 12: 9 the Lord told the Apostle Paul regarding his "thorn in the flesh" after Paul had asked for its removal, *"My grace is sufficient for thee: for my strength is made perfect in weakness."* My thought for today is that we praise the Lord! May we look beyond the problems of today and see the blessings of God in our lives. God has not forsaken us. God has blessed us with many promises. His grace is sufficient for the trials of the day. God bless and remember to praise the Lord!

August 12

When Sarah laughed at the announcement that she would bare a child in her old age, the Lord replied in Gen. 18:14, *"Is any thing too hard for the Lord?"* In Jer. 32:27 God asked the same question of the prophet Jeremiah: *"Behold, I am the Lord, the God of all flesh: is there any thing too hard for me?"* "The Circle Maker" by Mark Batterson is one of the best books I have ever read on the subject of prayer. In this book, the author conveys the power of prayer to see God provide beyond our greatest imaginations. He uses his own testimony as well as the testimony of others, but he also uses the testimonies of those in the Bible. One example is when God promised meat for the children of Israel in the desert, traveling to the Promised Land after their exodus from Egypt. In Num. 11:18-33 the people complained that they had no meat to eat. The Lord spoke to Moses and promised meat for a month. Moses questioned the possibility of that much meat being available for the nation of Israel. God's answer to Moses in verse 23: *"Is the Lord's hand waxed short? thou shalt see now whether my word shall come to pass unto thee or not."* God was saying, "Is there a limit to My power?" Today as you pray, dare to pray for that which only a God with limitless power could do or provide. God is pleased when we trust Him for the impossible. Remember that God answers prayer in His time and in His way. The answer may not come today, but keep praying. It may not come as you expected, but give God the glory no matter how it comes. Do not limit the power of God. Pray big, believe big, and watch God work! God bless you and have a great day.

August 13

I hate being sick or incapacitated. Being unable to function seems to be such a waste of time. The work of the Lord is never done. I remember a year or two ago when I pondered this as I sat confined to my chair, with one leg wrapped from knee surgery and the other knee holding a catheter bag. I asked the Lord for some thoughts that might encourage me as well as others who may be sick or having a rough time physically. My mind went to Rom. 5:3-4. *"And not only so, but we glory in tribulations also: knowing that tribulation worketh patience; And patience, experience; and experience, hope."* Of course, the *"tribulations"* referenced in that passage would include sickness and various health issues. *"Patience"* is another word for endurance. God uses every aspect of our lives to teach us to trust Him! There is no greater teacher than experience, and there is no greater blessing than hope, which for us believers is a certain reality. Simply stated, God uses these times in our lives to prepare us for the next task He has for us. He also uses these times to increase our faith. The days of sickness or incapacitation are not in vain. God has a plan and a purpose. So may we claim these verses and rejoice that he counted us worthy to experience this time to teach us to trust Him more perfectly. God is in control. God bless and have a great day!

August 14

Every situation provides an opportunity to share the Gospel with someone. The Book of Philippians was written by the Apostle Paul while he was in a Roman jail. His theme for the book is **joy**. The book instructs us on how to have joy in the midst of trials or regardless of how people may treat us, and it also warns us that material things do not provide joy. At the close of the epistle, in chapter 4, there are some verses that may give us a glimpse as to why Paul could rejoice in the Lord. In verse 22 he wrote, *"All the saints salute you, chiefly they that are of Caesar's household."* It seems reasonable to me that these *"saints"* were converts he led to Christ. As I read this verse, I thought about how often God puts us in particular circumstances so that we might be a witness for Him. I recall hearing of a nationally-known minister who was in the hospital with a back problem. He was in a semi-private room, and the gentleman in the other bed was sick unto death. That man's wife sat by his bedside praying for her husband. The minister approached the lady to offer comfort, and she told him, "I am praying for a miracle. My husband is not saved, and I am praying that he will trust Christ before he dies." The minister said, "Allow me to share the Gospel with him." Though the man seemed to be in a coma, the minister presented the Gospel and invited him to trust Christ as his Savior. The man seemed to respond and a tear ran down his cheek. Only eternity will reveal the destiny of that soul, but we can be sure that God had that minister there for that time. May all of us be sensitive to circumstances in which God places us. Every situation provides an opportunity to be a witness for the Savior. God bless and have a great day.

August 15

Everybody needs somebody at some time. God places us in situations that require the assistance of others. He also puts us in places to be a help and a blessing to others. One of my favorite illustrations of this truth is found in II Samuel 21. David was about to be killed by Ishbibenob, the son of Goliath. One of David's men, his nephew Abishai, came to his rescue in verse 17. *"But Abishai the son of Zeruiah succoured him, and smote the Philistine, and killed him."* Even the mighty King David needed someone to rescue him. We need to give thanks for the Abishais that God places in our lives, even though we all like to think we are independent and have no need of the help of others. I once had knee surgery and the ensuing complications really put me down. My Abishai at that time was primarily my wife Doris. Others were also a blessing during these days. I was made well aware of my need for help from others. Each of us also needs to be an Abishai for someone else at times. We are constantly coming across people who need a helping hand. Those situations give us the opportunity to be a blessing to others. God had Abishai in the right place at the right time. You and I must be conscious of God's allowing us to be in a place to help others. Give thanks for the Abishais God has placed in your life, and be an Abishai to someone today. God bless you and have a blessed day.

August 16

If ever there was a day that Christians need to heed the words of II Timothy 3, it is today. The first 7 verses read like today's newspaper, describing the condition of our society, beginning with verse 1: *"This know also, that in the last days perilous times shall come."* I don't have time to expound on them here but I suggest you read the remaining six verses. This chapter has three exhortations for the believer. First, expect **persecution**. Verse 12: *"Yea, and all that will live godly in Christ Jesus **shall suffer persecution**."* Any persecution for us in America cannot be compared to the suffering in many countries around the world. To restrain persecution here, Christians must be vigilant to let their voices be heard at the ballot box. We must engage in active efforts of evangelism, and we must pray faithfully for our country. Second, in verse 14 we are exhorted to **persevere** in the midst of these perilous times. *"But continue thou in the things which thou hast learned and hast been assured of ..."* As believers, we live every day expecting the return of the Lord, but until that day we must keep on serving and living for Jesus. The teachings of the Word of God are as relevant today as they were in the days of the early church. We must hold fast to those truths. Third, we are to rest on the **promises** in the Word of God. Verse 16 reminds us, *"All scripture is given by inspiration of God."* Every word is God-breathed and can be trusted. The strength to face the trials of these days is found in the promises of the Bible. My challenge for believers today is that we view the declining values of our society which is an opportunity for us to be light in the darkness. Why should we curse the darkness of the day, when we can light a candle? Yes, the days are dark, but I John 4:4 reminds us that *"greater is he that is in you, than he that is in the world."* Don't quit or give up hope. Stay faithful to the Lord and His Word. God bless and have a great day!

August 17

Everybody wants to feel special. We all desire to be the one who receives that special gift or attention. In John 5, one paralytic man was among a multitude seeking healing around the pool of Bethesada. He is described in verse 5: *"And a certain man was there, which had an infirmity thirty and eight years."* There were many afflicted people waiting for the moment so they could get in the pool with hope of being healed. Jesus did not heal all the people, just *"a certain man."* All we know about him is the length of his ailment and the fact that no one would help him get into the water for healing. Maybe these things got Christ's attention, but we know that the man was healed, not by an angel stirring the water in the pool, but by the words of the Son of God. It is vital that we acknowledge the grace of God in our lives. The word "grace" means "unmerited favor." You and I who know Jesus as Savior have been the recipients of His grace. It was His grace that saved us; we did not deserve His salvation and had no power to save ourselves. We are reminded in Eph. 2:8-9, *"For by grace are ye saved through faith; and that not of yourselves: it is the gift of God: Not of works, lest any man should boast."* It is by His grace that I serve Him. Out of the multitudes of the saved, I have a place of service for my Savior. Your place of service for the Lord is given you because of His grace. God has chosen you to be that Sunday School teacher, or that small group leader, or that usher, or that whatever position He has given you. Thank God today for His grace. Think of the many expressions of God's grace in your life. Recall those many "unmerited favors" bestowed upon you. I praise Him for His grace! God bless and have a great day.

August 18

It was 46 years ago today that God sent Doris and me a precious gift. It was the birth of our son Paul. God allowed us to enjoy him for 31 years. It was on Good Friday in 2004 that our Paul went home to be with the Lord, after 25 years of battling a brain tumor and all the complications it caused. We still miss him, but rejoice that he suffers no more and is with our Savior! As I thought of this day and the death of our son, I was reminded of David and the occasion of the death of his child as recorded in II Sam. 12:15-23. We can learn much from his actions in the wake of this tragedy. **He washed himself** (v. 20). David prepared himself for the future. There is no greater loss than the loss of a child. I have said many times that we never get **over** the death of a child, but by the grace of God we get **through** it. Life goes on, and so must we. **He worshipped in the Lord's house** (v. 20). David expressed his continued faith in his God and acknowledged God's sovereign will in the situation. We do not always understand the ways of God, but we can always trust His heart. God is good all the time, even in the valleys of life. **He knew he would see his son one day** (v. 23). He said, *"I shall go to him, but he shall not return to me."* Death may seem so final, but separation is but for a while for those who know the Lord as their Savior. So we wish our Paul a happy birthday and know it won't be long before we are together again, never to be separated. The comfort of the truths of this passage have blessed me, and I trust will bless you today. God bless and have a great day!

August 19

There are few people who can boast of doing any one thing for sixty years. It was around this time in 2017 that my friend Dr. Bill Pennell celebrated 60 years of ministry of the Gospel of Christ. That event caused me to think about servants of the Lord staying faithful over the years, and my mind went to II Cor. 4:8-10. *"We are troubled on every side, yet not distressed; we are perplexed, but not in despair; Persecuted, but not forsaken; cast down, but not destroyed; Always bearing about in the body the dying of the Lord Jesus, that the life also of Jesus might be made manifest in our body."* I am approaching 50 years of ministry, and I can testify that along the way you will encounter all the above while also having to face your own bad decisions. The Wise Man said in Prov. 24:16, *"For a just man falleth seven times, and riseth up again: but the wicked shall fall into mischief."* The key to spiritual success is **faithfulness**. Dr. Pennell has been an example of faithfulness. At that 60-year celebration event, there were glowing testimonies of lives that had been touched by this servant of the Lord. My thought for us today is that though we face adversity and trouble we just do not quit. I would remind each of us of the words of I Cor. 4:2. *"Moreover it is required in stewards, that a man be found faithful."* It is worth noting that after that celebration, Dr. Pennell at 78 years of age transitioned into another ministry, a new emphasis to raise support for Ukrainian missions. Ministry is not a vocation; it is calling to a way of life. Maybe your calling is to be a church worker, or a prayer warrior, or some other ministry. Do not quit. It will be worth it all when we see Jesus! God bless and have a great day!

August 20

    I awoke on a recent morning with the words of I Sam. 12:23 running through my mind. *"Moreover as for me, God forbid that I should sin against the Lord in ceasing to pray for you."* I must say that the prayers offered for me, especially in the past few months and years, have been so appreciated. As I have carried on with my ministry amid occasional health issues and struggles, I know it has been the prayers of many of you that have given me the strength to persevere and has brought me to this point of recovery. I am grateful for every prayer and desire continued prayer for good health. Your prayers for me have reminded me of the responsibility I have to pray for others. I have, for many years, prayed each morning for a long list of people. This is my pleasure and my duty. To not pray for others can be a sin against the Lord. How serious are we about praying for others? There was an old evangelist, Dr. Fred Garland, who had an unusual practice. If you approached him and asked him to pray for you, he would stop and pray that very moment for you. He said he feared that he would tell someone he would pray for them and then fail to do so. I think we all can learn a great lesson from Dr. Garland and not sin against the Lord by not praying for one another. God bless and have a great day!

August 21

This date in 2017 marked an historic day in the United States of America, as a total solar eclipse was seen across the entire land. The last such occasion was in 1918. People travelled to the best viewing sites with cameras and camping gear to see the moon totally veil the sun. As I thought of the hoopla surrounding this natural phenomena, I wondered how many observers would acknowledge that a Master Designer so ordered these events? One of the evidences of the existence of God is His creation. Rom. 1:20 tells us, *"For the invisible things of him from the creation of the world are clearly seen, being understood by the things that are made, even his eternal power and Godhead; so that they are without excuse."* The Bible says in Ps. 19:1, *"The heavens declare the glory of God; and the firmament sheweth his handywork."* As we hear and read so much about various natural events such as this, let it serve as a reminder to all of us of the awesome power of our God. We should also remember that such an awesome God, who designs such exciting and unbelievable things as an eclipse, is powerful enough to handle the affairs of men. Today, I lift my voice in praise to the living God that made Heaven and Earth and directs the movements of all the universe, but also directs the simplest and smallest events in my life. To the atheist and the agnostic, I would say that **there is a God.** If you want to get a glimpse of His majesty, just look to the heavens! God bless and have a great day!

August 22

School is back in session in nearly every city and town in our nation. For more than 35 years at teacher orientation, before the opening of our Christian school, I read Deut. 6:1-12. Today I emphasize verses 6-7a. *"And these words, which I command thee this day, shall be in thine heart: And thou shalt teach them diligently unto thy children."* These verses are part of what is known as the "shema," which according to Wikipedia is Hebrew for "a prayer that serves as a centerpiece of the morning and evening Jewish prayer services." My emphasis to the teachers was twofold. First, you cannot teach what you do not know. If you are to teach righteous living you must practice righteous living. If you are to teach Biblical principles, you must know those principles and live by them. Secondly, teach them diligently to the children. I always said that a teacher had not taught until someone had learned. This requires diligence in preparation as well as presentation. My fear for today is that our children are not being taught moral values and Biblical principles to guide their lives. Education today competes with social media and a philosophy of education that is void of God or the Bible. Therefore, it behooves parents to be more diligent in teaching these truths to their children. Whether children attend a Christian school or a public school, the ultimate teachers of morals, values and Biblical principles are the parents! Christian schools should seek to be an extension of the home, and the church certainly can reinforce those Biblical teachings, but God is going to hold the parents accountable for what is taught to their children. This school year, I challenge every parent to begin the day with your children with a short Bible study and time of prayer. God bless, and may your children grow up learning of the greatness and goodness of our God! Have a great day!

August 23

Did you ever wonder how in the world you would finish all you have been given to do? Well, regarding the things of God, we are given a promise to encourage us. It is found in Phil. 1:6. *"Being confident of this very thing, that he which hath begun a good work in you will perform it until the day of Jesus Christ."* Yes, thank God, this is true of our salvation. It is the Holy Spirit who began the work of salvation in us, and it is He who will "perform it" until the end. However, today my thoughts are concerning our service for the Lord. I live most of the time in Florida among a community that is largely retirement age. I see many of these retirees faithfully serving the Lord in their churches. The work begun in and through them years ago is still being performed. They move a bit slower, but they are still on the move for Jesus! My thought for today is that some of us need to **re-fire** in the work of the Lord. God is not finished with us. Recently, I watched two older men in our church strip a floor of old carpet and prepare the floor for new covering. One of the men was in in his late 80s. I was challenged to "keep on keeping on" in the work of the Lord. God began a good work in you. Now trust Him to continue to perform this work through you until He comes or you go to be with Him. God bless and have a great day!

August 24

I have been thinking and praying a great deal lately about the Book of Acts. It is our book of instruction as to how to carry out the Great Commission of our Lord. In the introduction of Acts in the King James Version printed by Thomas Nelson, the book is described as "the story of the men and women who took that commission seriously and began to spread the news of a risen Savior to the most remote corners of the known world." This "commission" is recorded in the Gospels and stated in the last words of Jesus, prior to His ascension into Heaven. These words are in Acts 1:8. *"But ye shall receive power, after that the Holy Ghost is come upon you: and ye shall be witnesses unto me both in Jerusalem, and in all Judaea, and in Samaria, and unto the uttermost part of the earth."* This commission given to the early church is the same commission given to the church and every believer today! My thought for today is how important is the Great Commission in your life and in the life of your church? Maybe I am missing something, but it seems to me that most churches and Christians today are engaged in a lot of good spiritual activities, but very little evangelism. The Great Commission has become replaced with all matter of activity in the church. Where are the programs to reach the lost with Gospel? What is the plan to carry the message of a risen Savior to our world? My challenge for today is that we begin to pray for a revival of evangelism in our churches and in the hearts of Christians everywhere. God bless you and may God help us "keep the main thing the main thing." The main thing is the Great Commission!

August 25

There is a statement at the beginning of the book of Acts that has always caught my attention. It is found in the opening verse of the first chapter. *"The former treatise have I made, O Theophilus, of all that Jesus began both to do and teach..."* The book of Acts is actually the second volume of a two-part work written by Luke, a disciple of Jesus (not one of the original twelve). The phrase "began to do and teach" indicates that Jesus is still doing and teaching. I am reminded of the words of Jesus in John 14:12. *"Verily, verily, I say unto you, He that believeth on me, the works that I do shall he do also; and greater works than these shall he do; because I go unto my Father."* We serve the same Jesus who walked upon the earth and showed Himself to be the Son of God through the miracles He performed. We who are His followers can also see the miraculous working of God in and through our lives. Though I do not believe in "faith healers," I do believe that Jesus still heals the sick! I have seen the miraculous provision of necessities of life come to me and to others. I have experienced the miraculous protection of the Lord in my life. Let's all strive to exercise our faith to see our God do the miraculous for us. He is able! He has not changed and is still doing and teaching. I need His power and strength every time I travel and speak, and he never fails to provide. As Phil. 4:13 says, *"I can do all things through Christ which strengtheneth me."* God bless you today.

August 26

I was on one of the several trips that I have made to the Holy Land in Israel. As we passed the Mount of Transfiguration, I commented to the group that it was here that Jesus was caught up into Heaven. One dear lady ask to speak to me privately. She said, "I have served in church all my life, and I never knew Jesus ascended back into Heaven!" In the first 11 verses of Acts 1 is recorded the statement of Jesus showing Himself as the **resurrected** Savior (v. 3); the question concerning the **restoration** of His kingdom (v. 6); the **reason** for the disciples being left behind, which is the Great Commission (v. 8); and His ascension to Heaven with the promise of His **return** for us (v. 11). The fact that our Lord ascended into the heavens is a declaration that our Savior is **alive**. The Bible says in Heb. 1:3b, *"Who being the brightness of his glory, and the express image of his person, and upholding all things by the word of his power, when he had by himself purged our sins, **sat down on the right hand of the Majesty on high.**"* We are reminded in Heb. 4:15-16, *"For we have not an high priest which cannot be touched with the feeling of our infirmities; but was in all points tempted like as we are, yet without sin. Let us therefore come boldly unto the throne of grace, that we may obtain mercy, and find grace to help in time of need."* My challenge for us today is that we call upon the living Savior to guide our lives. We can commit every need and every problem to Jesus. He lives to help us, to save us, and to give us hope for the future. I give Him praise today that He is alive now and for evermore! God bless and have a great day!

August 27

At the signing of the Declaration of Independence in 1776, Ben Franklin said to his fellow colonists, "We must, indeed, all hang together, or most assuredly we shall all hang separately." The same can be said today of Christians as we fight to protect our religious freedoms. In these days, when the very fabric of our Judeo-Christian heritage is being eroded by secular humanists and others, we need to stand together and seek to preserve our First Amendment freedoms. I am proud to be a part of the National Center for Life and Liberty, which is on the cutting edge of assisting churches and Christians in protecting their God-given liberties. As Acts 1 illustrates, two characteristics of the early church were unity and prayer. After the ascension of Jesus into Heaven, His followers gathered into *"an upper room"* (v. 13). Note their actions in verse 14: *"These all continued with one accord in prayer and supplication, with the women, and Mary the mother of Jesus, and with his brethren."* We could learn from this little band of believers how to respond to the challenges we face today. All of us who know Jesus need to band together in *"one accord"* for the cause of our Lord. Unity is not uniformity. We do not have to agree on every dot and tittle of theology to stand together for the right of all of us to worship according to the dictates of our own consciences. In the church, however, it is important that we be of *"one accord"* in doctrine and the practice of our faith. We also need to pray one for another. We need to pray for our government leaders and for our country. We ought to also pray for the salvation of souls. May God give unity and an unction for Christians everywhere to pray! We can see the great testimony and success of the early church in the following chapters of Acts. Let us not miss that their success was preceded by unity and prayer. God bless and have a great day.

August 28

God always has His man or woman for every task. In Acts 1:15-26 we have the record of the choosing of Mathias as the replacement for Judas Iscariot among the Apostles. Judas had betrayed our Lord and hung himself to escape his guilt (v. 18-19). There are two great lessons for us today from these verses. First, the guilt of sin is a horrible condition, but thank God we do not need to live with a load of guilt. There is forgiveness and restoration through the blood of Jesus, and I John 1:9 has a powerful message for all of us. *"If we confess our sins, he is faithful and just to forgive us our sins, and to cleanse us from all unrighteousness."* Isa. 55:7 declares, *"Let the wicked forsake his way, and the unrighteous man his thoughts: and let him return unto the Lord, and he will have mercy upon him; and to our God, for he will abundantly pardon."* Second, God always has His replacements for servants in His vineyard. When Judas was gone, God already had a replacement in the wings. There have been some great spiritual leaders who have graced our history and there were questions as to what would happen to the work of God when they were gone. The answer has always been God is raising up another spiritual leader or another ministry to replace the one that is gone. As the Bible says more than 40 times, *"his mercy endureth for ever."* Rid yourself of the guilt of sin. Confess it, repent and enjoy the joy of the Lord. God has not forsaken you; He loves you and desires to have a relationship with you. I would also encourage us to look beyond human servants of the Lord and know the work of God is in the hands of God. His Church shall live on, and God will raise up His servants to lead and serve His church! God bless you today and have a blessed day!

August 29

The purpose of these devotions is not to give an exegesis nor even an exposition of the Scriptures. The purpose is to encourage us to live for the Lord. Acts 2 is a much debated and discussed portion of Scripture. The one thing we can agree upon is the ultimate result of the Day of Pentecost as recorded there: *"And they were all filled with the Holy Ghost ..."* (v. 4) *"Then they that gladly received his word were baptized: and the same day there were added unto them about three thousand souls."* (v. 41) It is my opinion that Acts 2 was the empowering of the early church to carry the Gospel message to the world. This would require, and still requires, a supernatural power that can only come from the Holy Spirit of God. The ultimate evidence of the Spirit-filled life is the salvation of the lost. The word *"filled"* in verse 4 literally means "to be controlled." We are exhorted in Eph. 5:18, *"And be not drunk with wine, wherein is excess; but be filled with the Spirit."* To be filled is to be controlled by the Spirit. This should be the goal for those who know Christ as Savior. To be filled with the Spirit, we must empty ourselves of selfish and sinful desires. As a minister of the Gospel, I seek to be filled with the Holy Spirit each time I preach the Word of God. However, I must also seek that filling daily as I live. Join me today and ask the Lord to fill and control our lives. To have His presence and His power flowing through our lives and to be able to fulfill His purpose for our lives — this is my prayer and my desire. God bless and have a blessed day!

August 30

"That's good preaching, brother!" Every preacher has heard this remark, and it is surely appreciated. But a close look at the sermon preached on the day of Pentecost might make us question the quality of some of the sermons we have heard or preached. Peter's address focused on the death of Jesus on the cross and His bodily resurrection (Acts 2:14-40). Verses 23-24 are key: *"Him, being delivered by the determinate counsel and foreknowledge of God, ye have taken, and by wicked hands have crucified and slain: Whom God hath raised up, having loosed the pains of death: because it was not possible that he should be holden of it."* The message that brings men and women to salvation is the message of the Gospel — the death, burial and resurrection of Jesus Christ. It is my conviction that regardless of the sermon, the Gospel must be declared! Though I hear many good sermons, I do not hear a clear presentation of the Gospel in many of the sermons. It is the Gospel that brings people to a saving knowledge of Jesus Christ. The results on the day of Pentecost speak for themselves. There were more than 3,000 souls saved on that day. Could it be that we are not seeing the numbers of people coming to the Lord because we do not emphasize the death and resurrection of Christ in our preaching and our witnessing? Listen closely to the sermons you hear and see if there is an emphasis on the Gospel. Consider your witness to others; do you share that Christ died for the sins of every person, was buried, but rose from the dead and that Jesus can and will save all who come to Him? This is our message to a lost and dying world of sinners! God bless and have a great day.

August 31

The past few years have seen several natural disasters that have spurred people to go to great lengths to help those in need. Christians are to be compassionate to those in need. I am convinced that if the church really had a heart of compassion as commanded by the Bible, there would be little need of government welfare as we know it. The Bible says in I John 3:17, *"But whoso hath this world's good, and seeth his brother have need, and shutteth up his bowels of compassion from him, how dwelleth the love of God in him?"* The early church gives us an example of this in Acts 2:44-47. This was not redistribution of wealth mandated by the government of that day nor a requirement of church leadership. It was a voluntary act of believers to create a community of faith that cared for each other. In this passage, there are three characteristics seen in the early church. **Compassion**. Verses 45-46 tells us they sold their goods that the needs of all the people could be met. In the church, when one member hurts or is in need, all hurt and should feel a responsibility to meet the need. **Unity**. Verse 46: *"And they continued daily with one accord ..."* They agreed to take care of each other and there was no bickering about the practice. **Fellowship**. The verse continues, *"... breaking bread from house to house, did eat their meat with gladness and singleness of heart."* It is my opinion that more fellowship is needed within the congregation. This can include, as in the early church, eating together. It is these times that a bond of commitment to each other is established. The results of the early church are given in verse 47: *"And the Lord added to the church daily such as should be saved."* May God give us likeminded churches today. God bless and have a great day.

September 1

God desires to use you and me. This concept was made real recently when I read a commentary on the first 11 verses of Acts 3 — the record of the healing of the lame man at the temple gate. It was Peter and John who were going into the temple to pray when they encountered the lame man and spoke healing to him. In the commentary I was reading was a quote from Stott that reinforces that thought: **"The power was Christ's but the hand was Peter's."** In verses 6-7 we have the response of Peter to the request of the lame man for alms from Peter and John. *"Then Peter said, Silver and gold have I none; but such as I have give I thee: In the name of Jesus Christ of Nazareth rise up and walk. And he took him by the right hand, and lifted him up: and immediately his feet and ankle bones received strength."* The lame man walked! It was the power of Jesus that wrought the healing, but the hand that lifted the lame man was Peter's. God's power has not changed; only the hands are missing. My challenge for you and me today is that we be the hands God can use to bless others. We may not see the lame walk, but we can offer His salvation to a sinner. We can be the hands that provide food or raiment to the needy. Maybe God has given you silver and gold and you can bless the poor. Whatever we have to give must be given through the power of the Lord. An anointing of our deeds is essential for the miraculous to occur. In the passage from Acts 3, there was no healing without divine power, but also no healing without human hands. Will we be the hands used of God to bless others? May God help us to be His hands today! God bless and have a great day!

September 2

As I read the verses following the healing of the lame man in Acts 3:1-11, I am reminded of the words of the Apostle Paul in I Cor. 9:16. *"For though I preach the gospel, I have nothing to glory of: for necessity is laid upon me; yea, woe is unto me, if I preach not the gospel!"* The lame man in Acts 3 is said to have been, *"walking, and leaping, and praising God"* (v. 8). The people recognized him, and soon a crowd gathered (v. 9-11). My thought for today is found in verse 12. *"And when Peter saw it, he answered unto the people, Ye men of Israel, why marvel ye at this? or why look ye so earnestly on us, as though by our own power or holiness we had made this man to walk?"* This shows Peter's awareness of an opportunity to preach the Gospel — and in verses 13-26 we see Peter preaching. He first gave God the **glory** for the miracle of the healing of the lame man (v. 12-13), then spoke of the crowd's **guilt** for the crucifixion of Jesus (v. 13b-17) before speaking of the **grace** of God that used their acts of ignorance and violence to provide blessing to them. Verse 26: *"Unto you first God, having raised up his Son Jesus, sent him to bless you, in turning away every one of you from his iniquities."* We must embrace every opportunity to preach the Gospel. I have often said, "I will preach at the drop of a hat, and if given the opportunity, I will drop the hat!" An audience of one or of many is an opportunity. A crisis or a miracle can provide an opportunity to present the Gospel. While recently having a diagnostic test, I had the opportunity to share the Gospel with the technician. Remember the example of Peter and the words of Paul: *"woe is unto me, if I preach not the gospel!"* These words are for every Christian. God bless and have a great day.

September 3

It was a Saturday and our family was having our evening meal when we heard the cries of a man several blocks from our house. We rose from the table and went to see what the commotion was about. My dad walked to the doctor's office where a man paced up and down the sidewalk crying at the top of his lungs, "Lord, have mercy!" He returned to tell us that the man's little daughter had fallen from her high chair with a glass bottle, cut herself and was bleeding profusely. The little girl was being cared for by the doctor. I will never forget what my dad said that night. "We have tried to get that man and his family to come to church for years. To my knowledge, he has never darkened the door of the church, but tonight he calls on the God for whom he has never had time." Our national and local leaders, to their credit, often call for times of prayer in the wake of a natural disaster or some other tragedy. Praise the Lord for leaders who acknowledge the need for divine intervention in times like these. But this country also bans prayer from public schools and wishes to remove all evidence of the divine hand of God from other public places. Then, in a time of crisis our nation cries, "Lord, have mercy!" Could it be that God knows how to get our attention? I would challenge all of us today to pray more than ever for our country — that we return to the faith of our forefathers and the Judeo-Christian principles upon which this nation was founded. Remember the words of II Chr. 7:14, so often quoted by our current vice president: *"If my people, which are called by my name, shall humble themselves, and pray, and seek my face, and turn from their wicked ways; then will I hear from heaven, and will forgive their sin, and will heal their land."* Pray for our country, its leaders, and for a spiritual awakening in our land. God bless you today, and God bless America!

September 4

In the fourth chapter of Acts, we see for the first time the persecution of the Apostles as they proclaimed the Gospel. In the first seven verses, we note that it was the religious leaders who led the opposition to the ministry of these disciples. Verses 1-2: *"And as they spake unto the people, the priests, and the captain of the temple, and the Sadducees, came upon them, Being grieved that they taught the people, and preached through Jesus the resurrection from the dead."* Voices of truth have always experienced persecution. We, as Americans, have been fortunate not to know the violent persecution that other Christians have known. It is worth noting two things about the persecution of the early church. First, it did **not** stop them from preaching the Gospel. In verse 8 Peter took the opportunity to proclaim the Gospel as he stood before his accusers. Second, note how many were saved in the midst of persecution. Verse 4: *"Howbeit many of them which heard the word believed; and the number of the men was about five thousand."* Opposition to the Gospel is to be expected and will sometimes come from unlikely sources. But we must be faithful to proclaim the Good News that Jesus died for sinners, was buried and rose from the dead, and is alive today to save all who will receive Him as Savior! We should anticipate a great harvest of souls for the Savior in the midst of opposition! Do not lose hope. The message of the Gospel is still, as Rom. 1:16 proclaims, *"the power of God unto salvation to every one that believeth."* God bless and remain faithful to share the Gospel wherever you may be!

September 5

Why is Christianity so controversial? What is it about our message that seems to breed such animosity from unbelievers? I would suggest that one big reason is found in Peter's address in Acts 4:12. *"Neither is there salvation in any other: for there is none other name under heaven given among men, whereby we must be saved."* That statement was reminiscent of the words of Jesus in John 14:6. *"I am the way, the truth, and the life:* **no man cometh unto the Father, but by me."** We live in a society that desires to define God and the way of salvation according to its own philosophies or agendas. My response to the universalism of today is, *"let God be true, but every man a liar"* (Rom. 3:4). But the truth of the Word of God — that there is one way to Heaven and it is through the Lord Jesus — places a great responsibility upon those of us who have the truth of the Gospel. As I look at Acts 4:12, I am reminded of three things. First is the **urgency** of our message. The world must hear there is only one way, and that way is through the blood of Jesus. Second, I am moved by the **unbelievable truth** of the text. It defines us. Our work, our cause, our purpose in life is to get the message of the Gospel to the world. Third, it is easy to see the *unsettled reaction* of the world to this truth. Other religions find offense in the preaching of the Gospel. The unbelieving world rejects the thought that Jesus is the only way to Heaven, so we must expect rejection and often persecution. We must take seriously our responsibility to take the message of the Gospel to the world. Every person must hear the truth! Our responsibility begins with our family and friends and extends to *"all the world"* (Mark 16:15). May God give us the resolve and the commitment to take this truth to every person. God bless and have a great day!

September 6

The closing thought of each National Center for Life and Liberty seminar presented by attorney David Gibbs III, is taken from the prayer of Peter for persecuted believers of the early church in Acts 4:29. *"And now, Lord, behold their threatenings: and grant unto thy servants, that with all boldness they may speak thy word."* Though times have changed and there are attempts to hush the voices of the Gospel of Jesus, we must boldly speak the truth of the Bible. I am grateful for organizations like NCLL that come alongside churches and Christians to ensure our right to proclaim the message of the Word of God. It is interesting to note that the word *"boldness"* is used three times in Acts 4. The first time is when the accusers describe the character of Peter and John. *"Now when they saw the boldness of Peter and John, and perceived that they were unlearned and ignorant men, they marvelled; and they took knowledge of them, that they had been with Jesus"* (v. 13). The last time is in verse 31: *"And when they had prayed, the place was shaken where they were assembled together; and they were all filled with the Holy Ghost, and they spake the word of God with boldness."* According to Strong's Concordance, the word comes from a Greek word meaning "freedom or confidence." That is exactly how Christians and churches need to speak the truth of the Word of God — with freedom and confidence. Freedom will come when we speak with the power of the Holy Ghost on us. We can speak with confidence because we speak the unchanging Word of God. Times may have changed, but one thing has not. *"For ever, O Lord, thy word is settled in heaven"* (Ps. 119:89). Be bold. Stand and speak the truth of the Word of God with power and in the spirit of Christ! God bless and have a great day!

There is a sobering truth found in Eccl. 5:4. *"When thou vowest a vow unto God, defer not to pay it; for he hath no pleasure in fools: pay that which thou hast vowed."* This principle is played out in the book of Acts. In the last few verses of Acts 4, the people willingly sold their possession that the needs of all the people could be met. In Acts 5 we read of Ananias and Sapphira, a husband and wife who sold their land but did not give the proceeds to the Apostles as they had promised. Verse 3, *"But Peter said, Ananias, why hath Satan filled thine heart to lie to the Holy Ghost, and to keep back part of the price of the land?"* It is important to note that Ananias and Sapphira lost their lives not because they did not give their money, but because they lied to God. They *"vowed a vow to God"* but did not keep it. Aren't we grateful for God's grace that prevents judgment for our broken promises to Him? But this does not remove the seriousness of making vows to God and failing to keep them. I wonder how many of us have vowed to God to tithe but have failed to keep our promise. Others have promised to serve the Lord and have broken their vows. There are other vows that some of us have made and failed to keep. My challenge for today is that we renew our vows and keep our promises to God. I vowed to preach the Gospel as long as I have breath and the ability to do so. As I Cor. 9:16 says, *"Woe is unto me, if I preach not the gospel!"* What vows have you made to God? Are you keeping those vows? Today is the day to renew them and begin to live keeping your promises to God. God bless and have a great day!

September 8

It was about this time in 2017 that my wife and I were preparing for Hurricane Irma, which was bearing down on our home in St. Petersburg, Fla. I had to fly to Tennessee for a revival meeting, and we looked at several options for Doris to leave town as well, but none were feasible. After much prayer, our plans were settled and we were at peace that God would take care of both of us — which He did. Our house was without power for several days, but the storm did not damage our city nearly as much as it could have. Reflecting on this reminded me of several truths to note in times of crisis. **God is in control.** Our anchor in times of trouble is still Rom. 8:28. *"And we know that all things work together for good to them that love God, to them who are the called according to his purpose."* Not everything that happens is good, but everything that happens in the life of a believer is an ingredient to bring about a good result. **Good people rally in a time of crisis.** We experienced this in our lives when we went to get sandbags for our home. I was still a bit handicapped after my knee surgery, but my wife and I were filling our bags with sand when two people came up to us and began helping us. One gentleman literally filled our bags and then helped us load them in our car. Would it not be wonderful if we had this spirit of kindness all the time, not just in times of crisis? *Godly people need to pray for one another.* It is sad that it takes a crisis to drive us to our knees. But I thank God for the privilege of prayer. Let's not waste any opportunity to grow closer to the Savior. May we see each crisis as an opportunity to "love like Jesus." God bless and be safe!

September 9

While in college, I was required to memorize Psalm 46. My recent reflection on Hurricane Irma in 2017 brought the first three verses of this chapter to mind. *"God is our refuge and strength, a very present help in trouble. Therefore will not we fear, though the earth be removed, and though the mountains be carried into the midst of the sea; Though the waters thereof roar and be troubled, though the mountains shake with the swelling thereof. Selah."* Though the meaning of the word *"Selah"* is much debated, the most common interpretation seems to be, "think about that." When we face the uncertainty of severe weather or any other difficulty, we should think about these verses. Verse 1 reminds us to **seek God** in times of trouble. The word "refuge" is defined as "the place to flee for safety." In my childhood when a storm came up, my grandmother would tell us children, "Now sit down and be quiet until the storm passes." As I look back on her instruction, I see that in the time of trouble it is a good time to be quiet before the Lord and seek Him. Verse 1 also reminds us that **God is our strength.** None of us know what trouble the storm will bring, but we do know that God is bigger and stronger than any natural disaster. In the midst of the storm, we can rest in His strength. Later we can draw upon His strength to recover from the storm. The conclusion of the matter is summed up in the first statement of verse 2: *"Therefore will not we fear."* Yes, we must be concerned when threatened with storms and other troubles in life, but we have a God that is **present** and is more **powerful** than any storm that may come our way. Let's cast our cares upon Him. We can face the days of uncertainty with faith and assurance that *"God is our refuge and strength."* God bless you and be safe!

September 10

When severe weather strikes wherever you live, or temperatures reach extreme levels of hot or cold, our first instinct is to find shelter. But where do you find shelter during the storms of life? We can get direction and find encouragement in that regard from Psalms 91. Verses 1-2: *"He that dwelleth in the secret place of the most High shall abide under the shadow of the Almighty. I will say of the Lord, He is my refuge and my fortress: my God; in him will I trust."* Verses 4-6: *"He shall cover thee with his feathers, and under his wings shalt thou trust: his truth shall be thy shield and buckler. Thou shalt not be afraid for the terror by night; nor for the arrow that flieth by day; Nor for the pestilence that walketh in darkness; nor for the destruction that wasteth at noonday."* When friends and loved ones in various parts of the world must deal with natural disasters, we pray for their ability to find shelter. However, the storms I reference here are the storms of fear and concern they and all our families and friends are facing today. Our shelter is not made with brick and mortar. It is in the sovereign power and person of our God. It is in times like these that we must look to our God for protection and provision. May each of us today find shelter *"under the shadow of the Almighty."* He truly is *"my refuge and my fortress."* Let us join together in prayer for those in the path of whatever storm they may be facing. Let us seek shelter under the wings of our loving and all powerful God! God bless and have a great day!

September 11

On this date in 2001, our country was attacked when hijacked airliners were flown into the World Trade Center, the Pentagon and a field in Pennsylvania. Thousands were killed, and our nation was changed forever. As I think about the tragedies of the past and those we face today, I am reminded that even the difficult times are designed by God to make us **better** and never to make us **bitter.** My thoughts this morning are drawn from Ps. 46:10, *"Be still, and know that I am God: I will be exalted among the heathen, I will be exalted in the earth."* As Christians, storms and other attacks on us must be seen as opportunities for us to watch God work. As I think of the exhortation in this verse to *"be still,"* I know I do not want to miss what God is teaching us through the difficulties of life. The Lord said, *"I will be exalted among the heathen, I will be exalted in the earth."* Following the 9/11 attacks, there was a surge of increased church attendance. People sought God; even those who never had time for Him before called for prayers and acknowledged the need for God. The same thing happened amid major hurricanes in recent years. My prayer for today is that we will be reminded of our need for God in our lives and in our society. God is not a 911 number just to be called in emergencies. He is the God of the good times and bad times. Could it be if we sought Him in the good times that we could escape some of the bad times? Let's all take a moment to *"be still"* and seek God as we remember what happened to our nation in 2001. God is with us and will help us. He desires to be worshipped all the time. May the hard times serve to remind us of the greatness of our God. God bless and have a great day!

September 12

"Capture Your Town for Christ" was the theme of one of the Super Conferences that I attended many years ago at the Thomas Road Baptist Church. It later became the title of a book written by Dr. Elmer Towns and Dr. Jerry Falwell, with the testimonies of several churches that were making a difference in their cities. Today, I hear very little of churches with an intentional desire to reach their cities with the Gospel. I **have** heard criticism of the churches that are reaching multitudes and are making a difference in their cities. I do not think every church will be a large church. Google reports that 50 percent of all churches in the United States average 75 or fewer in attendance. But **every** church should have a burning desire to reach its town or county or city with the Gospel. If you take a casual glance of the account of the early church in Acts 1-5, it is obvious that those believers were committed to presenting the Gospel to Jerusalem and to other cities. They took seriously the final command of the resurrected Christ in Acts. 1:8. *"... and ye shall be witnesses unto me both in Jerusalem, and in all Judaea, and in Samaria, and unto the uttermost part of the earth."* If we follow the activity of these early believers, we find a continuous story of the salvation of people from Acts 2 until the amazing accusation levied against these believers in Acts 5:28 — *"... and, behold, ye have filled Jerusalem with your doctrine."* This should be the intention, and the goal of every church! Let's "be the church" and ask God for a burden to reach the lost with the Gospel. As His church, we ought to pray, plan, and promote a Biblical strategy to reach our city, our county, and our country with the Gospel of Christ. This is God's intended purpose for His church. It is the ultimate goal for your life and my life. May God give us a Biblical vision of His intended purpose for us. God bless and have a blessed day.

September 13

I remember standing behind the pulpit years ago at the Highland Park Baptist Church in Chattanooga where Dr. Lee Roberson was pastor. I was scheduled to speak to the student body of Tennessee Temple Schools for chapel. As I approached the pulpit, I noticed these words written on the pulpit: "Sir, we would see Jesus." These words were taken from John 12, when a group of Greeks sought an audience with Jesus after the resurrection of Lazarus and Christ's entry into Jerusalem. Verse 21: *"The same came therefore to Philip, which was of Bethsaida of Galilee, and desired him, saying, Sir, we would see Jesus."* I believe there are many people today who desire to see Jesus. They long to see Him in the lives of Christians and in the church. Be sure that there are people who are looking to see Jesus. It was Brennan Manning who wrote of the man that sought to minister to him while he was living on the streets as an alcoholic: "He was the only Jesus I ever knew." Will you be Jesus to someone today? We can allow Jesus to live His life through us and minister to others. Our churches can demonstrate the character of Jesus to others. Pastors, people do not need to hear from us, they need to hear from Jesus as we speak the Word of God from our pulpits. May each of us today be the feet of Jesus, the hands of Jesus, the voice of Jesus and, most of all, the heart of Jesus. There are multitudes who cry today, *"Sir, we would see Jesus."* May they see Him in us Christians and in His church! God bless you today and have a great day!

September 14

Every leader must have the assistance of others to carry out his or her duties. In the sixth chapter of Acts, we read of the first confrontation within the early church. Verse 1: *"And in those days, when the number of the disciples was multiplied, there arose a murmuring of the Grecians against the Hebrews, because their widows were neglected in the daily ministration."* I was a pastor for more than 43 years, and I can attest to the fact that there is always someone in the congregation who feels slighted by the pastor. In most cases, it is not intentional and sometimes the situation is overstated; however, the needs of the people must be addressed. In verses 2-7, we read of the choosing of the first deacons. It is worthy to note that these men were chosen to take the burden of the care of the widows off the disciples. They were to be helpers or servants. The disciples were to spend their time as outlined in verse 4: *"But we will give ourselves continually to prayer, and to the ministry of the word."* Many pastors today need to evaluate their priorities. The people in the church need to step up and assist in caring for the needs of the people, so the pastor can have time for prayer and the study of the Word. The work of the ministry requires the hands of all the people. By the way, I fear that too often, in many churches, it is widows who are neglected. What a blessing it is to be an encouragement and help to the widows! It may be that you are not a deacon, nor have had any formal appointment to a position in the church, but you can still minister to those in need and alleviate the pressure that is on the pastor. God bless and have a great day!

September 15

God uses men and often promotes according to their faithfulness. So it was with Stephen, whose testimony and message to the religious leaders of that day are recorded in Acts 6-7. As I read through these verses, I note in Acts 6 three things about this man of God. **His character** (v. 8). He is described as *"full of faith."* This defined Stephen's total trust in the Lord — not just his saving faith, but a living faith that could be observed. Stephen is also said to be full of *"power."* This was the power of the Holy Spirit working in his life, and it was manifested as Stephen *"did great wonders and miracles among the people."* His character was godly, and his actions demonstrated his relationship with the Lord. **His convincing message.** Stephen spoke with the power of God upon him. verse 10 says, *"And they were not able to resist the wisdom and the spirit by which he spake."* The message of the Gospel is still *"the power of God unto salvation to every one that believeth"* (Rom. 1:16) and is still available to be used today. **His countenance.** There was a look upon Stephen that announced his relationship with God. Note Verse 15. *"And all that sat in the council, looking stedfastly on him, saw his face as it had been the face of an angel."* Sometimes our countenance is the window of our testimony. I can think of some Christians I know or have known whose countenance announced their love for and dedication to the Lord. My thought for today is that we should seek God's power in and upon our lives — our faith should be spoken of, and our very countenance should speak of our relationship with the Savior. If I might borrow a familiar statement, "God is looking for a few good men and women." We need men and women who are full of His power and are people of faith, whose very countenance says they have been with Jesus. Oh, that today you and I might be that kind of person. God bless and have a great day.

September 16

What is the answer to the accusations levied against Christians? The answer is to proclaim the Word of God! In Acts 6:11, religious leaders alleged hearing Stephen *"speak blasphemous words against Moses, and against God."* The high priest then asked Stephen in Acts 7:1, *"Are these things so?"* Stephen offered as his defense a sermon beginning with God's dealings with Abraham (7:1-9), followed by a summary of the account of God raising up Moses to deliver the nation of Israel from the Egyptian bondage (7:1043). He then gave an account of the the people having the Tabernacle, and Solomon building the Temple (7:44-50). Stephen built a case of the continuous disobedience of Israel to the commands of God, reaching a peak in verse 51: *"Ye stiffnecked and uncircumcised in heart and ears, ye do always resist the Holy Ghost: as your fathers did, so do ye."* We can learn a great lesson from the example of Stephen in how he answered his critics. Stephen never allowed his accusers to divert him from proclaiming the Word of God. He did not attempt to defend himself, but rather took the occasion to preach Jesus to his accusers. I have always tried to stay away from defending myself and focus instead on doing the will of God for my life, which is to preach the Word. Satan will use anything to keep us from sharing the Gospel. I recall the advice given me by my pastor, Dr. Jerry Falwell, when I was a young pastor. I had heard another pastor make untrue accusations about him, and I was going to confront this pastor and set him straight. Dr Falwell said to me, "Don't you do that," Dr. Falwell told me. "You do not need to defend me. My enemies won't believe you and my friends don't believe it anyway." I have never forgotten that instruction. Instead of defending ourselves, let's take every opportunity to make much of Jesus. God bless and have a great day.

September 17

My prayer is that I will not only live well but also die well. Stephen's life was one of faith, lived in the power of the Holy Ghost (Acts 6:8). That was a great testimony, but maybe even greater is his testimony when dying as a martyr (7:54-60). He was stoned to death because of his preaching of the Gospel and was greeted by Jesus at his death. Even then, he manifested a godly spirit. Note in Acts 7:60 his last words: *"And he kneeled down, and cried with a loud voice, Lord, lay not this sin to their charge. And when he had said this, he fell asleep."* Stephen's dying testimony had a tremendous impact on one man in particular, as seen in subsequent chapters. I have witnessed the dying testimony of a couple of people that made a lasting impression on my life. One such testimony was that of my dad. He roused out of unconsciousness, pointed his finger at me and said, "Get them all." I knew what he meant, so I went and gathered the family together. As we stood around the bed, my Dad motioned with his hand to point to each of us and said with the last of his energy, "I love you all. Now go on." Those were his final words of farewell to the family he loved. He then returned to a state of unconsciousness and died a few minutes later. My mother prayed and thanked God for his life, and then asked me to pray. The memory of my father's death motivates me every day to cherish my family and to make the most of every day with them. Yes, I want my life to be lived to bring glory to God, but I also desire that my death will bring honor and glory to my Savior. Stephen's death was a victorious moment used by God to touch the life of a great sinner and bring that lost soul to Jesus. What a testimony! God bless you and have a great day!

September 18

After so many years in the ministry, it is not unusual to get a call at any time with news of an old friend or former church member who has gone to be with Jesus. They are still almost always unexpected and bring great sorrow, especially when it is someone I have seen serve faithfully over the years. The verse that came to mind on one such recent occasion is Rev. 14:13. *"And I heard a voice from heaven saying unto me, Write, Blessed are the dead which die in the Lord from henceforth: Yea, saith the Spirit, that they may rest from their labours; and their works do follow them."* Any time a loved one passes away should serve as a reminder to all of us of the uncertainty of life. We all need to take note of the words of James 4:13-14. *"Go to now, ye that say, To day or to morrow we will go into such a city, and continue there a year, and buy and sell, and get gain: Whereas ye know not what shall be on the morrow.* **For what is your life? It is even a vapour, that appeareth for a little time, and then vanisheth away."** We should live every day as if it is our last day to live. Surely, if Jesus does not return, one day will be our last. May each of us live faithfully for the Savior! God bless you today.

September 19

The Bible says in Rom. 8:28, *"And we know that all things work together for good to them that love God, to them who are the called according to his purpose."* Notice that it doesn't say "all things are good." The Lord ultimately makes everything — good and bad — work together for our good and His glory. There are times when bad things happen to good people. My dear friend Tracy Dartt put this truth into the song "The God of the Mountain." Here is part of the chorus.

> **And the God of the good times**
> **Is still God in the bad times.**
> **The God of the day**
> **Is Still God in the night.**

It must have seemed a bad thing when persecution came upon the early church. Acts 8:1 tells us, *"And Saul was consenting unto [Stephen's] his death. And at that time there was a great persecution against the church which was at Jerusalem; and they were all scattered abroad throughout the regions of Judaea and Samaria, except the apostles.* If we stop reading after the first verse we only see the bad. But a further reading reveals a good result, as God used persecution to spread the message of the Gospel. Verse 4: *"Therefore they that were scattered abroad went every where preaching the word."* We need to look for the divine opportunities that present themselves in the midst of our troubles. There are no disappointments in life; only His divine appointments. Though we often cannot see the purpose of some things that come in our lives, if we love God and are called according to His purpose, the God of the day will be the God of the night. God bless you today and have a great day.

September 20

You don't have to throw stones to be guilty of stoning. Note the opening statement of Acts 8:1. *"And Saul was consenting unto his [Stephen's] death."* Compare that to the words of Paul in Acts 22:20. *"And when the blood of thy martyr Stephen was shed, I also was standing by, and consenting unto his death, and kept the raiment of them that slew him."* As I read these verses, I was reminded of how many of us do not participate in many sins, but we stand by and do nothing to stop the injustices in our society. Some even hold the raiment of those who are carrying out the evil practices. I think of Christians who are opposed to abortion, yet stand by and say nothing. Some even hold the raiment of those who are guilty by voting for candidates who provide the funds (the stones) for the abortionists. You could apply this test to many other evil practices, such as same-sex marriage, legalization of drugs, or a system that does not provide affordable health care. No, we do not throw the stones, but we stand by and do nothing and sometimes even hold the coats of those who throw the stones. My thought for today is that we take heed to the motto of the National Center for Life and Liberty: "If it is wrong, fight it. If it is right, fight for it." May God give us the courage and wisdom to oppose evil. It is not enough for us to just not to be guilty of throwing stones; we must not consent to throwing stones, and we must not be seen as a sympathizer of those that do. God bless you and have a great day.

September 21

Isn't it interesting how it seems easier to be more concerned for reaching people of different racial and cultural backgrounds in foreign lands than reaching our neighbors who may have a different skin color or be from a different culture than us? Jesus left a command in Acts 1:8 for His followers to be *"witnesses unto me both in Jerusalem, and in all Judaea, and in Samaria, and unto the uttermost part of the earth."* The Samaritans were neighbors of Jerusalem, but were rejected and despised by the Jews. They had intermarried with Gentiles and were idol worshippers. There was a long history of strife between the Jews and the Samaritans. Jesus showed His love for the Samaritans in person when He met the woman at the well in John 4. In Acts 1:8 He left a command that the Samaritans were to receive a witness of the Gospel. We see this command obeyed in Acts 8:5. *"Then Philip went down to the city of Samaria, and preached Christ unto them."* There was an intentional effort to carry the message of Christ to the Samaritans! We, as individuals and churches, must intentionally reach out to the outcasts of our society, to the various races and different cultures around us with the Gospel. Several years ago, I had the privilege to speak in a church that truly was multicultural. There were different races, cultures and socioeconomic groups represented in that congregation. At the close of the service, a man dressed in the attire of his culture and obviously not from America came to receive Christ as Savior. The joy and the reception of that man by the people of the church spoke volumes as to why everyone, regardless of race or ethnic background, felt welcome in that church. Real mission-minded churches and Christians have the same burden to reach their Samaria as they do to carry the Gospel across the seas. May God burden each of us for our Samaria! God bless and have a great day!

September 22

I recall hearing evangelist Oliver B Greene saying, "Many people are going to miss salvation by 18 inches." He explained that many people have a head knowledge of the things of God but have never experienced believing faith that saves. In Acts 8:9-24 we see an illustration of one who says he believed the Gospel but never experienced true repentance and saving faith. This man was Simon, the sorcerer. He desired the power to do the supernatural like Phillip, but he had no desire to know Jesus. His true relationship with the Lord, or really the lack thereof, is seen in his attempt to buy the power of God. Verses 18-21: *"And when Simon saw that through laying on of the apostles' hands the Holy Ghost was given, he offered them money, Saying, Give me also this power, that on whomsoever I lay hands, he may receive the Holy Ghost. But Peter said unto him, Thy money perish with thee, because thou hast thought that the gift of God may be purchased with money. Thou hast neither part nor lot in this matter: for thy heart is not right in the sight of God."* There are many "religious but lost" among us. They want the benefits of knowing the Lord, but they have no desire to know the Lord! They desire Heaven but have no desire to turn from their sin and by faith, receive the death of Christ as the sacrifice for their sins. Dr. John Piper used the illustration of an infant in the arms of a mother. The mother sees a bird outside a window, and points to the bird and says, "Look, see the bird!" The infant points with its finger like the mother but never sees the bird. There are many who imitate Christian behavior but never see the Christ. They join the church, live right, even serve in the church, but they miss true salvation because they never see themselves as sinners in need of a Savior, and they never repent of their sin and personally, by faith, receive Jesus as their Savior. Let each of us examine ourselves to be sure we know the Savior, not just know about Him. God bless and have a great day.

September 23

The importance of one! This is but one of the many lessons we can learn from Acts 8:25-40. The text records the **call** of Philip away from a very successful evangelistic meeting in Samaria to take the Gospel to one Ethiopian eunuch. It also records the **conversion** of this African governmental official who evidently was religious, seeing he had made the trip from Ethiopia to Jerusalem to worship. We also note the **continuing** fulfillment of our Lord's last **command**, which was first given in Acts 1:8. The Gospel had been preached in Jerusalem (Acts 2), and then carried into Judaea (Acts 8:4); now the message was being given to the first Gentile from *"the uttermost parts of the earth."* Africa was believed by many in that day to be located at the end of the earth. Consider today the importance of **one.** God directed Philip to leave a successful citywide meeting to go and carry the Gospel to one Ethiopian eunuch. Sometimes God leads His servants from what may seem like the greater ministry to what appears to be a lesser place to fulfill His purpose. It is our responsibility to be where God directs us to be. In Acts 8:26, we note the undeniable leading of God in Philip's life. *"And the angel of the Lord spake unto Philip, saying, Arise, and go toward the south unto the way that goeth down from Jerusalem unto Gaza, which is desert."* Could it be that God is leading **you** to take the Gospel to **one?** Maybe a friend, maybe a neighbor, or maybe a stranger is the one God has for you to share the Gospel. It was not Peter or John who God chose to take His message to the eunuch. It was a layman, a deacon named Philip. God can and will use you to share the Good News of the Gospel. God bless and have a great day.

September 24

Jesus said to His disciples in John 4:35, *"Say not ye, There are yet four months, and then cometh harvest? behold, I say unto you, Lift up your eyes, and look on the fields; for they are white already to harvest."* I am convinced today that the fields are still white to harvest. I believe there are many who are **seekers** of peace with God and an eternal hope found only in Jesus. The problem today is the laborers are few. There is a great need for a **soul winner** to guide the seeker to the **Savior.** He alone is the answer to man's need, not religion or good works. A casual reading of Acts 8:26-40 identifies the three persons I mentioned above. Philip had been sent by God from Samaria to the south to be joined by an Ethiopian eunuch who was the seeker (v. 27-30). It was Philip who explained the scriptures to this eunuch and was the soul winner who led him to Christ. (v. 31-33, 35-40). Though the eunuch was reading the Scriptures, he could not understand them. Philip introduced this seeker to the Savior (v. 34-40). With all of the Bible teaching we have today, there are many who just need the simple Gospel of Christ. Many are like the eunuch — seekers who need someone to guide them to the Savior. We should be conscious of the searching hearts of those with whom we come in contact. Many seek peace in materialism, only to find that things do not satisfy. Others seek peace by using drugs or alcohol, only to find these lead to a life of addiction and heartache. Others seek peace in religion only to find empty rituals with no relationship to provide peace and assurance of eternal life. These and others are all seekers in need of a soul winner to tell them of Jesus, the Savior who gives peace and assurance of eternal life. God bless you today and keep an eye open for the seeker who may come across your path.

September 25

The closing verses of Acts 8 include the request of the Ethiopian eunuch to be baptized. It is interesting to note in verse 37 the prerequisite that Philip placed upon the eunuch for him to be baptized. *"And Philip said, If thou believest with all thine heart, thou mayest. And he answered and said, I believe that Jesus Christ is the Son of God."* Philip had just explained the scriptures to the eunuch, and it is evident that the message was received. Verse 35: *"Then Philip opened his mouth, and began at the same scripture, and preached unto him Jesus."* The eunuch knew and understood what he was to do once he trusted Christ. Today, I want to encourage all who have believed and received Christ as Savior to be obedient to the Lord and follow Him in believer's baptism. This is to be the first act of obedience for every believer. It is obvious from verses 38-39 that his baptism was by immersion. *"And he commanded the chariot to stand still: and they went down both into the water, both Philip and the eunuch; and he baptized him. And when they were come up out of the water, the Spirit of the Lord caught away Philip, that the eunuch saw him no more: and he went on his way rejoicing."* It is clearly stated here that these men *"went down both into the water"* and *"were come up out of the water."* Baptism is an outward symbol of the salvation we have received. I do not believe baptism saves, but I do believe that every believer should be baptized. Maybe there are some reading this who need to consider following the Lord in scriptural believer's baptism. God bless and have a great day.

September 26

The transforming effect of the Gospel in the life of a believing sinner still amazes me. I recently met an evangelist whose testimony written on a tract was entitled, "From the Prison to the Pulpit." He had received Christ as Savior while in prison, and now is a very successful preacher of the Gospel. We have an illustration of God's transforming work in Acts 9. This chapter records the conversion of Saul, who became the Apostle Paul. Prior to his conversion, Saul persecuted Christians and was present and consented to the stoning of Stephen. His conversion took place on the road to Damascus, where he was hoping to receive letters giving him the authority to arrest Christians and bring them to Jerusalem to be tried in the courts of law for their faith. Saul's conversion in Acts 9 is a clear illustration of Paul's words written later in II Cor. 5:17. *"Therefore if any man be in Christ, he is a new creature: old things are passed away; behold, all things are become new."* This truth gives hope to Christians who have wayward children or family or friends. There is hope that they may come to know Jesus and experience that transforming work of Christ. This truth behooves us to continue to pray for the lost and to continue to present the Gospel message to them. No sinner is so bad that God's grace cannot reach and change them. Thank God today for His grace and His transforming power. God bless and have a great day.

September 27

God has always had His man leading His cause in every generation. Many times throughout history there have been several notable leaders of the cause of Christ on the scene at the same time. The Apostle Paul, who persecuted early Christians before his conversion in Acts 9, became perhaps the most influential Christian leader of all time. He traveled across the Roman Empire preaching the Gospel and planting churches. He is credited with writing 13 of the 27 books of the New Testament. While reading about his conversion on the road to Damascus and reflecting on the amazing transformation in his life, I am persuaded to pray that God will raise up more spiritual leaders today. We need men of God to rise up and call our nation back to Him. That starts with a call for sinners to receive Jesus Christ as Savior. The challenge for Christians today is to establish Bible-preaching churches that will focus on reaching the world with the Gospel. There is a void of real spiritual leadership today in our society. There are men who are faithful to preach the Word, and thank God for each of them, but there is a need for a Pauline-styled leader to call our nation back to God. Thank God for those national voices that are faithfully proclaiming the Gospel. However, many of those voices are dying and the numbers of faithful proclaimers seems to be on the decline. I heard recently that in the United States, we are starting 4,000 churches per year, but there are 7,000 churches closing. My challenge for us today is found in II Chr. 7:14. *"If my people, which are called by my name, shall humble themselves, and pray, and seek my face, and turn from their wicked ways; then will I hear from heaven, and will forgive their sin, and will heal their land."* I believe as we pray, God will hear us and raise up godly leaders to champion the cause of Christ. God bless you and have a great day.

September 28

I was 18 years old, and I had just received Christ as my Savior. My pastor, Dr. Jerry Falwell, suggested that I attend a Bible college for a couple of years before pursuing a profession. God had different plans and called me into the ministry while I was in my first year at Tennessee Temple College. I enrolled at Temple as a new believer needing guidance and discipleship. God gave me a roommate I had known from his days of service at my home church, Thomas Road Baptist Church. His name is Dan Manley. He had dated my sister and was the son of a missionary family. Dan encouraged me in the faith. He was an example to me as he read his Bible and prayed daily. He often helped me understand the Christian life, and he was truly an influence in my life. As I read through the testimony of Paul's conversion, I was struck by the way God provided the people to bless and encourage Paul after his conversion. In Acts 9:10-18 we read of *"a certain disciple at Damascus, named Ananias."* It was this disciple that the Lord sent to minister to one Saul of Tarsus, who was to become known as the Apostle Paul. Then in verse 19, we note that before Saul begins his ministry, he was instructed and encouraged by other disciples: *"Then was Saul certain days with the disciples which were at Damascus."* Thank God for the mentors He places in our lives. Though I have been a Christian over 50 years, I still need the influence and encouragement of Godly men around me. I regularly speak and listen to those He has placed to speak spiritual guidance and wisdom into my life. Look for those Godly people in your life who will speak spiritual wisdom into your life and will be an encouragement to you. You may be the person God desires to be the voice of spiritual instruction and encouragement to someone. Seek to be used of God to bless some young believer today. God may send a "Saul of Tarsus" into your life that you may be a mentor and a blessing to him. God bless and have a great day!

September 29

It has been said, "When common sense makes good sense, seek no other sense." But there are times when God's will requires us to challenge common sense. I recall when God led me to go to the Roanoke Valley to plant a church. I was 23 years old, my wife was six months pregnant with our first child, and we had **no** money or financial support. I had offers to pastor and to serve on the staff of a large church. My mother said it made no sense to not take a position that could provide for the financial needs of my family. However, this was one time when the common-sense decision was not the will of God. These are the exceptions in the Christian life. Usually the common-sense decision is the right decision, as long as it does not violate the teachings of the Word of God. In Acts 9:22-25 we have the account of Jews seeking to quiet Saul of Tarsus from preaching the Gospel of Christ. They sought to kill him, so *"the disciples took him by night, and let down by the wall in a basket."* He could not leave through the gates because *"their laying await was known of Saul, and they watched the gates day and night to kill him."* It just made sense that the disciples would find a way to get Saul out of the city. My thought for today is that we must not allow the threats and persecutions of the enemies of the Cross to quiet our voices. We must use common sense approaches to continue proclaiming the Gospel of Christ. Look around you and see the opportunities that are available to us to spread the Gospel. Common sense led the disciples to lower Saul down the wall in a basket, so that he could continue preaching the Gospel. There are many opportunities available to us today, such as the printed book you hold in your hand. This is but one opportunity. There are many others. Look for your "basket" to be used to further the Gospel. God bless and have a great day!

September 30

"The church must stop shooting its wounded." I have heard this statement many times over the last few years. It simply means that the church must be willing to restore and accept a fallen believer. The restoration and acceptance includes servants of the Lord that have fallen but have repented and desire to live and serve the Lord. There is a challenge for the church to accept these fallen ones, and there has been a challenge for the church to accept outsiders that may come to the church with a past that is questionable. Saul of Taurus was not a fallen believer, but he had been a leader of Christian persecution. The believers in Jerusalem were slow to receive Saul and questioned whether he was truly a disciple of Jesus. There was one, Barnabas, who presented Saul and defended him before the apostles. The Bible says in Acts 9:27, *"But Barnabas took him, and brought him to the apostles, and declared unto them how he had seen the Lord in the way, and he had spoken to him, and how he preached boldly at Damascus in the name of Jesus."* The rejection of people today is often due to social status, to past sinful lives, or even racial or ethnic differences. There must be a Barnabas, or a few of them, in every church! That is, there must be those who vouch for and defend these who desire to be members of the church. My challenge for us today is that we see people through the eyes of Jesus. We should see every person as a soul for whom Jesus died. We must extend **grace** to all who desire to follow our Lord. Their past must be their past; we must love and receive people as they are **today.** May God help each of us to be a Barnabas to someone today. God bless and have a great day!

October 1

I was struck recently by a particular promise of God that is mentioned repeatedly in the Bible. John 14:14 says, *"If ye shall ask any thing in my name, I will do it."* The same promise is proclaimed in John 15:7. *"If ye abide in me, and my words abide in you, ye shall ask what ye will, and it shall be done unto you."* Then we see the words of Jesus again in John 15:16. *"Ye have not chosen me, but I have chosen you, and ordained you, that ye should go and bring forth fruit, and that your fruit should remain: that whatsoever ye shall ask of the Father in my name, he may give it you."* God has promised to hear and answer our prayers. There are times His answer is yes, and we receive what we ask. There are times He answers, "Not now," and we must patiently wait. Then there are times He answers, "No," and we must trust His wisdom. My thought for today is that, regardless of how hopeless our circumstances may seem, we have the privilege of prayer. Prayer is not only a privilege, it is a powerful resource as we journey through this life. Prayer is not about us pleading with God for what we want; it is about pursuing His plan for our lives. His plan will always result in a joyous life, as pointed out in John 15:11. *"These things have I spoken unto you, that my joy might remain in you, and that your joy might be full."* Today may be filled with uncertainty and fear, but God is waiting to hear from you. He has a plan, He has a purpose, and He will answer your prayers. God is only a prayer away! God has not forgotten you; He will hear you if you will only pray. God bless and have a great day.

October 2

The one defining characteristic of Christianity can be boiled down to the words of Christ in John 15:12. *"This is my commandment, That ye love one another, as I have loved you."* These were among the instructions given by Jesus to His disciples shortly before His crucifixion. It is certainly just as applicable to us today as it was then. For several years my former church used the phrase "Love Like Jesus" as its theme. The emphasis was that we show the love of Christ to others. As I read and meditate upon His words in John 15:12-13, I ask myself, "Just what kind of love does Jesus have for me?" His love for me should be the kind of love I have for others. I suggest His love is a **faithful love.** You can depend upon Jesus. This is the lesson taught by the illustration of the vine and the branches in John 15:1-6. I also observe that His love is a **forgiving love.** This is reiterated in Eph. 4:32. *"And be ye kind one to another, tenderhearted, forgiving one another, even as God for Christ's sake hath forgiven you."* It is a **forever love,** and it is unconditional as described in Rom. 8:35-39. Let's all ask God to love others through us. We should pray that we would be faithful to those God has put in our lives — faithful to share the Good News of His salvation and faithful to love at all times. We should love the unlovable. This can only be done as we allow the Spirit of Christ to create a forgiving spirit in each of us. Our love must be unconditional and a love that lasts forever. Oh, that we might "love like Jesus." God bless you and have a great day.

The ways of God will always be rejected by the world. Down through the centuries, persecution has repeatedly followed Christianity. Jesus warned His disciples in John 16:1-4 of their rejection of the religious world. *"These things have I spoken unto you, that ye should not be offended. They shall put you out of the synagogues: yea, the time cometh, that whosoever killeth you will think that he doeth God service. And these things will they do unto you, because they have not known the Father, nor me. But these things have I told you, that when the time shall come, ye may remember that I told you of them. And these things I said not unto you at the beginning, because I was with you."* Today we live in days of apostasy, which according to Webster means "a renunciation of our religious faith." The authority of the Word of God is questioned by religious leaders and denied by society. Jesus prepared His disciples, saying in John 16:1, *"These things have I spoken unto you, that ye should not be offended."* The word *"offended"* means "to not fall away." Believers often get discouraged by the rejection of the message of the Gospel. We become defeated and curse the darkness of a sinful society. But the greater the darkness, the brighter the light shines. The glorious Light of the Gospel still shines in this dark world of sin. Persecution gives opportunity for us to declare the truth of the Word of God. Our Lord is with us and will give us courage and strength to stand for the truth of the Word of God, just as He did for those disciples of the early church. Remember the warning of II Tim. 3:12. *"Yea, and all that will live godly in Christ Jesus shall suffer persecution."* God bless you today and remember the words of Dr. Bob Jones Sr., "Do right! If the stars fall, **do right!"**

October 4

Every believer has a companion who is constantly with him. That companion is the Holy Spirit of God who dwells **in** every believer. It was that same Holy Spirit who showed each of us our need for a Savior. Jesus said in John 16:8, *"And when he is come, he will reprove the world of sin, and of righteousness, and of judgment."* The word *"reprove"* literally means to convince or show. The Holy Spirit convicts us of our sin so that we see our need for a Savior, and also that we might confess our sin to maintain a right relationship with the Savior. This companion is also our spiritual teacher. Jesus said in John 16:13, *"Howbeit when he, the Spirit of truth, is come, he will guide you into all truth: for he shall not speak of himself; but whatsoever he shall hear, that shall he speak: and he will shew you things to come."* Anyone can learn the facts taught in the Bible, but the Holy Spirit is the one who guides the believer to the spiritual truths that God has for him. As you and I read the Word of God, we need to call upon the Holy Spirit to guide us to the truths God has for us in His Word. We must acknowledge the presence of the Holy Spirit in our lives and allow Him to be our guide. It was the Holy Spirit who drew us to the Savior that we might be saved, and that same Holy Spirit will direct our lives if we will but heed His leading. Thank God for the blessed Holy Spirit who leads and guides us through this life! God bless and have a great day!

October 5

I still am amazed how Jesus can take our sorrows and turn them into joy — not that we joy for the sorrow, but we joy in the midst of the sorrow. As Jesus was preparing His disciples for His death on the cross, He said in John 16:20, *"Verily, verily, I say unto you, That ye shall weep and lament, but the world shall rejoice: and ye shall be sorrowful, but your sorrow shall be turned into joy."* Jesus was speaking of the joy the disciples would experience at the time of His resurrection. Joy often follows pain. Jesus gives the example of this truth in verses 21-22. *"A woman when she is in travail hath sorrow, because her hour is come: but as soon as she is delivered of the child, she remembereth no more the anguish, for joy that a man is born into the world. And ye now therefore have sorrow: but I will see you again, and your heart shall rejoice, and your joy no man taketh from you."* He explained that just as the pain of a mother in childbirth is soon forgotten after the child is born, so would their sorrow at His death be forgotten quickly. My thought for today is summed up in the latter part of Ps. 30:5. *"Weeping may endure for a night, but joy cometh in the morning."* If today is a day of travail in your life, you can take hope in those words. There could have been no empty tomb if there had not been a cross. Have faith while in your hour of suffering; God has a plan and a purpose and *"your sorrow shall be turned into joy."* God bless and have a great day.

October 6

   "Pastor, would you pray for me? I am facing a difficult time in my life." I cannot tell you how many times I have heard those words or a similar statement coming from people having a hard time. As I write this I am reminded of the words of Jesus in John 16:33. *"These things I have spoken unto you, that in me ye might have peace. In the world ye shall have tribulation: but be of good cheer; I have overcome the world."* Dr. Bill Pennell's closing words in his daily devotion are, "Be kind to everyone. Everyone is having a hard time." Jesus knew his disciples were going to have a difficult time in the days following His death on the cross. Jesus also knew you and I would have some hard times in our lives. Though the disciples did not ask Jesus to pray for them to get through the coming days, Jesus prayed for them (John 17:9) and He prays for us (John 17:20). I am always honored to be asked to pray for anyone. I try to keep my word and pray for those I commit to pray for. At the same time, I need the prayers of others to help me through the trials of life. I thank God for the faithful prayer partners He has placed in my life. We must praise the Lord that He is our great Intercessor and is praying for each of us who know Him as our Savior. I challenge each of you today to read the 17th chapter of John and note the prayer of Jesus. Let's never forget to pray one for another. If you are facing difficult times, request prayer from those you know will pray for you, and know you have a Savior who is praying for you today! God bless and have a great day!

October 7

A former college classmate and pastor, Rev. Briggs King, called John 17 "the greatest prayer ever recorded. I have preached from it many times." Let's look at what made it so great. **Who prayed the prayer?** It is the prayer of the Son of God. He who was God yet man, was man yet God, felt the necessity to pray. How much the more should you and I feel the need to pray? **For whom did He pray?** First, He prayed for himself (v. 1-8). Our prayer should always include an evaluation of our motives and our personal needs. Second, He prayed for His disciples (v. 9-19). When we pray we need to pray for those that are close to us, such as family and friends. Third, He prayed for us — "for them also which believe on me through their word" (v. 20). This is a reminder that we often pray for those we do not know. We pray for missionaries, suffering saints, and lost sinners we do not know. **When did He pray?** This prayer was offered just before He was to leave His disciples and face His crucifixion. We need to pray before great trials come in our lives, and we need to pray for those who will be affected by what happens in our lives. Today, I would hope this prayer of our Lord humbles each of us when we think Jesus is praying for us. Yes, even today, *"we have an advocate with the Father, Jesus Christ the righteous"* (I John 2:1). He prayed for us before He went to the cross, and He is still interceding for us at the right hand of the Father (Rom 8:34). This prayer should help each of us face the challenges of today. Just think, you do not face the trials of the day alone. Jesus is praying for you. Praise the Lord. God bless and have a great day.

October 8

"Divide and conquer" is one of the tactics of Satan. He seeks to bring division among the brethren — church against church and Christian against Christian. Surely we must stand for right, but we need to stand together with those who know and serve our Lord. Jesus prayed for His disciples in John 17:11. *"And now I am no more in the world, but these are in the world, and I come to thee. Holy Father, keep through thine own name those whom thou hast given me, that they may be one, as we are."* Verses 20-21: *"Neither pray I for these alone, but for them also which shall believe on me through their word; That they all may be one; as thou, Father, art in me, and I in thee, that they also may be one in us: that the world may believe that thou hast sent me."* More than ever we need unity among the brethren. We will have our differences on secondary doctrines, and we will differ on methods of worship and what is a worldly standard as opposed to what is righteous. But can we agree on the fundamental doctrines of the Word of God? I'm talking about the virgin birth, the deity of Christ, His vicarious suffering on the cross for the sins of mankind, His bodily resurrection from the dead, and the promise of His second coming. Can we agree that salvation is by grace through faith? If we can agree on these and other cardinal doctrines, surely we can serve and live in unity and we can be as one. The days of persecution are upon us. The forces of evil would quiet our message and confine us to our churches. Moral teaching of the Bible is being portrayed as "hate speech." Religious liberty is questioned and attacked. Our only hope is that we stand together for these doctrines and practices. May our unity begin with us praying one for another. We do not have to agree on everything. Unity is not uniformity, but it is a command of our Lord! God bless you today and have a great day!

October 9

What is faith? We talk often about having faith. In Heb. 11:1 we find the Biblical definition: *"Now faith is the substance of things hoped for, the evidence of things not seen."* But what do these words really mean? To me, it means to believe what I cannot see and to possess what I do not have. To see an illustration of this, one needs only to read the account of the healing of the nobleman's dying son in John 4:46-54. This nobleman sought Jesus for healing. Verses 50-51: *"Jesus saith unto him, Go thy way; thy son liveth. And the man believed the word that Jesus had spoken unto him, and he went his way. And as he was now going down, his servants met him, and told him, saying, Thy son liveth."* The nobleman believed what he could not see, and then he possessed what he did not have. Biblical faith is based on a **Person** — Jesus, the Son of God. My faith is not a leap into the dark. It is a confidence that Jesus is able to do more than I can see and provide what I do not possess. Biblical faith is founded upon the **promises** of God. What Jesus said to the nobleman— "Go thy way; thy son liveth" — was a promise, and it was all the nobleman needed to possess what he did not have, which was the healing of his son. It is Biblical faith that *produces* in our lives what we cannot see and allows us to possess what we do not have. May we all seek to walk by faith and not by sight. The faith life is an exciting adventure, watching God work to give us what we cannot see and allowing us to possess what we do not have. God bless you and have a great day!

October 10

Can a true believer lose his or her salvation? Simply stated, this is an age-old question that divides believers. Judas Iscariot, the disciple who betrayed Jesus, is often cited as an example by those who would argue that you can lose your salvation. With that in mind, read John 17:12. *"While I was with them in the world, I kept them in thy name: those that thou gavest me I have kept, and none of them is lost, but the son of perdition; that the scripture might be fulfilled."* The key word in the text is *"but."* This little word is a word of contrast, meaning one of another kind. Judas never was saved; he was never a true follower of Jesus. We might say he was **a professor but not a possessor** of eternal life. My thought for today is that we be certain we are both professors and possessors. God's salvation is a free gift to all who believe. It is based upon Christ's finished work on the cross, not anything we have done. Recall the familiar words of Eph. 2:8-9. *"For by grace are ye saved through faith; and that not of yourselves: it is the gift of God: Not of works, lest any man should boast."* Because it is all about what He has done and not about anything we have done, we can rejoice in the promise of Rom. 8:38-39. *"For I am persuaded, that neither death, nor life, nor angels, nor principalities, nor powers, nor things present, nor things to come, Nor height, nor depth, nor any other creature, shall be able to separate us from the love of God, which is in Christ Jesus our Lord."* Praise God for His gift of **eternal** salvation! God bless and have a great day!

Do you have that special place where you go to pray? I heard of one well-known Preacher who had a small closet that was his prayer closet. Others have a chair or a special place in an office. The point is that we all need a place we can go to be alone with God. After teaching His disciples (John 13-16) and praying with them (John 17), Jesus left the upper room with them as the time for His arrest was near. Notice John 18:1-2. *"When Jesus had spoken these words, he went forth with his disciples over the brook Cedron, where was a garden, into the which he entered, and his disciples. And Judas also, which betrayed him, knew the place: for Jesus ofttimes resorted thither with his disciples."* Judas was aware, as were the other disciples, that Christ had a few specific places where He would go in times of need. There are several accounts in the Gospels of how He went into the mountains to pray. Obviously, this garden spot near the brook Cedron was another favorite. My challenge for us today is that we set aside those special places to go and fellowship with our Lord. Maybe it will be a place to pray and read His Word, or a getaway for extended times of communion with the Lord. We all need those places of refuge to prepare us for the trials of life. God bless and have a great day!

October 12

It really hurts to be betrayed by a friend. An account of the most infamous betrayal in history is found in John 18:2-5. *"And Judas also, which betrayed him, knew the place: for Jesus ofttimes resorted thither with his disciples. Judas then, having received a band of men and officers from the chief priests and Pharisees, cometh thither with lanterns and torches and weapons. Jesus therefore, knowing all things that should come upon him, went forth, and said unto them, Whom seek ye? They answered him, Jesus of Nazareth. Jesus saith unto them, I am he. And Judas also, which betrayed him, stood with them."* Luke's account records that Judas sought to place a kiss upon the cheek of our Lord to identify Him to the Roman soldiers. This was the disciple whom Jesus had given the position of treasurer of His followers. Yet it was Judas who turned on Him and led the soldiers to the garden to arrest Him. In Matt. 26:14-15 we are told, *"Then one of the twelve, called Judas Iscariot, went unto the chief priests, And said unto them, What will ye give me, and I will deliver him unto you? And they covenanted with him for thirty pieces of silver."* My thought for today is that if Jesus could choose 12 and one of them be a Judas, why do we think we will not have those in our lives who hurt and disappoint us? It is interesting to note that Jesus knew Judas would betray Him, yet Jesus continued to allow him to serve and even washed his feet along with those of the other disciples (John 13:1-5). This was a demonstration of forgiveness. We must learn to forgive those who abuse and misuse us. You will be the loser if you do not have a forgiving spirit. The bitterness will eat away at your joy and rob you of a blessed life. Do not let the Judas in your life be the thief of your victorious life in Christ! God bless and have a great day!

October 13

As I read the account of Jesus' arrest, His hearings before Annas and Caiaphas the high priest, then his appearance before the Roman governor Pilate, I am reminded of the unjust treatment of our Savior. The conclusion of Pilate regarding the charges levied against Jesus was, as stated in John 18:38, *"I find in Him no fault at all."* Yet the religious crowd cried for His death. As I read this account, I was reminded of the false accusations that are often said of Bible believers today. We are called homophobic because we hold to the teaching of the Word of God regarding sexual relations between same sex partners (Rom. 1:26-27). We are accused of denying women their rights because we believe life begins at conception and that life in the womb has a right to live. These and other Biblical positions may not be politically correct, but they are the teachings of the Word of God. As believers, we should seek to help and be a blessing to those who are homosexual. We may not agree with their lifestyles, and we will not condone their sin, but we love them and pray for them and seek to win them to a saving knowledge of our Lord. We truly do support women's health and are concerned about the children born out of unwanted pregnancies. We should strive to follow the example of Jesus and accept the fact that we are going to be "crucified" by the world and often by the liberal religious crowd. Stand for right, but be sure to stand in the right way. When accused or persecuted, we must maintain the spirit of Christ, who according to Isa. 53:7 was *"brought as a lamb to the slaughter, and as a sheep before her shearers is dumb, so he openeth not his mouth."* May God give us strength to stand, grace to stand with a right spirit, and let it be said of us, "We find no fault in them." God bless and have a blessed day.

October 14

Good men, even at their best, are just men. It is both refreshing and encouraging to see the honest reporting of the failures of the characters of the Bible. The **bad judgment** of Peter is on display in John 18:10-11. *"Then Simon Peter having a sword drew it, and smote the high priest's servant, and cut off his right ear. The servant's name was Malchus. Then said Jesus unto Peter, Put up thy sword into the sheath: the cup which my Father hath given me, shall I not drink it?"* There are times in our lives when we seek to do good, but bad judgments cause us to make mistakes, just as Peter did here. Later in the same chapter we also see Peter's **blatant denial** that he was a follower of Jesus. This denial had been predicted by Jesus in John 13:38. I fear there are times we also deny the Lord, either by words or deeds. We are all just sinners saved by grace. Most of us who know Christ as Savior desire to live for Him and to stand strong in our faith. But the truth is that we still contend with the fears and weakness of the flesh every day. The encouraging word is that God does not forsake us. Peter was so ashamed of his failures that he returned to his old profession of fishing after the crucifixion of Jesus. Even though Jesus had shown Himself to His disciples after the resurrection, the Bible says in John 21:3, *"Simon Peter saith unto them, I go a fishing."* But Jesus came to them there as well to reassure and encourage them, especially Peter, to continue in their service to the Lord. My challenge for us today is God is **not** finished with you or me. Regardless of our mistakes or our sin, he still has a plan for each of our lives. As Dr. Henry Blackaby has said, "Find out what God is up to in your life, and join Him." God bless you and have a great day.

October 15

It just does not seem right that the guilty should go free and the innocent be condemned. Yet that is exactly what happened in John 18:39-40. Pilate had heard the cries of the people for Jesus to be put to death. It was the time of the Passover, and the custom was that the Roman government would release one prisoner for the Jews at this season. Saying that he found no fault in Jesus at all, Pilate made one last offer to free Him. But the Jewish mob would not have it. Verse 40: *"Then cried they all again, saying, Not this man, but Barabbas. Now Barabbas was a robber."* We might be quite judgmental of these Jews, but I would remind each of us this is a picture of what Jesus was going to do on the cross for us. He was the sinless who died for the sinful. He was the innocent who died for the guilty. The Bible says in Rom. 5:8, *"But God commendeth his love toward us, in that, while we were yet sinners, Christ died for us."* This thought is expressed again in II Cor. 5:21. *"For he hath made him to be sin for us, who knew no sin; that we might be made the righteousness of God in him."* The innocent dying for the guilty does not seem right, but thanks be to God that Jesus, the sinless One, died for the guilty that we might go free from the penalty of our sin. We all are just like Barabbas, guilty but free, because of the sacrifice of the Savior. Give thanks and praise today for the sacrifice of Christ on the cross for your sin! God bless and have a great day!

October 16

Words matter! According to Prov. 25:11, *"A word fitly spoken is like apples of gold in pictures of silver."* I met a lady a few years ago who told me that when she was an 11-year-old girl, riding a bus to Sunday School, I shared a few words that stayed with her throughout her childhood, also reminding her of God's care for her later in life. Those words were from Prov. 18:24. *".. there is a friend that sticketh closer than a brother."* This little girl felt she had no friends. Her home life was not good, and she felt all alone. She said of these simple words spoken to her when she was 11, "It was a seed planted that others would water over the years of my life." Today, this dear lady is a committed servant of our Savior. In just the past few years, she has come to hear me speak. Words matter, so let's be sure our words are words of encouragement and help to others. May we speak often of the love and concern of the Savior for even the least of people. Those words not only blessed that 11-year-old girl when first spoken, but I can tell you they blessed a 69-year-old preacher much later. As was said by this dear lady, words are "seeds," and they do grow and bring forth fruit. I want my words to bring forth fruit that will bless others and glorify my Savior! God bless you and thank you, dear lady, for sharing with me this wonderful testimony!

October 17

The hub of all we believe as Christians is the cross. From the hub of the cross extends our hope, our salvation, and the major doctrines of our faith. In John 19:1-37 is an account of the crucifixion of Jesus. The night I received Christ as my Savior, I read Luke's account of the crucifixion. My prayer that night was that I would never take Jesus' death on the cross for my sin for granted. It is a good thing for all of us to read and meditate upon the suffering of the Savior for our sins — and that suffering quite some time before He was placed upon the cross. As we are told in John 19:1-3, *"Then Pilate therefore took Jesus, and scourged him. And the soldiers platted a crown of thorns, and put it on his head, and they put on him a purple robe, And said, Hail, King of the Jews! and they smote him with their hands."* My thought for today is that each of us should not fail to give thanks to Jesus for the suffering He endured for our sake. Oh, how He must love us! Oh, that we would love Him and serve Him regardless of the suffering we might be called upon to suffer for Him. It is said that there are more Christians suffering and being put to death for their faith today than any other time in history. That kind of suffering could very easily come to America. May each of us be willing to suffer for Him who suffered so much for us! God bless you and have a great day!

October 18

The fifth of the Ten Commandments is recorded in Ex. 20:12. *"Honour thy father and thy mother: that thy days may be long upon the land which the Lord thy God giveth thee."* It is noteworthy that Jesus remembered His mother when He was dying on the cross. The Bible records this exchange in John 19:26-27. *"When Jesus therefore saw his mother, and the disciple standing by, whom he loved, he saith unto his mother, Woman, behold thy son! Then saith he to the disciple, Behold thy mother! And from that hour that disciple took her unto his own home."* In Exodus we have the **exhortation** given as a commandment, and in John we see the **example** of Jesus on the cross. Knowing all of this, we certainly must honor our parents. If children are not taught to honor the parents they can see, how will they ever honor a God they cannot see? I am appalled at the disrespect I see in the market place demonstrated by children toward their parents! Is it any wonder we have so much rebellion in our society? I live in Florida, and I see the thousands of older people who seem to be forgotten by their children. God has promised the blessing of longevity to those who honor their parents. My mother is in a memory care facility. She does not remember that I visit her, but I remember, and God remembers. If your parents are living, honor them today. Call or go by and see them. Let them know you love and appreciate them. God bless and have a great day.

October 19

"When common sense makes good sense, seek no other sense." There are seven sayings of Jesus recorded while He was on the cross. I have preached, and I have heard many sermons on them. As He hung on the cross, His body lacerated from the scourging (John 19:1) and the crown of thorns upon His head, Jesus suffered such physical agony and pain. Death on a cross was an excruciating death. One would pull himself up by the arms that were nailed to the cross at the wrist or hands while pushing up with his body to get a breath. Death was certain, but it was also painful. When Jesus cried out, *"I thirst,"* in John 19:28, it was a cry of agony and pain. It was a cry of His humanity. He suffered as a man for our sins. Yes, He was God, but He was in the flesh and suffered physical pain as a man. My thought today is for those who may be suffering from physical pain. Maybe your pain is from a disease or illness. It could be you have suffered an accident that has left you with great pain. Whatever it is, God knows your pain and He has experienced the greatest of pain. He can heal! He can give grace to you as you suffer through your pain. We are reminded in Heb. 2:18, *"For in that he himself hath suffered being tempted, he is able to succour* [help] *them that are tempted."* God bless and know God loves you and sees you just where you are! Have a great day!

October 20

It has often been said, "A picture is worth a thousand words." Think about the picture painted by three simple words from Jesus on the cross: "It is finished." That phrase shows us the completeness of His death for our sins. The three words are but one word in the Greek language, *"tetelestai."* This word is actually a word picture. According to bible.org, it was a word "written on business documents or receipts in New Testament times to show a bill had been paid in full." Christ's death on the cross **paid in full** the sin debt of the world. All who will repent of their sin and receive His payment, by faith, for their sin can be saved from their sin. There are no works nor sacrament necessary for us to be saved. As the old song states:

> *Jesus paid it all; all to Him I owe.*
> *Sin had left a crimson stain;*
> *He washed it white as snow.*

What a vivid reminder that our salvation was purchased in full on the cross of Calvary. We live right and do right not to be saved, but because we are saved. We who have trusted Jesus as Savior have been purchased with His precious blood. Now we are to live for Him. May we all give Him praise for His salvation, so freely offered to all or any that will receive it. God bless and have a great day.

October 21

Never forget that day — the day you met Jesus and He became your Savior. In John 19 we read of the death of Jesus on the cross. After His death, there came a man named Joseph of Arimathea to Pilate to ask for the body of Jesus that he might bury Him (John 19:38). We also read of another man who came to help prepare the body of Jesus for burial. John 19:39 tells us, *"And there came also Nicodemus, which at the first came to Jesus by night, and brought a mixture of myrrh and aloes, about an hundred pound weight."* Nicodemus never forgot his encounter with the Christ, which is described for us in the third chapter of John. Jesus was speaking to him when He spoke the words we now know as John 3:16. *"For God so loved the world, that he gave his only begotten Son, that whosoever believeth in him should not perish, but have everlasting life."* It was the night Nicodemus first met the Lord that motivated him to assist in the burial of Jesus, even though it could have been dangerous. I am sometimes asked why I keep going and preaching. It is the memory of that Thursday night in 1965 when I met Jesus and He became my Savior! Never forget the day you met Jesus. It is the memory of that hour and that day that will keep you keeping on for the Lord. God bless and have a great day!

October 22

Several years ago during the Easter season, I heard a TV commentator ask a very prominent preacher, "What do you believe is the significance of the teachings of the resurrection?" I was appalled by the answer given by this pastor and teacher. His response was, "Well, the significance of the resurrection is that something good can come out of bad." Something good certainly resulted from our Lord's resurrection, but the real significance is that the empty and bodily resurrection of Christ are the proof of our salvation. As described in Rom. 4:25, *"Who was delivered for our offences, and was raised again for our justification."* The death of Jesus on the cross paid the sin debt for mankind, and His resurrection is the proof that He was God's sacrifice for our sin. When Mary Magdalene ran to Peter and John with the report of the empty tomb she said, *"They have taken away the Lord out of the sepulchre, and we know not where they have laid him"* (John 20:2). Her perception of the situation was wrong, but today I fear there are many who do not truly understand that our God lives. The empty tomb was more than a good thing resulting from a bad situation. His body had not been taken away; He arose from the dead. We cannot see Him, but we can talk to Him through prayer and we feel His presence as we walk through this life. I encourage you today to meditate on the reality that we serve a **living** Savior! God bless and remember to spend some time with the Lord today.

October 23

I was saved as a high school senior. After my conversion I had a desire to share what had happened to me with others. My friends could not believe the difference in my behavior. Some were glad for me, while others mocked and said it would not last. But when you have truly met the Master, there is a natural desire to introduce your friends to Him and His gift of salvation. Mary Magdalene could not keep quiet about seeing the resurrected Christ. The Bible says in John 20:18, *"Mary Magdalene came and told the disciples that she had seen the Lord, and that he had spoken these things unto her."* My challenge for today is that we be witnesses to what we have experienced and what we know about Jesus. A witness is "one who tells what he knows." I know I trusted Jesus as my Savior, and He changed my life. I have seen Him with the eye of faith. I know He is alive and will save all or any who will call upon Him. Rom. 10:13 says, *"For whosoever shall call upon the name of the Lord shall be saved."* If you have "seen" Him — not with the physical eye, but with the eye of faith — you have a story to tell. May God give each of us the courage and motivation to share Jesus with others.

October 24

"I won't believe it until I see it." That was the attitude of the disciples and especially Thomas, who has been dubbed "Doubting Thomas." The truth is that there are many things in life that we believe, yet we cannot see. Think about it. Can you see love? Can you see the wind, or electricity? No, we only see the results of each of them. Yet we do not question that they are real. In verse 20 of the 20th chapter of John we read, *"And when he had so said, he shewed unto them his hands and his side. Then were the disciples glad, when they saw the Lord."* They **saw**, and they **believed**. Verses 24-25: *"But Thomas, one of the twelve, called Didymus, was not with them when Jesus came. The other disciples therefore said unto him, We have seen the Lord. But he said unto them, Except I shall see in his hands the print of the nails, and put my finger into the print of the nails, and thrust my hand into his side, I will not believe."* I have never seen the resurrected Savior. I have not seen the print of the nails in His hands nor thrust my hand into His side, but I witness the fact that He is alive every day. I see the witness of His resurrection every Sunday. We worship on Sunday rather than Saturday because Sunday is Resurrection Day! We have the testimony of the many witnesses recorded as seeing the resurrected Christ (I Cor. 15:3-8) and we see His power to change the lives of those who believe and receive Christ through repentance and faith in Him. I do not have to see it to believe it; I just have to know it is true! Our Savior rose from the dead and lives today! Give Him praise today!

October 25

There are many verses in the New Testament to remind us who know Christ as Savior that the Holy Spirit lives *in* us. For example, the Bible says in I Cor. 6:19, *"What? know ye not that your body is the temple of the Holy Ghost which is in you, which ye have of God, and ye are not your own?"* In John 14:16 Jesus promised His disciples *"another Comforter"* and described that comforter in more detail in verse 17: *"Even the Spirit of truth; whom the world cannot receive, because it seeth him not, neither knoweth him: but ye know him; for he dwelleth **with** you, and shall be **in** you."* When Jesus showed Himself after His resurrection and appeared to His disciples, He gave what in the Greek language is a judicial command: *"And when he had said this, he breathed on them, and saith unto them, Receive ye the Holy Ghost"* (John 20:22). It is my opinion that this is the time **all** believers were first indwelt by the Holy Spirit, and every believer since has been indwelt by the Holy Spirit of God. If you are saved, God the Holy Spirit dwells **in** you! Let's all remember to call upon Him who dwells in us to guide us and teach us, that we may live to bring glory to our Savior. Remember that we are never alone. The blessed Holy Spirit is with us every moment of our lives. He is as close as a breath! He will **never** leave us. He convicts us when we go astray, comforts us in times of trouble, and is a constant guide as we walk through this life. Acknowledge His presence in your life. God bless and have a great day.

October 26

God is interested in every aspect of our lives. He cares about your physical needs. He cares about those disappointments that come. He cares about the failures we experience. Our God cares about us in every possible way. We see this exemplified in the resurrected Christ's appearance on the shore of the Sea of Galilee (Tiberias) in John 21. Some of the disciples were fishing but had caught nothing. That changed after Jesus spoke to them in verse 6. *"And he said unto them, Cast the net on the right side of the ship, and ye shall find. They cast therefore, and now they were not able to draw it for the multitude of fishes."* Isn't it amazing how Jesus **always** shows up when all of our efforts seem in vain? These were professional fishermen. They knew how to fish, but they had not caught a thing until Jesus spoke to them and they followed His instructions. Jesus always knows on what side of the ship we should cast our nets for a catch. He will show up when we least expect and He will bless us beyond our greatest expectation. Listen today for His voice, look for His presence and enjoy His provisions. God has not forsaken you. On the contrary, He is interested in your every need. He knows where the fish are and He will direct you to them for a catch. God bless and have a great day.

October 27

I was saved after hearing the preaching of an old Texas evangelist named Lester Roloff. He had a unique way of delivering a sermon. Sometimes he would break into a song in the midst of his message. One of his favorites was "Come and Dine." The chorus of the song goes like this:

Come and dine, the Master calleth, Come and Dine;
You may feast at Jesus' table all the time.
He who fed the multitude, turned the water into wine,
To the hungry calleth now, Come and Dine.

The song is a reminder of the resurrected Christ's appearance to His disciples on the shore of the Sea of Galilee in John 21. After Jesus had directed these fishermen in verse 6 to a spot where they would be assured a catch, He invited them to come to the shore and meet with Him. The exact phrase at the beginning of verse 12: *"Jesus saith unto them, Come and dine."* The simple application of this text for us is a reminder that Jesus desires to fellowship with His followers. The words of verse 12 could be aimed directly at us. *"Jesus saith unto* [your name], *Come and dine."* Jesus is calling you and me today to fellowship with Him. He has a spiritual table spread for each of us. We only need to come and dine. As you begin your day, take a few minutes and come to the spiritual table of our Lord and dine and fellowship with the living Christ. God bless and have a blessed day.

October 28

As I read the account of Jesus with His disciples on the shore of the Sea of Galilee in John 21, I noted with interest the words of Jesus to Peter in verse 15: *"Simon, son of Jonas, lovest thou me more than these?"* Jesus asks the same question of each of us. The key thought for us here is the word *"these."* I believe Jesus was asking Peter, "Do you love me more than the nets, the boat, more than the the things of the world?" I wonder what our answer would be to the question, "Do you love me more than your profession, more than the things of this world?" Be careful how you answer. God just may ask you to leave your job and the comforts you enjoy to *"feed my sheep"* (v. 16). I recall being in college with numerous men who had left good-paying jobs and lives of comfort and security to come to Bible school or college to prepare to go to the mission field or other places of service. Do you love Jesus more than the comforts and security of this world? God could be calling you to leave your comfort zone in a major way. There is no greater privilege than to be a minister of the Gospel of Christ. It may be His call for you is to give of your time to be a Sunday School teacher or work in some other place of service — one that will require a sacrifice of some pleasure or even a change of profession that you might fulfill His calling for your life. May God give each of us the grace and commitment to hear and heed His calling in our life. God bless and have a great day.

"I'm jealous." We all have expressed feelings of jealousy at times in our lives. Jealousy is defined as "resentment against a rival, a person enjoying success or advantage." It is also a sin. There was one disciple who is described in John 21:20 as the one *"whom Jesus loved."* John had a special place at the Passover table, described in that verse as the one *"which also leaned on his breast at supper, and said, Lord, which is he that betrayeth thee?"* Peter had been the center of our Lord's attention on the shore of Galilee. In verses 18-19 Christ had just given some insight as to Peter's future. Seeing John, Peter asked in verse 21, *"and what shall this man do?"* There is an indication that there was a little envy or a bit of jealousy in the heart of Peter. Note our Lord's response in verse 22: *"If I will that he tarry till I come, what is that to thee? follow thou me."* Simply put, Peter was to follow Jesus, and it was none of his business what happened in the life of John. We need to rejoice when others are blessed and not be envious of their blessings. We must recognize that each of us has a particular place in the plan of God. Peter's place of service was not the same as John's place. May each of us guard our hearts from jealousy. It is God who raises up and brings down. I will rejoice in my position in Christ, giving Him praise for my blessings and also for the blessings in the lives of others. God bless and have a blessed day!

October 30

The Gospels — Matthew, Mark, Luke, and John — give us a glimpse of the life and ministry of Jesus. This book contains selections from every chapter of John. It is interesting to note John 21:25, the final verse of the book: *"And there are also many other things which Jesus did, the which, if they should be written every one, I suppose that even the world itself could not contain the books that should be written. Amen."* As I read these words I began to think of all that the Lord does for us today. It could be said if we really gave Him the credit for all He does, it would be impossible for us to recount all of His blessings to us. He shows Himself mighty in creation. He shows Himself merciful in His dealings with us in life's circumstances. He bestows multitudes of blessings on us every day. Surely we could say His benefits and blessing to us are more than we could ever say or think. With this in mind, now would be a good time to take a few minutes and acknowledge the **greatness** of our God. We need to to give Him praise for His goodness to us. The depths and wonders of our salvation alone go beyond our deepest understanding. Think about it; the Creator of the universe, the most Holy God, loved us so much, He sent His only begotten Son to die for our sin that we might have a home in Heaven. What a Savior! God bless you today and have a great day.

October 31

There is so much we can learn from other people. My pastor and I were visiting with a paraplegic man at a veterans' hospital. This man knows the Lord. He was disabled in an accident. We went to visit him to encourage him but left blessed and encouraged far more than we encouraged him. As we talked with this man, he said regarding his life of total dependence upon others and the passing of his days, "I have lived between two worlds long enough to know as much about one as the other." As I heard this man whose life seemed to be so restricted and helpless, I thought that he was truly living out the words of Paul in Phil. 4:11. *"Not that I speak in respect of want: for I have learned, in whatsoever state I am, therewith to be content."* This man also said, "I walk through a routine everyday. I pray for a list. When it is time for me to go, I have no fears." Here was a man, who by my standards, had no reason to rejoice in his life, but he had found a purpose and God's plan and was satisfied. I am sure he would like to be able to walk and to feed himself, but he had found peace with his plight. All of us need to seek God's purpose for our lives and be content with His will for us. From a secular point of view, we might say that if life hands us a basket of lemons, we need to make lemonade. The words of Rom. 8:28 are still true. *"And we know that all things work together for good to them that love God, to them who are the called according to his purpose."* God bless you today and have a blessed day!

November 1

I recently heard a TV commentator indicate that the whole of the population has grown discouraged and even despondent during these days of political debate here in America. I have purposely not commented on political issues in this book because that is not my purpose here. I wish to concentrate on messages that uplift readers. But as every November is election season in the United States, I feel I must address some Biblical exhortations regarding the role of government. According to Romans 13, government is to be our protector and not our provider. Verses 3-4: *"For rulers are not a terror to good works, but to the evil. ... For he is the minister of God to thee for good. But if thou do that which is evil, be afraid; for he beareth not the sword in vain: for he is the minister of God, a revenger to execute wrath upon him that doeth evil."* This passage also reminds us where the true powers lies. Verse 1: *"For there is no power but of God: the powers that be are ordained of God."* In America we choose those who will represent us and administer our God given responsibilities in our society. Therefore, it behooves every American to vote — and to vote our values. It has been said often that America will get the government it deserves. My prayer is that we deserve the continued blessing of God upon our nation. No political candidate will be without sin, but I must choose the candidate who is the closest to my values. I must choose the candidate who holds to the Biblical teachings on the life of the unborn and the moral values as taught in the Word of God. We all must remember that we the people are the government, and God will hold us accountable for what kind of *"minister of God"* (verse 4) each of us will be. God bless you and go vote!

November 2

According to Wikipedia, "The first Thanksgiving was celebrated by the Pilgrims after the first harvest in the New World in 1621. The feast lasted three days, and as accounted by attendee Edward Winslow, it was attended by 90 Native Americans and 52 Pilgrims." As I read this account of the first Thanksgiving, I thought of the many blessings in my life over the past year. I know there are still three weeks to go before the celebration of Thanksgiving, but I was moved to single out one thing each day for the next 22 days and give thanks especially for that one thing each day. Consider the exhortation in I Thess. 5:18. *"In every thing give thanks: for this is the will of God in Christ Jesus concerning you."* As I look back over my life, even the past year, I am so thankful for my **salvation.** The Apostle Paul stated it so plainly yet so eloquently in II Cor. 9:15. *"Thanks be unto God for his unspeakable gift."* It is easy to go through the years and never really give thanks to God for His gift of eternal life. As I grow older and my days grow fewer, the more I appreciate the hope in me for a place called Heaven. No, I am not wanting to go now; in fact, I have asked God for 15 more years to serve Him. But if today is the last day of my life here on Earth, I can say with the Apostle Paul in II Cor. 5:8, *"We are confident, I say, and willing rather to be absent from the body, and to be present with the Lord."* Thank you, Jesus, for this promise! Give God thanks today for His unspeakable gift of salvation. God bless and have a great day!

November 3

While spending the month of November identifying things for which to be thankful, it is no surprise that one of the first to come to my mind is my *spouse*. Today is my wife's birthday. Yes, she is just 39 years old again. Seriously, Doris is a faithful wife who has stood by me through the hard times and the good times. I am so thankful for her faithfulness to the Lord and to me. As I think about the 50-plus years we have spent together, I am reminded of the words of Prov. 18:22. *"Whoso findeth a wife findeth a good thing, and obtaineth favour of the Lord."* While I wish my wife a happy birthday today, I can say that she and I both thank God for health and the ability to continue serving Him together. It is so important that we not take our spouses for granted. I regularly see widows and widowers in churches and other places, and the emptiness in their face is reflected as they walk alone through life. Each of us needs to share a loving thought with our spouse. Men, we need to thank God for our wives. Happy Birthday, Honey. May God grant you many more that we can spend together. God bless and remember to give thanks for that special person God has placed in your life.

November 4

Today I want to say with the Apostle Paul, *"And I thank Christ Jesus our Lord, who hath enabled me, for that he counted me faithful, putting me into the ministry; Who was before a blasphemer, and a persecutor, and injurious: but I obtained mercy, because I did it ignorantly in unbelief"* (I Tim. 1:12-13). I want to thank God that He allows me to **serve** Him. The joy of life is to be used of God. It was the above verses that God used to speak to me about surrendering my life to serve Him. I have never regretted what happened the night of Jan. 25, 1966, when I publicly made my decision to surrender my life to preach the Gospel. I thank God for allowing me to serve Him! Indeed, God has called every believer to serve Him. It may not be a call to preach or to be a missionary, but God has a place of service for every one of His children. You may be a Sunday School teacher, an usher, a prayer warrior, or a greeter. Maybe God has given you the gift of hospitality. You may have a special ministry or place of service in a ministry of helps. There are no insignificant places of service for our Savior. Every place of service is equally blessed by our Lord if it is His place for you to serve. Give God thanks today for the privilege of serving. God bless you today and keep on keeping on serving the Lord!

November 5

As we approach the Thanksgiving season, I want to thank God for the **Scriptures**. Actually, we should be thankful every day that He has given us the Bible. The psalmist wrote in Ps. 119:103, *"How sweet are thy words unto my taste! yea, sweeter than honey to my mouth!"* Someone has said about the Bible, "This Book will keep you from sin, or sin will keep you from this Book." There are 176 verses in Psalms 119. The majority of them are exhortations about the Bible, beginning with verse 1: *"Blessed are the undefiled in the way, who walk in the law of the Lord."* I challenge you to take a few minutes today and read Psalms 119 and make note of all it says about *"the law of the Lord."* I am so thankful for the fact that God gave us written instructions on how to live. My thought for today is how thankful I am that God gave us instructions on how to live. He included words of comfort and the message of salvation. There are warnings and promises throughout the Bible to direct our paths. Thank you Lord, for your holy Scriptures! Truly they are sweet to my taste! However, the Bible must be read and meditated upon for it to be effective in our lives. I heard of one old saint who said he would never place a morsel of bread into his mouth until he had fed his soul from the Word of God. Today, let us give thanks for the Word of God. Let's commit to spend time every day reading and digesting that which is *"sweeter than honey."* God bless you and have a great day.

November 6

   I want to thank God for the **seasons of life.** As I think back over my life, I surely can see the different seasons and the blessings of God in each period of time in my life. As a child, I was privileged to be raised in a Christian home. My parents taught me the value of work and the necessity of worship. I never knew what it was not to go to church. As a teen, I strayed from the Christian values of my parents, but the Lord saved me as a teenager. My early adult years were spent as a pastor. The Lord allowed me to found a church at the age of 23. This season of founding and watching God build His church over 19 years was the springtime of my ministry. I traveled in evangelism for three years after that, and for a while, my wife and I struggled with finding the direction God had for our lives. I guess this could be considered the summer of my life. I then went on to pastor three other churches. These years could be the autumn of my life. A few years ago, I entered the winter, leaving the pastorate and committing the rest of my life to helping churches and encouraging pastors. No one season is greater or better than the other. My thought for today is found in Eccl. 3:1. *"To every thing there is a season, and a time to every purpose under the heaven."* I am trusting God for a long winter with many years of continued service for the Savior! Wherever you are in life, it is but a season. Make the most out of every season of life. Allow God to use today. You are where you are for a reason. As Dr. Henry Blackaby said, "Find out what God is up to in your life and join Him." God bless you today.

November 7

I often say, "God is in control," and I believe that. Today, I truly want to thank God for His sovereignty. The psalmist wrote in Ps. 135:6, *"Whatsoever the Lord pleased, that did he in heaven, and in earth, in the seas, and all deep places."* This thought is confirmed again in Job 42:2. *"I know that thou canst do every thing, and that no thought can be withholden from thee."* We live in days of uncertainty. Our political future is uncertain; our economic future is uncertain; and our very lives are uncertain, for we do not know the hour of our death. There is one thing about which we can be certain — God is in control. I do not know what tomorrow may hold, but I know Who holds my tomorrows. I may not know how I will meet my financial needs or my physical needs, but I know Who has an inexhaustible supply for every need. I do not know who will be elected to political office, but I do know Who controls every office holder. According to Prov. 21:1, *"The king's heart is in the hand of the Lord, as the rivers of water: he turneth it whithersoever he will."* Yes, my friend, our God reigns! My thought for today is that we give God thanks for His sovereign power. We can trust Him for He has all power. Surely we must do all we can do to assure we have good government. We must do our part in providing for our financial and physical needs, and we must live until we die. However, when we have done all we can, God will take care of the rest. When we cannot, He can and does according to His sovereign will. Today and every day, I will rest upon the wisdom and power of a sovereign God. There is no need of worry, no need of anxiety. God is in control. He is sovereign! God bless and have a great day.

November 8

Today I want to thank God for **statesmen** who molded and made our country the home of the brave and the land of the free. I fear that in our nation today we have very few, if any, true statesmen (or women) seeking office. The word "statesman" means "a skilled, experienced, and respected political leader." The single word that defines statesmanship to me is the word "respected." The men who signed the Declaration of Independence and then the Constitution were respected men of their day. They were not perfect, and not all were Christian, but they sought to build a better country with freedom and liberty as their goal. Today I see too many of those seeking office for their own gain of wealth or power. I am reminded of the words of Prov. 29:2. *"When the righteous are in authority, the people rejoice: but when the wicked beareth rule, the people mourn."* Though we may not have a righteous person seeking to be elected, I would remind each of us that **we are the authority.** We the people are the government; therefore, we are to vote our values. We are to be the statesmen and stateswomen of our country. I challenge each of us to vote our values. My values are the values of the Word of God. That means with any important issue, including abortion or same-sex marriage, I must ask the question, "What does God say? And what does God say about the role of government in our lives?" I must vote, because God will hold me accountable for my vote. May each of us vote respecting the values of the Word of God. May we conduct ourselves as statesmen.

November 9

Today I want to remind each of us to thank God for our **system of government.** Some of you have probably voted in a local election in the past few days, as is typically done at this time of year in many cities and towns. In certain years at this time, we elect state legislators, governors, members of Congress and a president of the United States. Each time a leader of our nation is chosen in a free election without violence, expressing the will of the people, we witness democracy in action. We the people chose our elected represenatives at every level — local, state and national. We are a government "of the people, by the people, and for the people," as Abraham Lincoln said so eloquently in his timeless Gettysburg Address. It would be wise, however, to remember the words of Ps. 75:7. *"But God is the judge: he putteth down one, and setteth up another."* We are also reminded in Dan. 2:21, *"And he changeth the times and the seasons: he removeth kings, and setteth up kings: he giveth wisdom unto the wise, and knowledge to them that know understanding."* We who live in the United States of America should thank God for our country. It is the greatest country on Earth. We enjoy the freedom of religion, the right to choose our leaders, and the right to pursue our dreams in a land of prosperity and possibilities. It is God who has raised up the land. We are to use our prosperity and possibilities to preach the Gospel to every creature. We are to give God the glory and the praise for preserving our nation. Today, we Thank God for His blessings on America. God bless and have a great day.

November 10

As we approach Thanksgiving, and we continue our thoughts of the things for which we should be thankful, my mind goes to Ps. 136:1. *"O give thanks unto the Lord; for he is good: for his mercy endureth for ever."* There are 26 verses in Psalm 136 and each verse ends with the phrase, *"for his mercy endureth for ever."* Someone has said that mercy is our not receiving what we actually deserve. The dictionary defines mercy as "compassion or forgiveness shown toward someone whom it is within one's power to punish or harm." Because of our sin, God has every right to judge and punish us, but thank God that *"his mercy endureth for ever."* My thought for today is that we give thanks to God for His mercy. I give Him thanks that He is **sensitive** to the fact that in my flesh I am weak. I fall and I fail to measure up to His standard of holiness. Yet He has mercy on me and showers me with blessings that are so undeserved. I read a book some years ago about the most often-prayed prayer in the Bible. That prayer is, "Lord have mercy on me." It is a prayer that God always answers *"for his mercy endureth for ever."* Do not live today in the failures of your past — *"for his mercy endureth for ever."* If you have fallen, get up and start anew — *"for his mercy endureth for ever."* Oh, thank God for His mercy! God bless and have a great day!

November 11

We should thank God for those who have served our country in the military. Today is Veterans Day, the day we honor all the men and women who have served in our military. All of us enjoy the benefits and blessings of freedom at the expense of those men and women who have fought (and many who have died) for our country. Our liberty and freedom are not free! It is our military that ensures and protects our liberty. We are exhorted in Rom. 13:7, *"Render therefore to all their dues: tribute to whom tribute is due; custom to whom custom; fear to whom fear; honour to whom honour."* So today we say "thank you" to all who have served in our armed forces. May I encourage each of us to take a few minutes and pray for our service men and women. Also pray for the thousands of veterans who are still suffering from the scars of conflict. Some of these scars are seen with the eye, but many suffer with emotional issues from their time of service. They need and deserve our encouragement and prayers. May God bless every man and woman who has served our country in the military. Today, we salute you and may God help us to never forget the price you paid for our liberty. God bless, and happy Veterans Day to all our veterans!

November 12

Today I want us to thank God that He is the **supplier** of our every need. The Apostle Paul wrote under the inspiration of the Holy Spirit in Phil. 4:19, *"But my God shall supply all your need according to his riches in glory by Christ Jesus."* A few years ago, my wife and I began a new journey of faith. I retired from the pastorate to begin a ministry of itinerant speaking in churches. I did not have one scheduled meeting. My ministry was to be and still is a ministry of helps and encouragement to pastors and churches. We had very little retirement income and knew God would have to meet our needs. After these past few years I can give God the glory and thank Him for meeting our every need. Today we still walk by faith. God has given me the opportunity to expand our ministry to work with the National Center for Life and Liberty. I assist attorney David Gibbs III in legal seminars. This has opened the door for me to minister in many churches and encourage the pastors and churches in these trying days of ministry. God has provided meetings, but He has also provided money for our ministry's operations as well as our living expenses. Every time we have a financial need, God provides through the generosity of His people. I can also report that we have spoken in churches 48 to 50 weeks every year and have been able to go on seven mission trips. We have seen hundreds of people saved and been able to help many churches and pastors. We give God thanks for His supply for every need! My challenge for all of us is that we take a moment and thank God for supplying our needs. Whatever it is today, God can meet your need. Give Him glory for His abundant supply! God bless you and have a great day!

November 13

Today I want to thank God for the **serenity of the morning.** The word "serenity" means "the state of being calm, peaceful and untroubled." The quiet times of the mornings have been my time to prepare myself for the day. The psalmist said in Ps. 5:3, *"My voice shalt thou hear in the morning, O Lord; in the morning will I direct my prayer unto thee, and will look up."* During those years that my wife and I cared for our severely mentally and physically handicapped son, the mornings were my refuge — the time I could be quiet before the Lord. The demands of the pastorate along with the oversight of a childcare facility and Christian school often seemed more than I could handle. The constant demands of the day were met each morning with a quiet, calm, peaceful and untroubled time with the Lord. Today, I still must have that time of serenity in the morning with Him. My challenge for today is that each of us thank God for the calm, the peaceful and untroubled moments we can have with Him. It is these moments that prepare us for the challenges of the day and also serve as a reminder of His presence. God's presence is never so real as in the quiet moments we spend with Him. Today I thank God for the quiet time; the serenity of the morning. God bless you and have a great day.

November 14

One night I was blessed to hear a missionary speak and share how he had personally led many people to Christ. As he did that, my mind began to wander, and I thought of those who I had seen saved in my ministry. The emphasis of the speaker was the importance of everyone telling others about the Savior. I had spoken earlier from Rom. 10:13-17 and made a point to emphasize verse 14: *"How then shall they call on him in whom they have not believed? and how shall they believe in him of whom they have not heard? and how shall they hear without a preacher?"* The word "preacher" literally means "proclaimer." The one thing I want to thank God for today is that everyone who knows Christ can share the Gospel and win souls to Christ. Soul winning is everyone's business! My challenge for us today is that we share Jesus with someone. It is not up to us to save anyone, but we are responsible to share the love of Christ with others. Someone said, "If you tell the story to enough people, you will eventually tell it to someone who desires to hear it." There is no greater joy than seeing someone come to know Jesus as Savior. I thank God that He has chosen all of us who know Him as Savior to be His voice to share His great love with others. Everybody needs to hear about Jesus! God has chosen you and me to be His voice to tell the world that Jesus saves! Be His voice today! God bless and have a great day.

November 15

I'm proud to an American! I have refrained from making any political comment during these most recent days of political activity. I hope my devotions each day are words of exhortation and encouragement to those who read them. However, I must say I believe God has blessed America with an opportunity to preserve our religious liberties and rebuild our our country's economic systems. There are many things that I thank God for in America. One of those is freedom of **speech** — the right to express my views without fear of judgment from the powers that be. I am reminded of the words of Prov. 18:21. *"Death and life are in the power of the tongue: and they that love it shall eat the fruit thereof."* Words matter. For one thing, they can change the destiny of a soul. Rom. 10:13 says, *"For whosoever shall call upon the name of the Lord shall be saved."* Words can console the hurting. Words can convey a message that determines the direction and ultimately the destiny of a society. It is time that the silent majority of Christians speak the message of salvation to the world. It is time for the silent majority of freedom-loving Americans to exercise their freedom of speech and speak out for the values that have made our country great. Thank God we have the right of freedom of speech. Now let's exercise that right and speak out for Jesus and for Christian values in our country! God bless and have a great day!

November 16

In 1624 the English poet John Donne wrote, "No man is an island." As I begin each day, I often think of how thankful I am for the **strength** I receive from others. Many times in my life I have felt that all was lost and there seemed no way out of my circumstances. Then God would send a friend or an acquaintance to speak words of encouragement or someone to help lift my burden. I thank God for those special someones God has placed in my life at just the right moment. I am reminded of the words of Eccl. 4:9-10. *"Two are better than one; because they have a good reward for their labour. For if they fall, the one will lift up his fellow: but woe to him that is alone when he falleth; for he hath not another to help him up."* My thoughts for today are twofold. First, take a minute and thank God for those special people the Lord has placed in your life. Then call or send a message to that special friend and thank them for just being there in your time of trouble. Surely it is true that no man is an island. We need each other. Second, seek to be that special someone in the life of a person you know who needs a friend. This season is an awfully depressing time for many people. Thanksgiving and Christmas are difficult for many who have lost love ones or those who are going through difficult times in their lives. We can be that special someone to speak words of comfort, or maybe offer a hand to help them. Everybody needs somebody at some time in their lives. Seek to be that somebody. God bless and have a blessed day.

November 17

We live in an uncertain world. Every day, we face the uncertainties of life. Our health is uncertain. Just one phone call from the doctor can change your life forever. One shooting pain, one accident, or one change in your job can change your life. Uncertainty breeds fear and anxiety. Today, I thank God for the **security** we have in Jesus! The security of our salvation rests upon Him. We are promised in Heb. 7:25, *"Wherefore he is able also to save them to the uttermost that come unto God by him, seeing he ever liveth to make intercession for them."* The word "uttermost" means "all the way to the end." In other words, my salvation is secure and certain in Jesus. There are other certainties in Christ, too many to mention. One of those is the certainty of His presence. My security in the midst of the uncertainties of life is that Jesus walks with me. The Bible says in Deut. 31:6, *"Be strong and of a good courage, fear not, nor be afraid of them: for the Lord thy God, he it is that doth go with thee; he will not fail thee, nor forsake thee."* Consider the parting words of Jesus to His disciples and to us in Matt. 28:20. *"And lo, I am with you alway, even unto the end of the world."* Someone has said the word "alway" can be translated as "the whole of every day." Whatever the day may bring, I am secure in Jesus. I am certain that He is with me! I thank God my security does not rest in me nor my circumstances. I am secure in Christ. God bless and have a great day.

November 18

Sunday should be a special day in the life of any child of God. I thank God for **Sundays.** We refer to Sunday as the Lord's Day, and surely it is. It is the day we gather to worship our resurrected Lord. It was on the first day of the week that our Savior was raised from the dead. The Bible says in John 20:1, *"The first day of the week cometh Mary Magdalene early, when it was yet dark, unto the sepulchre, and seeth the stone taken away from the sepulchre."* Each Sunday we are called to remember that our Savior lives. Today, I give thanks that I do not have to walk through this life alone. My Savior walks with me. He is my guide, my helper, and my strength. I can talk with Him anytime about anything. All other religions have a dead founder and are left with just a stated dogma to live as their religion. We have a faith that is built upon a living relationship with the resurrected Christ! Yes, He has given us teachings and commandments, but He is with us to help us live by those teachings and commandments. I know He is alive! I just talked to Him. I cannot see Him, but I can surely feel His presence. Thank God for Sunday, the reminder that Jesus is alive! God bless and have a great day!

I want to thank God for **spiritual songs**. We cannot put enough emphasis on the value and blessing of music. In my darkest hours, I listen to music. When the burdens of life are great, I sing. No, I do not have a musical bone in my body, but when I am alone I sing old hymns like "My Jesus I Love Thee." When our son Paul was in pain or was sick to his stomach as a result of his brain tumor, he would sing "Jesus Loves Me." There is just something about music that eases the pain and lifts the burden. One of the characteristics of a Spirit-filled life is singing. The Bible says in Eph. 5:18-19, *"And be not drunk with wine, wherein is excess; but be filled with the Spirit; Speaking to yourselves in psalms and hymns and spiritual songs, singing and making melody in your heart to the Lord."* To be filled with the Spirit is to be controlled by the Spirit. So ask God today to give you a song to sing. If you have no song, listen to some spiritual songs and allow the music to soothe your hurts and lift your spirits. Thank God today for spiritual songs! God bless and have a great day.

November 20

There will always be people around us who never seem to be happy. They enjoy good health and have plenty of money, yet they are never satisfied. I am not referring to the desire to do better or having goals to accomplish. I am speaking of having a spirit of discontent. As we approach the holiday season, there will be those who fall into despair and discouragement. I thank God for the full **satisfaction** that is in Christ Jesus. We are reminded in Ps. 107:8-9, *"Oh that men would praise the Lord for his goodness, and for his wonderful works to the children of men! For he satisfieth the longing soul, and filleth the hungry soul with goodness."* In the New Testament, the Apostle Paul expressed the same truth in Phil. 4:11. *"Not that I speak in respect of want: for I have learned, in whatsoever state I am, therewith to be content."* My thought for today is that we all should thank God for the total sufficiency we have in Jesus. He supplies our every need. He saves us from our sin and is the security of our future. He is the strength of my life. I find in Him great satisfaction for living. I may be losing my health and I may have no wealth, but if I have Jesus I can *"praise the Lord for his goodness, and for his wonderful works to the children of men."* Today I pray that each of us will thank God that He is the source of satisfaction for our lives. God bless and have a great day.

November 21

History tells us that the first Thanksgiving was celebrated by the Pilgrims in 1621, after their first harvest in the New World. According to Wikipedia, it was President Abraham Lincoln who proclaimed a national holiday of "Thanksgiving and Praise to our beneficent Father who dwelleth in the Heavens." Today I want each of us to thank God for the **spiritual sensitivity** of our forefathers. I do not propose that many of them were saved or Christians, but they had a sense of the reality of the existence of God. They honored God and gave Him the credit for their blessings and safety. Their moral compass was based on their belief in God. The mores of that society reflected a humble respect for holiness. We would do well to put God back into our society rather than attempt to remove Him from our schools and other public places. Today, let's join together and thank God for our spiritual heritage. We give God thanks for the spiritual sensitivity of our founding fathers. Let us pray that God will raise up a generation of national leaders who will return to the faith of our founders — leaders who will call upon us as a nation to thank God for His benefits. May the words of Ps. 103:2 be our cry: *"Bless the Lord, O my soul, and forget not all his benefits."* May we not forget James 1:17. *"Every good gift and every perfect gift is from above, and cometh down from the Father of lights, with whom is no variableness, neither shadow of turning."* Thank God that our forefathers had spiritual sensitivity and paused to thank God for all their blessings! God bless you and have a great day.

November 22

Happy Thanksgiving to each of you! As I write this for today, I have so much for which to be thankful. I have tried to focus on one thing each day for the past 20 days for which to thank God. On this final day of giving thanks for one particular thing, I feel compelled to thank God for each of you. Yes, each of you, my **supporters**. Some of you support me by reading the devotional thoughts I post each day via social media. It is for you I write them. Others not only read them but also pray for me and for our ministry regularly. It is your prayers that give us the Lord's strength and guidance to carry out His work. There are others who support us in prayer and with financial support. It is you who make it possible for us to go and minister. Each of you share in the ministry in your own way. This Thanksgiving I wish to say "thank you" for your investment in our ministry. Paul's said to his friends in Phil. 1:3, *"I thank my God upon every remembrance of you."* I can say the same for each of you reading this. Yes, I am thankful for my family. I am thankful for my friends. I am most thankful for my Savior. But today I thank God for those who support our ministry in any way. God bless each of you and have a happy Thanksgiving.

November 23

We are told that a couple of days this week will be the most traveled days of the year. People everywhere are traveling to be with family and friends for Thanksgiving. As I thought of what to thank God for today, one of the things that came to mind was *safety*. I know that there will be accidents this week and possibly some casualties as the roads are filled with so many travelers. This motivates me to pray for safety for those that are traveling. I travel most weeks of the year, and I know there have been many times that God has kept me safe and provided an escape from what could have been a serious accident. Today I thank God for safety on the road. Prov. 18:10 reminds us, *"The name of the Lord is a strong tower: the righteous runneth into it, and is safe."* My thought for today is that those who will be on the road pray for safety. Those of us who are anxiously waiting for our families and friends to arrive should pray for those on the road. It is the Lord who is our refuge. It is God who will keep us safe. I want to thank God in advance for His protection of my family that will be traveling today. It is God who is our *"strong tower"* and our refuge, and it is God who will keep us *"safe."* Thank God for His hand of protection and the safety that we have in His care. God bless you today and be safe!

November 24

Are we really supposed to be thankful for everything? It would seem so according to I Thess. 5:18. *"In every thing give thanks: for this is the will of God in Christ Jesus concerning you."* I certainly have gone through some experiences of life for which I did not thank God. However, that verse reminds us that we are to *"give thanks"* in everything. In the midst of sorrow and hurt, we can find something for which to thank God. Today I do not want to thank God for the sorrows of life, but I do want to thank God for His **sovereign purpose** for every sorrow. The will of God for me to "give thanks" is the will of God for my life. As my good friend Tracy Dartt so wonderfully penned in the lyrics of the song, "God On The Mountain":

> **For the God on the mountain**
> **Is the God in the valley**
> **When things go wrong,**
> **He'll make them right**
> **And the God of the good times**
> **Is still God in the bad times**
> **The God of the day**
> **Is still God in the night**

What we need to give thanks for is God's divine purpose **for** everything that happens **in** our lives — even our sorrows. Surely He has a sovereign purpose for every sorrow that comes along. Today I do not thank the Lord for everything in my life, but I do thank Him in everything. I know my God has a purpose and plan for my life. Surely He is the God on the mountain and the God of the valley. God bless and have a great day.

November 25

We can learn so much from our children and even our grandchildren. On a recent Thanksgiving holiday our daughter's family came to stay with us. My wife gave each of our two grandchildren $20 to spend during that time, as it has been Mema's custom for many years to give them some cash when they visit. Later, I went to the store with my daughter and grandson, who went back to the car first as we paid for the items we had purchased. When we got to the car my grandson informed us he had given a homeless man a couple of dollars from what we had given him. My heart was warmed as I saw his concern for others. Later that day, he wanted to go to the 7-11 store to get a Slurpee (a frozen drink). His dad gave him three dollars to spend on that and other snacks. When my grandson returned from the store, he informed us that the clerk gave him the Slurpee free of charge. His two-dollar gift had become three. I could not help but mention to him that God will always bless us if we give. May each of us strive to live to be conduits of blessing to others. We cannot out-give the Lord. The promise of Jesus in Luke 6:38 is for you and me: *"Give, and it shall be given unto you; good measure, pressed down, and shaken together, and running over, shall men give into your bosom. For with the same measure that ye mete withal it shall be measured to you again."* We should never give simply to get, but we can know that as we give we will receive. God bless you today and have a blessed day.

November 26

I recall hearing a well-known old preacher, Dr. B.R. Lakin, make this statement: "You hear people say and sing they are homesick for Heaven. Well, it's just not so. Every time they get sick, it is off to the doctor they go. If they were homesick for Heaven, they wouldn't be so concerned about getting well." The truth is that we all want to live as long as possible. The desire to live is instilled in each of us, but there is a reality of our own morality that we all must face. The Bible clearly states in Heb. 9:27, *"And as it is appointed unto men once to die, but after this the judgment."* Every time we visit with family and think about how our children and grandchildren are growing up, or take note of the aging of friends, we are reminded of the passing of years in our lives. The words of James 4:14 are so true: *"For what is your life? It is even a vapour, that appeareth for a little time, and then vanisheth away."* With that mind, let me encourage you to live every day to the fullest for the Savior. Make decisions with Heaven in mind. Acknowledge the reality of eternity. This world is not our home. We are just pilgrims passing through in search of what II Cor. 5:1 calls *"an house not made with hands, eternal in the heavens."* The longer I live the more I think about heaven. Thank God for the hope that we have for a place beyond this life free of pain and disappointment. God bless and have a great day.

November 27

Loyalty is a forgotten virtue! When I think of loyalty, I think of David's loyalty to Saul, who sought to kill David due to his envy and jealousy. David had opportunities to kill Saul, yet he would not. His feelings were expressed in I Sam. 26:11. *"The Lord forbid that I should stretch forth mine hand against the Lord's anointed."* He recognized that God had placed Saul as the king and had given David a place of service in the kingdom, waiting for his time to be king. Until it was God's time for David to take the throne, he would remain loyal to Saul, even though Saul was not loyal to him. A few thoughts about loyalty: **Our loyalty to others will determine the loyalty others show us.** Paul warns in Gal. 6:7, *"Be not deceived; God is not mocked: for whatsoever a man soweth, that shall he also reap."* Because of his loyalty, David was blessed later in life with loyal servants. We often wonder why we do not have loyal friends. We may need to check our loyalty to others. **Loyalty never condones wrong, but it does not give reason for disloyalty.** God had taken his hand of blessing from Saul, but David remained loyal to him. He understood that God would judge Saul but his responsibility was to be a humble servant to the king. God calls upon us to humble ourselves and be faithful to our callings even when we are betrayed. **Loyalty frees me from the responsibility of being the judge.** Again, loyalty does not mean we condone evil, but it does give place to God to be the judge in the affairs of others. My prayer is that my loyalty will first be to the Savior. My second responsibility is to be loyal to my family, and then to be loyal to my friends. God bless you today!

November 28

"In the beginning God created the heaven and the earth." This is the first verse in the Bible. As I awoke one recent morning these words just kept going through my mind. I had just read the first chapter of Genesis and the thought occurred to me that every single thing had and has a beginning — except God. How awesome is that? When we wrap our heads around that thought, it makes sense that God can do anything and everything in your life and mine. If He could speak the worlds into existence, He can speak, and my needs will be supplied. His abilities are never the question; only my faith in Him to do all that is needed and all I cannot do. As I get older, there are more and more things I cannot do. However, I serve an ageless God whose power will never change. The God of creation is **my** God! Look around you today at the beauty and the wonder of creation. Remember that the God who had no beginning, and who made everything on earth and in the heavens, is the same God who cares for you. I stand in awe of His power and majesty today. To Him be all glory and honor. God bless you and have a great day.

November 29

I am **His.** I belong to God. Though He did not create me as He did the first man and woman, I am a creation of God. In Gen. 1:26-31 we have the account of God creating the first man and woman. The detail of this creation is given again in Gen 2:7, 21-25. Our key thought today is found in Gen. 1:27. *"So God created man in his own image, in the image of God created he him; male and female created he them."* What does it mean to be created *"in the image of God"*? That phrase means "a shadow or likeness of God." No, we are not little gods, nor do we possess a spark of deity in us. We are sinful and need a Savior. However, our creation gives us a glimpse of our true purpose in life. We are to be God-like. We are to live in the likeness of our God. One writer, Dick Staub, who I do not know, points out in an article in Relevant magazine that God is creative, so we should be creative. All of us "make things," he said, and some are better at making things than others. Also stated is, "You are spiritual because God is spiritual." Other attributes are listed, but I think we get the point. We are created in the image and likeness of our Creator. If God created me, then He owns me. I belong to God. My life is to be lived in the likeness of Him. I can only live like Him if I am living surrendered to Him. Because I am a sinner by nature, I must be saved and have the Holy Spirit living in me that I might live as a shadow and in the likeness of my Creator. My greatest desire is that others might see Christ in me and through me. I truly want to live in the image of God. God bless you and have a great day.

November 30

Did you ever wonder why God rested on the seventh day of creation? Surely an omnipotent God does not get tired and need rest. But the Bible says in Gen. 2:2-3, *"And on the seventh day God ended his work which he had made; and he rested on the seventh day from all his work which he had made. And God blessed the seventh day, and sanctified it: because that in it he had rested from all his work which God created and made."* God did not rest because He was tired. The words of Jesus in Mark 2:27-28 help us understand why God rested. *"And he said unto them, The sabbath was made for man, and not man for the sabbath: Therefore the Son of man is Lord also of the sabbath."* The sabbath is a reminder to all of us that **we** get tired. God did not need rest because He was tired, but He rested to teach us that when we become weary, we need to take time to rest. There is also the lesson from the sabbath that we need to give time for worship. Note Ex. 20:8-11. *"Remember the sabbath day, to keep it holy. Six days shalt thou labour, and do all thy work: But the seventh day is the sabbath of the Lord thy God: in it thou shalt not do any work, thou, nor thy son, nor thy daughter, thy manservant, nor thy maidservant, nor thy cattle, nor thy stranger that is within thy gates: For in six days the Lord made heaven and earth, the sea, and all that in them is, and rested the seventh day: wherefore the Lord blessed the sabbath day, and hallowed it."* All of us need some "down time." Our physical makeup requires rest. I also would remind us that God expects one seventh of our time to be spent worshipping Him. Private worship, as well as public worship, is a requirement of our Creator. So rest if you must, and be sure to take the time to worship the Lord. God bless and have a great day.

December 1

"Decisions are the hinges upon which the doors of our future swing." I have used this quote many times in sermons and devotions, but the truth of the statement is ever before me. Every decision has consequences and affects the rest of your life in some way. Every decision has an effect upon the lives of others. When God created man and woman, He gave them the power of choice. He made a perfect environment for Adam and Eve in the Garden of Eden and placed them there. God gave the fruit of every tree to man to enjoy, except one. Gen. 2:17 says, *"But of the tree of the knowledge of good and evil, thou shalt not eat of it: for in the day that thou eatest thereof thou shalt surely die."* Adam was given a choice. He could obey God and live in innocence and plenty or He could eat of the forbidden tree and die. This death was both physical and spiritual. God still gives us choices. We can obey His Word and live in victory, or we can choose the forbidden fruits of this world and suffer the consequences. My challenge for us today is that we choose to obey God. His way is the best. God's will leads to joy and the fullness of life. Beware of your choices today! They truly are the hinges upon which the doors of your future swing. God bless and have a great day!

December 2

As we have previously noted, our decisions affect others as well as ourselves. God placed Adam and Eve in the Garden of Eden and gave them the benefit of every tree in the garden, except one. The decision of Adam and Eve had consequences for all mankind. They decided to listen to the voice of temptation from the serpent. The Bible says in Gen. 3:6, *"And when the woman saw that the tree was good for food, and that it was pleasant to the eyes, and a tree to be desired to make one wise, she took of the fruit thereof, and did eat, and gave also unto her husband with her; and he did eat."* Time does not allow us to discuss all the consequences of this decision, but we can easily see how it impacted every person who has ever lived. The consequence for you and me of Adam's and Eve's decision to eat of the forbidden fruit is conveyed in Rom. 5:12. *"Wherefore, as by one man sin entered into the world, and death by sin; and so death passed upon all men, for that all have sinned."* Because of sin, the choice of Adam and Eve, we **all** are born sinners. This may seem unfair until we see another Man's choice that brought deliverance and hope. Rom. 5:17 says, *"For if by one man's offence death reigned by one; much more they which receive abundance of grace and of the gift of righteousness shall reign in life by one, Jesus Christ."* Verse 19: *"For as by one man's disobedience many were made sinners, so by the obedience of one shall many be made righteous."* Thank God for the decision to send His Son Jesus to die for our sin. Praise the Lord for His free gift of salvation made possible through His decision to die on a cross for our sin. Yes, decisions are the hinges upon which the doors of our future swing. God bless you and have a great day.

December 3

Jesus said of Satan in John 8:44, *"... for he is a liar, and the father of it."* The first mention of Satan in the Bible (Gen. 3:1) describes him as *"the serpent."* The occasion is a conversation with Eve in the Garden of Eden where he tempted her to eat of the forbidden fruit of the Tree of the Knowledge of Good and Evil. In Gen. 2:16-17 God warned, *"And the Lord God commanded the man, saying, Of every tree of the garden thou mayest freely eat: But of the tree of the knowledge of good and evil, thou shalt not eat of it: for in the day that thou eatest thereof thou shalt surely die."* When the serpent came to Eve to tempt her to eat of the fruit, he lied. He said in Gen. 3:3, *"But of the fruit of the tree which is in the midst of the garden, God hath said, Ye shall not eat of it, neither shall ye touch it, lest ye die."* God **never** said they would die if they touched it. The second lie is found in verse 5: *"... ye shall be as gods, knowing good and evil."* Beware of the lies of Satan. God's Word is still true. What God calls sin is still sin, and the consequences of sin is still spiritual death and sometimes physical death. Satan will add to the Word of God or even deny the truth of His Word to tempt us to eat of the forbidden fruits of sin. But the results are always traumatic. Beware of the lies of the devil and flee temptation. God bless you and have a great day.

December 4

Sometimes I will speak in Sunday services at a church, so that church's pastor can have time to attend to health or family issues. I remember one particular Sunday when I preached in Florida for a pastor who had taken his wife to Missouri to visit family. The wife had Stage 4 cancer and was no longer able to accept treatment. It was likely to be her last visit with her family. As I awoke that Sunday morning, I thought of the uncertainty of life. We never know what a day will bring in our lives. But whether health or sickness, wealth or poverty, we can be sure of the presence of our Lord. He promised in Matt. 28:20, *"and, lo, I am with you always, even unto the end of the world."* Thank God we do not face the trials of this life alone! God is with us! We also face every problem in life in His **power.** Though the burdens seem too heavy to bear, He has promised in II Cor. 12:9, *"my strength is made perfect in weakness."* Our times of weakness give occasion for us to experience His **strength.** It is in the times we do not understand that our faith reaches beyond what we can see, and we trust Him for a **purpose** we cannot see. In every situation God has a plan, and Rom. 8:28 is still true. *"And we know that all things work together for good to them that love God, to them who are the called according to his purpose."* So today whatever your circumstance, remember that God loves you and has neither forsaken nor forgotten you. Follow the admonition of I Pet. 5:7 — *"Casting all your care upon him; for he careth for you."* God bless you and have a great day.

December 5

I have heard a new convert say, "I found the Lord," when in reality it was the Lord that found him. God has always sought man in the time of man's need. Even in the earliest days of the existence of man, God sought him in the hour of man's disobedience. It was after Adam and Eve had eaten the forbidden fruit that God came to the garden seeking them. Look at Gen. 3:8-9. *"And they heard the voice of the Lord God walking in the garden in the cool of the day: and Adam and his wife hid themselves from the presence of the Lord God amongst the trees of the garden. And the Lord God called unto Adam, and said unto him, Where art thou?"* I believe God has been asking that question of men and women ever since. God knew of the physical location of Adam, and He was aware of the disobedience of Adam and Eve. The question was not for His information, but to bring Adam to the realization as to **where he was!** Adam was "naked," his fellowship with God had been broken, and there were to be consequences for his disobedience. Many of us have been disobedient to God, naked in our sin and having no fellowship with Him. Yet there is still a voice that cries out to us, *"Where art thou?"* That is the voice of God. Though there may be consequences that cannot be escaped and there seems to be no hope, God loves you and He is seeking you. He still cries, *"Where art thou?"* If we will acknowledge where we are, God will provide reconciliation. We may suffer the consequences of our decisions, but God will be there for us to provide a way of escape that we might be able to bear them (I Cor. 10:13). God is seeking you and me today! May each of us heed His voice. He truly cares for us wherever we may be! God bless and have a great day.

December 6

"It's beginning to look a lot like Christmas!" Did you know that the first mention of the virgin birth is in Genesis? This is what theologians call the "protoevangelium," which is defined by Wikipedia as "God's statement to the serpent in the Garden of Eden about how the seed of the woman would crush the serpent's head." The passage to which I refer is Gen. 3:15. *"And I will put enmity between thee and the woman, and between thy seed and her seed; it shall bruise thy head, and thou shalt bruise his heel."* The reference to the virgin birth can be found in the phrase "her seed." Human procreation is accomplished with the seed of the man fertilizing the female egg. The seed of procreation comes from the male, not the female. Jesus birth was a miraculous birth without the seed of a man. He was born of a virgin. The virgin birth was necessary to declare His deity. He was the God/Man. As a man he could experience all the hurts and disappointments of being a human. He could be tempted as we are tempted. As God, He could live without sin and be the sin sacrifice for the sins of every man. If there is no virgin birth, there is no sacrifice for our sin! My thought for today is that, as we prepare for Christmas, we remember this season as a celebration of the virgin birth of our Savior. Truly, He is the reason for the season.

December 7

A most interesting event is conveyed in Gen. 3:21. *"Unto Adam also and to his wife did the Lord God make coats of skins, and clothed them."* This verse is often used as proof that the shedding of blood was necessary to provide a covering for man's sin. That idea is supported by Heb. 9:21. *"And almost all things are by the law purged with blood; and without shedding of blood is no remission."* The picture here in Genesis is true and is an excellent illustration. But today, I want to focus on another aspect of this event, which is the fact that God provided the needs of Adam and Eve. The verse says specifically that it was God who provided the coats of skin. The needs of our lives are not hidden from God. He knows it all, and we can trust Him to meet our needs. My life has been an ongoing drama of watching God provide for my needs. When I have patiently waited, He has always provided the coats of skin I needed. When I have stepped out of His will to try to make my own way, I have created unwanted and unnecessary circumstances. Even in the times when we have fallen or failed, God wants to provide our coverings and can always do it. Wherever you may be in life today, look to God for your need. Trust Him to provide your coats of skin. He still cares for you. He still desires to meet your need. Oh how I thank God for His tender mercies and continual supply for every need in my life. God bless you and have a blessed day.

December 8

Why do you think Christianity is so despised by other religions? Why are so many Christians being put to death for their faith? I recently heard someone give an explanation for the persecution and the desire to quiet the message of the Gospel that really makes sense to me: "Christianity teaches that Jesus is the **only** way to heaven." As I thought about the explanation, I was reminded that the first murder ever recorded took place because there was only one sacrifice acceptable to God. Adam and Eve had two sons, Cain and Abel. Both brought offerings to the Lord as noted in Gen. 4:3-5. *"And in process of time it came to pass, that Cain brought of the fruit of the ground an offering unto the Lord. And Abel, he also brought of the firstlings of his flock and of the fat thereof. And the Lord had respect unto Abel and to his offering: But unto Cain and to his offering he had not respect. And Cain was very wroth, and his countenance fell."* Abel's offering was a blood offering, which is what God required. The Lord provided Cain with a chance to submit the required offering, but instead Cain became angry with Abel and killed him (v. 8). Christians can expect persecution because we are not politically correct. We **do not** believe there are many ways to God. We believe, and the Bible declares, that the offering of Jesus on the cross is the **only** sacrifice for sin. We believe the words of Jesus in John 14:6. *"I am the way, the truth, and the life: no man cometh unto the Father, but by me."* Therefore, do not be surprised if you are persecuted for the sake of the Gospel. God bless and have a great day.

December 9

One cannot deny that sin has its consequences. So it was with Cain. In Gen. 4:11-14 we read of the consequences placed upon him for his sin of killing his brother, Abel. It is worth noting that though there were great consequences for his sin, God also showed great compassion when Cain thought he would have to live as a marked man. In verse 14 Cain expressed his fear: *"Behold, thou hast driven me out this day from the face of the earth; and from thy face shall I be hid; and I shall be a fugitive and a vagabond in the earth; and it shall come to pass, that every one that findeth me shall slay me."* In verse 15 God eased that fear: *"And the Lord said unto him, Therefore whosoever slayeth Cain, vengeance shall be taken on him sevenfold. And the Lord set a mark upon Cain, lest any finding him should kill him."* This should serve as a reminder to us that God is a God of mercy, meaning that we do not receive what we most certainly deserve. He is a God of forgiveness and compassion. Though the consequences of sin may linger, God still has a plan and purpose for every life. He is also a God of grace, meaning that we receive favor we do not deserve. Cain did not deserve the protection of God, yet in His mercy and grace God showed compassion on him. Oh that we might have the same forgiving spirit toward others that God has toward us! May God endow each of us today with holy compassion for the fallen, the guilty, and the hurting. God bless and have a great day.

December 10

The year was 1984. The occasion was a mass meeting of Baptists in Washington, D.C. There were a number of speakers, but one remains in my memory, even though I do not remember his name. His assigned subject had to do with the brevity of life. I remember vividly his opening statement: "You got to live until you die!" As I read the genealogies in Genesis 5, it is interesting to note how often the statement *"and he died"* is used. If I counted correctly, it is used eight times in the 32 verses of the chapter. Though in the days of the Old Testament the length of their lives was longer, they still died. Regardless of the number of years we live, all of us will die, if Jesus does not return first. In Heb. 9:27 we are reminded, *"And as it is appointed unto men once to die, but after this the judgment."* My challenge for today is that not we focus on death, but rather we live until we die. Every single day is another opportunity to serve Jesus and others. I fear that as we grow older, we lose the enthusiasm to live productive lives. But until we die, God has a plan for us. There is purpose in every day that we live. Our energy levels may change, but our usefulness never leaves. Live until you die. Don't quit; stay active for the Lord. Seek to be a blessing to someone each day. It is not until death that we stop living, and **real** living is serving Jesus. God bless and have a blessed day.

December 11

The one attribute of God that amazes me is His **grace.** No matter how wicked man might be, God still extends his grace to him. In the sixth chapter of Genesis is recorded the time when mankind had become exceeding wicked and the judgment of God was about to come. Verse 7 says, *"And the Lord said, I will destroy man whom I have created from the face of the earth; both man, and beast, and the creeping thing, and the fowls of the air; for it repenteth me that I have made them."* Then, in verse 8: *"But Noah found grace in the eyes of the Lord."* The word "grace" means "unmerited favor." In other words, God does for us that which we do not deserve. For example, no one deserves to be saved. Yet, God in His grace offers salvation to sinful men through the sacrifice of Jesus' death on the cross (Eph. 2:8-9). The blessings we enjoy in this life come because of His marvelous grace. Though the times we are living seem to be so wicked and godless, our God still extends His grace to us. We are a blessed people! God in His grace has provided us with His salvation. He has blessed us with provisions of life, protection in this life, and His presence to be with us as we travel down life's road. I hear preachers compare these days with the days of Noah. Maybe they are correct. If so, I want to be the Noah of today who *"found grace in the eyes of the Lord."* God bless you and have a great day.

December 12

During the years of our son's illness and other trials of life, the song "God Will Take Care of You" has always blessed and encouraged me. Whenever the Gethsemane Quartet came to our church, Penny Andrews always sang this song.

Be not dismayed whate'er betide
God will take care of you
Beneath His wings of love abide
God will take care of you.

God will take care of you;
Through every day o'er all the way
He will take care of you
God will take care of you

Through days of toil; when heart doth fail
God will take care of you
When dangers fierce your path assail
God will take care of you.

As I read about the building of the ark in Genesis 6-8, I was reminded of the care provided Noah and his family during the flood. After the rains ceased and the waters subsided, the word came to Noah in Gen. 8:16, *"Go forth of the ark, thou, and thy wife, and thy sons, and thy sons' wives with thee."* Sometimes, you and I would do well simply to stop and remind ourselves that God will take care of us. Through the storms of life, we have an ark of safety in Jesus our Lord. Every need supplied, all protection provided, and the promise of a new day with opportunities to serve our Lord are ours because God does take care of us. God bless and have a great day!

December 13

I am a blessed man. Today is my birthday, and I have gone beyond the *"threescore years and ten"* cited in Ps. 90:10. Looking back, I was blessed to be born in a great country to godly parents who taught me to honor God and to work hard. Church was always a central part of our lives, and they loved and honored our pastor. I was blessed to go to a great church with a great pastor. God blessed me with a great wife. Through more than 50 years of marriage, she has stood with me and supported me through thick and thin. She has been and still is my number-one prayer warrior and encourager. God has given me a wonderful family — a daughter who loves me but most of all loves God; a son-in-law who has a heart for God; and two wonderful grandchildren. Though our son was mentally and physically handicapped due to a brain tumor, he was the joy of our lives for the 31 years the Lord allowed us to have him. Through the pain, he always loved Jesus and demonstrated that childlike faith that taught me so much about trusting God. God has allowed me to pastor four churches and to travel to many others to speak, both in America and abroad. I have seen many, many people come to know Jesus as Savior. Today, I am in good health and still traveling and preaching. God has allowed me to join the National Center for Life and Liberty as its pastoral care coordinator. I speak in churches around the country presenting the Gospel and assuring pastors that NCLL is there to assist them and to fight for their religious liberties. I still encourage pastors and churches through PRH Ministries. God has still given me the "fire in my belly" to serve Him. Thank you for indulging me today as I praise the Lord for His blessings. I have asked God for 10 more years to serve Him, and then I want to negotiate for five more. But if today were my last day to live and to serve Him, I truly can say I have been and am a **blessed man**! God bless and have a great day.

December 14

The Bible says in Rom. 3:23, *"For all have sinned, and come short of the glory of God."* The word *"all"* literally means **all**. I am impressed with the honest reporting of the Word of God concerning the actions of various Bible characters we have read about so many times. We note in Gen. 6:8, *"But Noah found grace in the eyes of the Lord."* We read of Noah's great faith as he built the Ark though it had never rained on the earth. He was greatly used of God to preserve his family and the entire animal Kingdom during the flood. Noah is listed among the honor roll of the faithful in Heb. 11:7. With all these accolades, you would think Noah surely would never fall into sin. But Gen. 9:20-21 says, *"And Noah began to be an husbandman, and he planted a vineyard: And he drank of the wine, and was drunken; and he was uncovered within his tent."* All of us need to be conscious of the weakness of our flesh. Though we be saved, we still must contend with the temptations of this world and our flesh. Because all of us are subject to the enticements of sin, we all should show compassion to those who fail. At some point in our lives we will need the forgiveness of others. I would remind each of us of the words of Jesus in Matt. 6:15. *"But if ye forgive not men their trespasses, neither will your Father forgive your trespasses."* The failures of the characters in the Bible and the lives of others should serve to caution each of us. Surely if men like Noah can fall, we need to carefully live our lives that we not fall into Satan's trap. God bless you today and have a great day!

December 15

One of the most notorious stories in the New Testament regarding the Christ child is a reminder for us not to let the opposition stop us from doing the will of God. Shortly after Jesus was born, it became evident that Herod wanted to kill him. The wise men were warned of this, and Joseph took Mary and the baby to Egypt for safety. The brutal tactics of Herod are displayed in Matt. 2:13-16. *"And when they were departed, behold, the angel of the Lord appeareth to Joseph in a dream, saying, Arise, and take the young child and his mother, and flee into Egypt, and be thou there until I bring thee word: for Herod will seek the young child to destroy him. When he arose, he took the young child and his mother by night, and departed into Egypt: And was there until the death of Herod: that it might be fulfilled which was spoken of the Lord by the prophet, saying, Out of Egypt have I called my son. Then Herod, when he saw that he was mocked of the wise men, was exceeding wroth, and sent forth, and slew all the children that were in Bethlehem, and in all the coasts thereof, from two years old and under, according to the time which he had diligently inquired of the wise men."* As Herod tried to destroy Christ physically, men have been trying to destroy His teachings through the ages. Society tries to take God out of public organizations and remove manger scenes hoping to make Christmas just a winter holiday with no spiritual significance. What are we to do? We are to protect the message. Mary and Joseph fled to Egypt for a while, but they returned, and Jesus lived to fulfill His Father's will. Look for ways to share the real meaning of Christmas with your friends and fellow workers. This season is a great time to share the Gospel and see people come to know the Christ of Christmas. Have a great day and remind someone of the reason for the season today!

December 16

"How can I know the will of God for my life?" This is a question I have often been asked by young people and sometimes from folks not so young. My response is often, "Are you in the will of God right now?" If the answer is yes, I would instruct them to stay in the will of God for the rest of the day. If they remained in the will of God for that day and continued in God's will every day, they would stay in God's will. The Bible says in Ps. 119:105, *"Thy word is a lamp unto my feet, and a light unto my path."* God guides us step by step. There are times we know our destination, and there are times we walk totally by faith one day at a time. As I read the account of Abram being led to leave his country for a land that God would show him, I was reminded that faith obeys and does not always know the destiny of that obedience. In Gen. 12:1 we read, *"Now the Lord had said unto Abram, Get thee out of thy country, and from thy kindred, and from thy father's house, unto a land that I will shew thee."* The knowledge of the will of God begins with the faith to obey the leading of God in your life. There are times when we do not understand the where nor the how, but if God calls or leads we must obey. We walk by faith believing the will of God will bring glory to God and be for our good. Note the promise given to Abram in Gen. 12:2. *"And I will make of thee a great nation, and I will bless thee, and make thy name great; and thou shalt be a blessing."* My challenge for each of us is to live one moment at a time, one day at a time - obeying the will of God for our lives. We can rest assured God will bless those that walk by faith and obey His will. God bless and have a great day.

December 17

    Just one week from tomorrow we celebrate Christmas. As we approach that day, I want us to spend the next week thinking about Christmas, from tomorrow through Christmas Day. We will explore seven specific thoughts pertaining to this season:

    1. The prophecies of the virgin birth.
    2. The place of the virgin birth.
    3. The people involved with the virgin birth.
    4. The unusual participants of the occasion.
    5. The purpose of the virgin birth.
    6. The promises that are ours because of the virgin birth.
    7. Putting your presence under the tree.

Today, I begin my thoughts of Christmas with a warning to all of us to remember that He is the reason for the season. Christmas is not about giving and receiving gifts, but about **the gift** given that first Christmas morning. The greatest Christmas verse in the Bible is John 3:16. *"For God so loved the world, that he gave his only begotten Son, that whosoever believeth in him should not perish, but have everlasting life."* Do not allow the commercial emphasis to squeeze out the real meaning of Christmas. My challenge for each of us is that we take a few moments each day and read some verses in the Bible that relate to the birth of Christ. I would suggest we spend a few moments each day in prayer and praise to our God for His glorious gift that first Christmas morning. Then, I challenge each of us to share the real meaning of Christmas with others during this season. Let's let the whole world know Jesus was born on Christmas Day! God bless and Merry Christmas.

December 18

The miraculous virgin birth of Jesus had been prophesied in the Old Testament. There are two prophecies that come to mind. The words of Gen. 3:15 are known as the Protoevangelium, meaning "the first mention of the Gospel." *"And I will put enmity between thee and the woman, and between thy seed and her seed; it shall bruise thy head, and thou shalt bruise his heel."* These words were spoken to the serpent that had tempted Eve in the Garden of Eden. The first mention of the virgin birth is implied in the reference to *"her seed."* The seed of procreation always comes from the man, not the woman. Thus, there is the prediction, the prophecy of the virgin birth implied. The second prophecy is found in Isa. 7:14. *"Therefore the Lord himself shall give you a sign; Behold, a virgin shall conceive, and bear a son, and shall call his name Immanuel."* There is little doubt as to the clear meaning of the text. There are some who translate the word *"virgin"* as "young woman." I would refer them to Matt. 1:18. *"Now the birth of Jesus Christ was on this wise: When as his mother Mary was espoused to Joseph,* **before they came together,** *she was found with child of the Holy Ghost."* Yes, the virgin birth was prophesied and then verified. Jesus was born of a virgin on that first Christmas morning. As we approach Christmas Day, may we rejoice that God the Father planned the coming of the Christ child to be a miraculous event that Jesus might be able to provide Himself a sacrifice for the sins of all mankind. On Christmas, we celebrate His birth, a **virgin birth** as prophesied in the Old Testament and verified in the New Testament. God bless you and have a great day.

December 19

The meaning of the word "Bethlehem" is "house of bread." With that in mind, take note of John 6:35. *"And Jesus said unto them, I am the bread of life: he that cometh to me shall never hunger; and he that believeth on me shall never thirst."* Spurgeon said, "In the blessed Bread of Heaven, made of the bruised body of our Lord Jesus and baked in the furnace of His agonies, we find a blessed food." It was in this little town named Bethlehem, just six miles from Jerusalem, that a virgin would give birth to the Son of God. Just as bread is often spoken of as the symbol of the substance of life, so Jesus is the source of our spiritual life. Jesus said in John 14:6, *"I am the way, the truth, and the life: no man cometh unto the Father, but by me."* My thought for today is that even the place of His birth gave an announcement to who He was and what His purpose in life was to be. Even the prophets told of the place of His birth in Micah 5:2. *"But thou, Bethlehem Ephratah, though thou be little among the thousands of Judah, yet out of thee shall he come forth unto me that is to be ruler in Israel; whose goings forth have been from of old, from everlasting."* As we celebrate the birth of the Savior, may we never forget that He came to be the giver of life. Yes, He came to save us from our sin and give us eternal life, but He also came that we might have life *"more abundantly"* (John 10:10). Today, let us partake by faith, of the Bread of Life and find strength for the struggles of life. May we have fullness of joy from this bread. As we celebrate His birth, may we feast upon Him who is the the Bread of Life. God bless and have a great day.

December 20

God chooses to use mankind to accomplish His will, even when providing a Savior for sinful man. God chose to use a virgin maiden to be the vessel to give birth to the Son of God. Mary does not deserve to be deified, or worshipped, or to be seen as some special conduit to God for us. However, we must pause and give thought as to this humble Jewish maiden and the great purpose God had for her life. Luke 1 describes the announcement to Mary that she would be the one to give birth to the Christ child. Verse 28: *"And the angel came in unto her, and said, Hail, thou that art highly favoured, the Lord is with thee: blessed art thou among women."* Verse 31: *"And, behold, thou shalt conceive in thy womb, and bring forth a son, and shalt call his name JESUS."* There are several things about Mary that we should note and seek to imitate. **Her character.** God uses people of character — not perfect people, but those who are pure in life and thought. God could use Mary because she had remained sexually pure. **Her faith.** The call of God upon her life was to be and do what had never been done. She was to give birth to a child that was not conceived with a man. Her explanation for being with child would make no sense to anyone who asked. Her faith had to be without question and firmly fixed upon a God of promise. **Her obedience.** She was willing to be the one to deliver the hope of the world in Bethlehem's manger. She heard the call from the angel and was willing to obey. There will never be another virgin birth. God is not looking for another Mary, but He is looking for people to do His will. You and I have a purpose for our lives. May God help each of us to be men and women of character, of faith, and be obedient to that purpose. May Mary be an example for each of us to allow God to use us for His purpose and glory. God bless and have great day.

December 21

I have had the privilege of being invited to some special occasions in the life of some prestigious people. The significance of the individual who is recognized is often reflected by those in attendance at the event. So it was with the birth of Jesus. Yes, He was born in a stable and of lowly parents. Who would believe He was born of a virgin? Would not this be humanly impossible? It would be a miracle. God surrounded this occasion with the miraculous appearance of the *"angel of the Lord"* (Luke 2:9), who appeared to the shepherds and with the *"multitude of the heavenly host"* (Luke 2:13) that joined the angel of the Lord for the announcement to the shepherds. Then the shepherds came to Bethlehem that first Christmas day. Luke 2:16 says, *"And they came with haste, and found Mary and Joseph, and the the babe lying in a manger."* They were just ordinary men with humble vocations, yet were invited to attend the greatest event in the history of mankind. Even at Christ's birth, His deity was declared by God. His birth was attended by the *"angel of the Lord,"* and God sent a delegation of a *"multitude of the heavenly host"* to announce it. The attendees also gave indication of the babe's destiny — shepherds who cared for the lambs that would be offered as sacrifices for the sins of the people. Let us not forget that we celebrate the coming of the Son of God to earth to become the sacrifice for our sins. God bless and have a great day.

December 22

I was at a Christmas dinner a few years ago and heard something very interesting. The hostess told me that her young granddaughter had put up a Christmas greeting with a most unusual inscription. It simply read, "Peace and Quiet." No doubt she was thinking of the words of the angels in Luke 2:14 on the occasion the birth of Jesus. *"Glory to God in the highest, and on earth peace, good will toward men."* That this young girl settled on the phrase "Peace and Quiet" for a Christmas inscription is somewhat amusing, but the truth is that with the hustle and bustle of the holiday season we could all use some time to just stop and enjoy a little peace and quiet. There are plenty of passages in the Bible that suggest our need to slow down at times and listen to the Lord. Perhaps the most well-known verse in that regard is Ps. 46:10. *"Be still, and know that I am God: I will be exalted among the heathen, I will be exalted in the earth."* Especially at this time of year, the admonition to *"be still"* is good advice. Find a quiet place this Christmas and allow God to fill your heart with His peace. We know from Phil. 4:7 that it *"passeth all understanding."* Nearly all of the devotional entries in this book were written in the early morning hours. I enjoy the peace and quiet of that time of day when I can sit quietly with my Lord and enjoy the peace only He can give. Take a few minutes this Christmas and sit quietly with the Lord and enjoy His peace. God bless you today!

December 23

The celebration of the birth of Jesus is a celebration of promise. The virgin birth of the Christ child comes with the promise of salvation. It also comes with the promise of a God who has lived in the world and knows our hurts and disappointments. There is also the promise that one day this baby born in Bethlehem will rule the world in peace and prosperity. The commercial emphasis of today has taken away the real meaning of Christmas. The secularism of today has attempted to replace the real meaning of this celebration with one of bright lights, parties, and a few days off from work. With just two days to go before Christmas Day, I am praying that God will remind me of the promises that are mine because of the birth of Jesus. Think with me for a few moments about His promises to us from that manger in Bethlehem. **We have a Savior.** *"... he shall save his people from their sins"* (Matt. 1:21). **We have Someone who gives help and relief.** *"For in that he himself hath suffered being tempted, he is able to succour them that are tempted"* (Heb. 2:18). **We have a sovereign King to reign over us.** *"For unto us a child is born, unto us a son is given: and the government shall be upon his shoulder ..."* (Isa. 9:6). Every Christmas light we see, every Christmas song we hear, and every gift we receive or give should remind us of the promises that are ours because Jesus came by way of a virgin to be born, to live, and to die that we might live a life with promises. These are the promises that give us hope in the days of trouble. They are the promises that ring out this Christmas season. God bless and have a blessed Christmas.

December 24

    I remember as a child singing that old song, "All I want for Christmas is my two front teeth." Now that it's Christmas Eve, let me ask you this: What do you think Jesus wants from us this Christmas? Remember, this is **His** birthday. Surely we would not celebrate His birthday without considering a gift for Him. Now I know many churches will have a special offering for Jesus and that is fine. But I am speaking of a gift that all of us can present to Jesus this Christmas. More than money, more than anything Jesus asks *"that ye present your bodies a living sacrifice, holy, acceptable unto God, which is your reasonable service"* (Rom. 12:1). Jesus wants our lives to be lived for Him and for His purpose. I guess we could say this Christmas Eve that we should **put our presence under the tree**; that is, humbly place our lives beneath the cross (the tree) to conform to His will. My challenge for each of us this Christmas is to remember that it is not all about us and not even all about family and friends. It is all about Him. It is His birthday. We celebrate His birth. The most important gift given today will be the gift of each of us to serve the Lord. This Christmas I challenge each of us to present ourselves to the Lord to be and to do what He desires of us. God bless you this Christmas and remember that He is the reason for the season.

December 25

Merry Christmas to each of you! This is the day that we celebrate the birth of our Savior. It has become a day of gift exchanges and family gatherings with plenty of good food and fellowship with dear friends. These are all wonderful things, but we must not forget the babe in Bethlehem's manger who was born on Christmas Day. Most of us have heard or have read for ourselves the record of the birth of Jesus according to the Gospels of Matthew and Luke. There are two verses in Galatians that are often overlooked as a reminder of **how** Jesus came and **why** He came. Notice Gal. 4:45. *"But when the fulness of the time was come, God sent forth his Son, made of a woman, made under the law, To redeem them that were under the law, that we might receive the adoption of sons."* Jesus was born, *"made of a woman,"* just like any other person. The only difference was He had no earthly biological father. As we see in Matt. 1:20, *"that which is conceived in her is of the Holy Ghost."* His purpose in life was to die for the sins of all men — *"redeem them ... that we might receive the adoption of sons."* Today as you open your gifts, let them be a reminder of God's gift to us; the gift of His Son. As you give your gifts, remember how God freely gave His Son to be the sacrifice for our sins. As you enjoy family and friends today, please invite the celebrant, Jesus, to be a part of your celebration. Speak of Him often and speak to Him often, throughout the day. This is His day! God bless and have a great day!

December 26

The day after Christmas can mean a lot of different things to various people. Some are just glad they made it through another year with family members (not all family gatherings are fun). For many people this is a day to make the long trek back home, return those gifts that don't fit or just aren't quite what they wanted, or stay at home and take down the decorations. Whatever the case, the day after such a big day can be a downer. That's right, we can feel a bit depressed or blue. The excitement has passed. But the truth is, for those of us who know Jesus as our Savior, the day after is as exciting as the day we celebrate. We understand the birth of Christ was just the beginning. That babe in Bethlehem's manger would walk among men. He would suffer all the aches and pains of life, yet without sin. He would live for 33 years and then die on a cross for our sins. The birth is where it started, but surely not where it concluded. With that in mind, we should strive to continue with a spirit of Christmas throughout the year — a spirit of giving and of the reality of the life and death of Jesus for our sin. He was born on Christmas Day, but His birth marked the beginning, not the end. May we allow the spirit of yesterday, Christmas Day, be the spirit of every day in the coming year. Once again, let me wish you all a Merry Christmas, and I guess we now can begin to say Happy New Year! God bless and have a great day.

December 27

These few days between Christmas and the end of the calendar year are naturally a time for many of us to think about the end of one year and the beginning of another. For many, this past year was a year for fears, failures, and failings. Others will look at it as a year of successes, service, and stability. I would encourage all of us today to seek a fresh vision for the new year. On a recent day, while I was driving alone in my car, I listened to a nationally-known pastor and teacher as he was speaking on the life of David. For the portion of his program that I heard, his emphasis was on how David mishandled his sin. He tried to cover it up and attempted to deny it (II Sam. 11:1-17). David's sin started with **laziness.** Verse 1: *"But David tarried still at Jerusalem."* Next came **lust**. Verse 2: *"And from the roof he saw a woman washing herself; and the woman was very beautiful to look upon."* From there he moved to **adultery.** Verse 4: *"And she came in unto him, and he lay with her."* The final step was **murder**, as evidenced in verse 17. *"And Uriah the Hittite died also."* Why do we mention this horrible series of events today? Because David repented to the Lord and, although there were consequences, he continued to serve as king. He got a fresh start. I challenge all of you who have fallen or failed, to repent and return to the work God has given you. Today is a new day with a fresh start for all of us. To those who have been successful and served faithfully, start the year with a fresh vision with enthusiasm for the privilege to live and serve our Lord. God bless you and Happy New Year to each of you.

December 28

Albert Einstein once said, "Learn from yesterday, live for today, and hope for tomorrow." The last few days of each year always cause me to begin to think about what I feel God wants for my life in the coming year. It has also been my practice to set goals for each year — not resolutions, but life goals for the ministry, for my personal life, and for my family. The words of Einstein written above give good advice for these closing days of this year. **Learn from yesterday.** We cannot change our yesterdays, but we can allow our yesterdays to change us. My prayer is that I can honestly say, "I know I am not what I ought to be, but thank God I am not what I used to be." **Live for today.** Today is the only day we have to live. Yesterday is gone; tomorrow may never come. Heb. 13:5 reminds us, *"Let your conversation be without covetousness; and be content with such things as ye have: for he hath said, I will never leave thee, nor forsake thee."* To covet means to be "greedy or showing a strong desire for material possessions." This is not to say we should not work hard to obtain the things we desire in life. It is to say that the material things we have in life should never define our lives. For me, living for today is about being a blessing to someone and fulfilling God's plan for my life. **Hope for tomorrow.** Our hope for tomorrow is looking for the coming of Lord. We are to be living according to Tit. 2:13. *"Looking for that blessed hope, and the glorious appearing of the great God and our Saviour Jesus Christ."* As we approach the close of a year, and anticipate the dawning of the new year, let's plan like everything depends on us, pray like everything depends on God, and put our trust in God for strength for today. God bless and have a great day.

December 29

The Bible is filled with promises. Someone has said that there is a promise for every day. I have never counted them, so I do not know the actual number. But as I read through my Bible, God gives me promises upon which to live. We can trust His promises. A good example of a promise given that is being kept is found in Genesis 12:23. This is a promise given to Abram. *"And I will make of thee a great nation, and I will bless thee, and make thy name great; and thou shalt be a blessing: And I will bless them that bless thee, and curse him that curseth thee: and in thee shall all families of the earth be blessed."* God kept and is keeping His promise to Abram and to his seed, Israel. I believe God has blessed America largely because America has blessed Israel. As I noticed some of the decisions of our government in recent years that were less than pro-Israel, I feared the promise from God to *"curse him that curseth thee."* God is a **promise keeper.** As we face the close of another year and anticipate the new year, I would suggest that each of us ask God for a promise for the new year. One that I have claimed for a new year is found in Jer. 33:3. *"Call unto me, and I will answer thee, and show thee great and mighty things, which thou knowest not."* I am sure that when Abram left his homeland he had no idea just how and to what extent God was going to bless him and his seed. Today, I challenge you to claim a promise from God to be His promise to you, and watch God work. The coming year can be our year of promise. God bless you and keep holding on to the promises of God!

December 30

While reading some end-of-the-year inspirational quotes I came across this statement from Mark Twain: "Twenty years from now you will be more disappointed by the things you didn't do than the ones you did do. So throw off the bow lines. Sail away from the safe harbor. Catch the trade winds in your sails. Explore. Dream. Discover." I thought of the many people described in the Bible accomplishing great things for God because they explored, dreamed, and discovered. Abram dreamed of a land God would show him and heeded His command in Gen. 12:1. *"Get thee out of thy country, and from thy kindred, and from thy father's house, unto a land that I will shew thee."* Nehemiah, when he heard of the condition of the walls of Jerusalem, sought to go and rebuild the walls. His dream led to exploring, and his exploring led him to discover the provision of God for the task and people to assist in building the wall. As we come to the close of another year, let us determine that the coming year will be a year of **doing** and not a year of regret for the things we did not do. I know Jesus could come any day, but until He comes may we be found faithful doing the work and the will of God. As we come to a new year, what is it you plan to do for the Savior in the next 12 months? It has been my experience that we only do what we plan to do. We need to **explore** our opportunities; we need to **dream** of that thing God has for our lives; and then we will **discover** that God will empower us to do his will. God bless you and have a great day.

December 31

To some people, today is the **last** day of the year. To others it marks the **beginning** of a new year. Oprah Winfrey once said, "Year's end is neither an end nor a beginning but a going on, with all wisdom that experience can instill in us. Cheers to another year and another chance to get it right." Though I certainly would not put a lot of trust in Oprah's spiritual insight, I wholeheartedly agree with her statement. I believe you and I should take a few moments and recount the blessings of the past year. We should begin to plan for the coming year, but most importantly we must live **today**. I am reminded of the words of Ps. 118:24. *"This is the day which the Lord hath made: we will rejoice and be glad in it."* Last year was a great year for Doris and me. The Lord allowed me to speak in dozens of churches across the United States and participate in a number of seminars with the National Center for Life and Liberty. Many came to know the Lord and we were able to encourage pastors and congregations in their time of need while offering through NCLL legal advice to protect religious liberties. However, yesterday is gone. We must plan for next year, but most importantly we must learn from yesterday and live for the Savior today. I have often repeated the statement, "Yesterday is a canceled check; tomorrow is a promissory note. Only today is legal tender to be spent." My thought for today is to live one day at a time. God blessed you with a yesterday, and He alone will provide the opportunities for tomorrow. Today is the day we have to live and serve Him. Let's all *"rejoice and be glad"* for today! God bless and have a great day.

Koiné Press is a division of
Baptist Training Center Publications.

BAPTIST TRAINING CENTER PUBLICATIONS

WINTER HAVEN, FLORIDA

Moments of Inspiration and other great Christian book titles
are available on Amazon.com and other online retailers.

Made in the USA
Middletown, DE
30 November 2018